10/97

WITHDRAWN

THE
UTE INDIANS
OF COLORADO
IN THE TWENTIETH CENTURY

THE
UTE INDIANS
OF COLORADO
IN THE TWENTIETH CENTURY

By Richard K. Young

UNIVERSITY OF OKLAHOMA PRESS
Norman and London

Library of Congress Cataloging-in-Publication Data

Young, Richard K. (Richard Keith), 1958–
The Ute Indians of Colorado in the twentieth century /
by Richard K. Young
p. cm.
Includes bibliographical references and index.
ISBN 0-8061-2968-9 (cloth : alk. paper)
1. Ute Indians—History—20th century.
2. Ute Indians—Government relations.
3. Ute Indians—Social life and customs.
I. Title.
E99.U8Y68   1997
978.8'0049745—dc21   97-2381
CIP

Text design by Cathy Carney Imboden.
Text is set in Goudy Old Style.

1 2 3 4 5 6 7 8 9 10

For my mother and father

CONTENTS

ILLUSTRATIONS

MAPS

PHOTOGRAPHS
Following page 38

PREFACE

The story of the Indian peoples of the American West does not end with the military clashes at the Little Bighorn or Wounded Knee or with the surrenders of such renowned leaders as Chief Joseph or Geronimo. Nor does the story of the Ute people conclude with the so-called Meeker Massacre of 1879. By that time, tribes such as the Utes had been pushed to the periphery of Euro-American civilization and forced to reside on newly created reservations. Here began a new and important chapter in Ute history, one that is often overlooked by those interested only in romanticized tales of "noble savages" or accounts of frontier warfare. Here the Ute Indians encountered a federal government that confronted them not with guns but with schools, plows, and bibles. Here, on the reservation, they faced a daunting challenge — to survive as a tribe, as a culturally distinct people, in the midst of an overwhelmingly powerful and populous foreign civilization.

This book, which examines the twentieth-century experiences of the two Ute tribes of Colorado, traces the journey of the Southern Utes and the Ute Mountain Utes through this challenging period. I have endeavored to produce the most comprehensive history possible for a volume of modest length. Political, economic, social, and cultural dimensions are all considered here. This is a comparative history, chronicling the stories of two neighboring and culturally similar tribes as they each struggled to find their place in twentieth-century America. I have also attempted to place the experiences of these two tribes in a larger context by addressing the broad implications of U.S. Indian policies and modern socioeconomic forces for reservation-dwelling tribes in general.

In considering these two tribes and their leaders, I am neither a partisan nor a critic. This book takes an objective perspective on its subject, and I seek to dispassionately recount and interpret— but not judge—the modern story of the Ute people of Colorado. To this end, I have taken great pains to utilize the widest possible variety of sources, both Indian and non-Indian. This book draws on a healthy mixture of documents, both tribal and federal, and also on oral history information gleaned from a large array of interviews with tribal members. An extensive collection of secondary sources has also been consulted.

Many people have kindly provided assistance over the course of this project. I am particularly grateful to Thomas J. Noel of the University of Colorado, Denver, for his advice and constant encouragement from start to finish. Mark S. Foster also aided in the early stages of my work. I am deeply indebted to a number of scholars who reviewed early drafts of the manuscript. The critical comments of Richard O. Clemmer of the University of Denver and David Rich Lewis of Utah State University were invaluable in helping to correct inaccuracies and omissions; and extensive feedback from Katherine M. B. Osburn of Tennessee Technological University enabled me to refine my analysis and attain a greater degree of objectivity.

My research was made much easier through the generous help of many individuals. Records manager Debra R. Frost provided much-needed assistance with my research in the Southern Ute

Tribal Records and Archives; and the staffs of both tribal news-papers, the *Weenuche Smoke Signals* and the *Southern Ute Drum*, went out of their way to aid me in my work. The Bureau of Indian Affairs employees at the Ute Mountain Ute Agency in Towaoc were very kind in providing me access to the agency's records. I also wish to express my gratitude to Joan Howard and Eileen Bol-ger at the National Archives (Rocky Mountain Region) in Den-ver and to the research staffs at the following institutions: the Western History Collections at the University of Colorado's Norlin Library, the Colorado Historical Society, and the Denver Public Library's Western History Department.

I am especially grateful to those tribal members who shared their recollections and views with me through often-lengthy in-terviews. John E. Baker Sr., Sunshine Cloud Smith, and Bertha Grove offered valuable insight into developments on the South-ern Ute Reservation; Ernest House Sr., Terry Knight, Norman Lopez, and Arthur Cuthair provided a window into life at Ute Mountain. I am particularly in debt to Arthur Cuthair for grant-ing me access to an extensive collection of oral history interviews with tribal members.

Finally, I want to thank my wife, Mary Taylor Gray Young, for her encouragement and proofreading assistance and for her pa-tience over the course of this lengthy project.

RICHARD K. YOUNG

Denver, Colorado

THE
UTE INDIANS
OF COLORADO
IN THE TWENTIETH CENTURY

INTRODUCTION

One hundred five members of the Southern Ute Tribe gathered in their Council Hall on the banks of the Los Pinos River about 1 mile north of the town of Ignacio, Colorado. They had come to this General Council meeting on September 28, 1951, to consider a plan, formulated by tribal officials, delineating how the tribe would expend a large sum of money currently being held by the U.S. government—money for which the tribe had waged a prolonged legal battle. The struggle had not ended during the previous year when the U.S. Court of Claims awarded nearly $7 million to the Southern Utes. These funds, part of a $31,761,206 land claims judgment in favor of the Confederated Ute Bands, were to remain in the U.S. Treasury until such time as the tribe developed—and Congress approved—a long-range plan specifying how the money would be spent. The question before the Southern Ute people on September 28 was whether or not to approve the "rehabilitation plan" devised to satisfy this requirement.

One of the prime architects of the proposed plan was thirty-three-year-old tribal member John E. Baker. Raised on a farm located downriver from Ignacio, Baker was one of five sons born to

Julian Baker, who combined farming with periods of service on the Tribal Council and as tribal judge. The elder Baker grew wheat and oats on his allotted land in the fertile Los Pinos River valley, and he also raised sheep, goats, and cattle. Julian Baker put a premium on education, and as a result all five of his sons graduated from high school. John Baker graduated from the Sherman Indian School in California in 1938.[1] After serving as an army medical corpsman in England from 1942 to 1945, Baker returned to the reservation at the end of World War II and eventually headed for Chicago to study architecture and building construction at Chicago Technical College.[2] Having already participated in the creation of one tribal rehabilitation plan, a document that was subsequently rejected by the Bureau of Indian Affairs (BIA), John Baker was back at school in Chicago in early 1951 when he received a letter from former tribal chairman Sam Burch requesting his assistance in the formulation of a new plan. Baker responded immediately, sending off a letter of withdrawal to the college, packing his belongings, and catching a bus out of Chicago that same afternoon.[3]

Now on September 28, after laboring for several months as chairman of the Planning Committee, John Baker stood before an assembly of tribal members to read the rehabilitation plan produced by his committee. Already endorsed by the elected Tribal Council, the plan had been referred to the General Council, an assembly of adult tribal members, for final approval. Baker had read through most of the lengthy document with no response at all from the audience when, with fourteen pages to go, a tribal member questioned how the land claims money would be distributed. Then, as if a dam had burst, the crowd unleashed a flood of angry invective on John Baker and the Tribal Council. The people were angry that only a portion of the judgment money was to be distributed directly to the membership, angry that their use of this money would be subject to restrictions, and angry that the Tribal Council had kept them in the dark about all of this until after the plan had been completed. The discussion grew increasingly heated. Personal attacks were leveled at Baker, and comments such as "Well, that plan stinks!" echoed throughout the Council Hall. At one point, a group of tribal members rose to propose an alternative plan. After continued acrimonious debate, one supporter of the second plan called for a show of hands by all who favored this alternative. As many of the assembled Indians raised their hands in an untallied vote, the tumultuous meeting was finally adjourned.[4]

The Southern Ute Tribe of 1951 stood uneasily on the brink of fundamental political, economic, and social change, and the prospect was unsettling to many members of the tribe. The debate over the rehabilitation plan—and over the future direction of the tribe—was breeding confusion, disagreement, and anger among the people. Yet the tribe was able to overcome these internal divisions and apprehensions to ultimately unite behind the rehabilitation plan that had provoked such furor at the September meeting. As tempers cooled and people began to comprehend the plan more clearly, tribal opposition to the committee's plan waned. On December 27, 1951, the General Council was reconvened, and after extensive discussion—at times quite animated, but not so heated as three months earlier—tribal members approved the proposed plan by an overwhelming 74–6 vote.[5]

Although congressional approval of the Southern Ute Rehabilitation Plan was still more than two years off, the job for which John Baker had been called back from Chicago was now largely completed. But Baker, the aspiring engineer, did not return to his studies. What had initially been described by Sam Burch as a six-month job ended up becoming a lifetime assignment for the strong-willed and outspoken young World War II veteran.[6] With only a few brief interruptions, John E. Baker Sr. would continue to serve his tribe, first as rehabilitation director, then as tribal chairman and as a member of the Tribal Council and a host of other tribal entities, until his retirement from the council in 1982.

THE UTE MOUNTAIN UTES

Several years later and roughly 85 miles to the west, the governors of four southwestern states were seeking to bring change—in the form of a modern highway—to the vast open stretches of the Ute Mountain Ute Reservation. The governors of Colorado, Utah, Arizona, and New Mexico had assembled in the town of Cortez, just to the north of the reservation, in May 1958. They hoped to obtain approval of the highway proposal from the chief of the tribe. Chief Jack House, however, proved to be less than accommodating. The aging Ute patriarch of some sixty-eight years—he did not know his date of birth but estimated it to have been around 1891[7]—refused to meet with the governors either in Cortez or at his own home in the reservation town of Towaoc.

Jack House had lived his entire life amid the arid isolation of the Ute Mountain Ute Reservation. Born in the canyon of the Mancos River in the final decade of the nineteenth century, he had spent most of his years raising livestock in these same rugged canyons that cut deeply into Mesa Verde and the surrounding upland.[8] Like most people of the Weeminuche band—the Ute band that constituted the Ute Mountain Ute Tribe—he raised sheep and horses, and later cattle, in this desert land of canyon and mesa. Before moving into a small house in Towaoc, the House family had lived a seminomadic existence, moving seasonally with its animals up and down Mancos Canyon. For several years the Houses had lived in an earthen hogan, but more often they resided in tents, free to move whenever and wherever they pleased. Jack House never went to school, and like most Utes of his generation he spoke little English.[9]

Jack House had always played an active role in the affairs of his people, serving as a member of the Ute Mountain Council as early as 1920.[10] The Weeminuche did not have a hereditary chieftaincy; rather, the chief was chosen for his personal character and abilities, often by his predecessor.[11] John Miller had been chief since the death of Chief Ignacio in 1913, and Jack House served under Miller as a subchief. Shortly before his death in 1936, Chief Miller tapped House as his successor.[12] Throughout the ensuing thirty-five-year period of his chieftainship, House would be much more than just a symbolic leader of his tribe; Chief House wielded substantial power in the conduct of tribal affairs until the time of his death. In addition to occupying the traditional leadership position of tribal chief, House continued to serve without interruption on the elected Tribal Council until the mid 1960s. Although he was never again chairman of this body after 1939, he continued to play a predominant role in its deliberations. Thus, it was not from Chairman Albert Wing or the other members of the Tribal Council that the four governors needed to win approval of their highway proposal; it was from Chief Jack House.

Despite the rebuff from House, Colorado governor Steven L. R. McNichols drove from Cortez to Towaoc, the secluded reservation town on the dusty valley floor that gently sloped upward from Navajo Wash to the foot of Sleeping Ute Mountain, to call on the chief at his home. Chief House was not swayed by the governor's visit.[13] McNichols and the other governors wanted a road across the barren, semidesert grassland in the southwestern section of the reservation for access to the rich oil fields around Aneth, Utah; but tribal opinion was against the highway. As a result, House was holding firm in his position. He argued that the highway would split the reservation and that it would damage too much of the tribe's grazing land.[14] A year and a half later, the chief changed his mind and assented to construction of the new road; however, he did so only after the tribe had been awarded $500,000 from the Colorado State Highway Department for the purchase of the right-of-way for this extension of U.S. Highway 160 from Chimney Rock, on U.S. Highway 666 south of Cortez, to the Four Corners.[15]

The "old man" with the cowboy hat and long braids of gray

hair continued to play an important advisory role in tribal affairs
even after he retired from the Tribal Council. Tribal officials continued to seek the aging chief's blessing for major decisions.[16]
Chief Jack House, the last chief of the Ute Mountain Utes, died
on August 19, 1971.

COMMON HERITAGE, DIFFERENT PATHS

John E. Baker Sr. and Chief Jack House both helped chart the
courses that their respective tribes would follow through a sea of
changes—a sea that was often quite stormy. Both men sought to
navigate through wave after wave of change, be it the prospect of
new wealth—and the government-mandated strings that came
attached—or plans for a new highway across the reservation or
any one of an endless array of developments that modern America might place in the path of a Native American people in the
mid-twentieth century.

Both John Baker and Jack House were strong leaders, and both
were Utes; but there the resemblance stops. The stark contrast
between these two individuals and the lives they led is representative of the larger dichotomy between the two neighboring Ute
tribes. Up until the late nineteenth century, the Southern Utes
and Ute Mountain Utes, as they would later come to be called,
shared for the most part a common past and a common culture.
As white settlers intruded on their land and the U.S. government
forced the Utes to yield most of their traditional territory, they
were pushed onto a common reservation. But as the nineteenth
century drew to a close, events pulled the Ute bands of southwestern Colorado apart and led them to embark on two strikingly
divergent paths. The result was the establishment of two separate
reservations—the Southern Ute Reservation in the east and the
Ute Mountain Ute Reservation to the west. Although the two
newly created reservations shared a common border, the starkly
different lives led by their respective inhabitants gave the ap-

pearance that the two reservations were worlds apart. This immense gulf between the two tribes would still be discernible a full
century after its initial appearance in the 1890s. And yet these
two tribes are not without their similarities. They have both been
subjected to the same political, economic, social, and cultural
forces and have had to confront many of the same problems.

This volume will trace the divergent paths followed by the
Southern Utes and the Ute Mountain Utes during the twentieth
century, with particular emphasis placed on the experiences of
the two tribes since the early 1930s. This period witnessed a fundamental transformation in these two groups—and in most other
American Indian nations as well. The forces that unleashed this
transformation were largely set in motion by the advent of the Indian New Deal, a shift in U.S. Indian policy implemented during
the presidency of Franklin D. Roosevelt. The centerpiece of this
new approach to Indian affairs was the Indian Reorganization
Act (IRA), passed by Congress in 1934. The IRA, however, was
merely one piece in the ever-changing puzzle of twentieth-
century U.S. government Indian policy. This study will chronicle
the often contrasting responses of the two Ute tribes of Colorado
to both government policies and socioeconomic forces.

A NEGLECTED STORY

One reason for focusing on the Ute experience of the middle and
late twentieth century, aside from the revolutionary transformation that took place during this period, is the scant historiographical attention that has been paid to this subject. The literature
pertaining to the history of Colorado's Ute Indians is far from extensive. Historians have lavished much more attention on the
Utes' neighbors to the south, such as the Navajo, Hopi, and Pueblo
peoples, and also on their rivals to the east on the Great Plains—
the Sioux, Cheyenne, Arapaho, Comanche, and Pawnee. Why
have the Utes, who once roamed throughout a vast mountain

and desert domain covering over 130,000 square miles and stretching over parts of present-day Colorado, Utah, and New Mexico, not stimulated a similar level of interest? A number of factors might be responsible: the relatively small population of the Utes; the eclectic ambiguity of the Ute way of life, which during the nineteenth century combined cultural elements from the Great Basin, Southwest, and Great Plains; the Utes' lack of significant contact with Anglo Americans until relatively late in the scheme of western settlement; and the Utes' generally peaceful relations with the United States.[17]

Neither the two Colorado Ute tribes nor the Ute people as a whole ever represented a large Native American population in comparison with other Indian nations. The total population of all Great Basin Indians—the Ute, Paiute, Shoshone, Bannock, Washoe, and other tribes residing in the rugged and dry area between the Sierra Nevada and the Rocky Mountains—amounted to roughly 8 percent of the nationwide Indian population in 1890. This figure decreased to about 5 percent by 1910 and to a mere 2 percent in 1980.[18] The Ute people in turn constituted approximately 28 percent of the total Great Basin Indian population in 1873, but for most of the twentieth century their share of the regional population hovered around only 18 percent.[19] In 1974 the combined population of all three modern Ute tribes comprised 3,815 members, in comparison with tribal populations of 96,743 for the Navajo nation, 47,825 for the Sioux, and 6,872 for the Cheyenne.[20] Since the Southern Ute and Ute Mountain Ute tribes together constitute only three out of a total of seven Ute bands, the relatively small size of these two tribes becomes clear. Consider, for example, the beginning of the 1930s, when Southern Ute and Ute Mountain Ute tribal populations numbered only 369 and 444, respectively.[21]

Regardless of these limited numbers, the twentieth-century experience of the two Colorado Ute tribes is quite revealing and worthy of study. The story of the modern Ute Mountain Ute and

Southern Ute Tribes is a microcosm of American Indian history in the twentieth century. The relatively small size of the populations involved does not diminish the fact that these two tribes were subjected to the same fundamental internal and external forces afflicting all Native American peoples during the modern period. They felt the same assimilationist pressures, they confronted the same issues of cultural change, and they endured the same sequence of U.S. Indian policies—allotment of Indian land and efforts to promote an agricultural economy at the turn of the century, tribal reorganization during the 1930s, formulation of tribal rehabilitation plans and discussion of tribal termination during the 1950s and 1960s, and subsequent policies directed toward economic development and tribal self-determination. The federal government implemented such policies on small reservations, such as the two Colorado Ute reservations, with as much vigor and determination as it did on large jurisdictions, such as the immense Navajo Reservation. The small size of the Ute Mountain Ute and Southern Ute Tribes did not preclude their becoming the objects of constant scrutiny by a host of federal officials, from the local agent or superintendent on up to the commissioner of Indian affairs.

The lack of scholarly attention paid to the Ute experience invites additional study of the history of this people. This is particularly true with respect to the modern period: Ute historiography, while generally thin, is especially sparse with regard to the twentieth-century experience of these tribes. It is as if the Ute Indians of Colorado simply disappeared after the much-celebrated Meeker Massacre of 1879.

The Ute Mountain Ute Tribe in particular has suffered historiographical neglect with respect to the current century. Most studies of the Utes in Colorado have focused primarily on the Southern Utes. Although some works have dealt with both tribes, historians have rarely focused their attention on the Ute Mountain Utes. This preference for investigating the Ignacio Utes is

not surprising given the relative amounts of data available. With
the vast collection of material accumulated by the Tri-Ethnic Research Project of the 1950s and 1960s, and with a large assort-
ment of tribal and BIA documents assembled since the early
1970s in the tribe's own archives, the researcher of Southern Ute
history has access to a large volume of primary source material.
No similar treasure trove exists in Towaoc. Moreover, the more
isolated and closed nature of Ute Mountain Ute society and of
the tribal government in Towaoc has made it exceedingly difficult for historians to research the history of this people.

EXISTING IN A DILEMMA

The two Ute tribes of Colorado, like all Indian peoples in the
United States, faced a complex and difficult situation throughout
the twentieth century. They confronted the daunting challenge
of reconciling a series of conflicting goals: to survive in a world
dominated by an alien socioeconomic system and yet retain their
unique cultural traditions and identity; to provide for the needs
of tribal members while also conserving the tribe's finite financial resources; to enable tribal members to remain on the reservation where they could live together as a people while also
ensuring that individual members could function and support
themselves in mainstream American society; to obtain the benefits of economic and social development while minimizing the
accompanying social problems; and to maintain cooperative and
productive relationships with federal, state, and local governments while asserting tribal sovereignty and self-determination.

    As the Ute Mountain Utes and Southern Utes confronted the
dilemmas posed by their place in twentieth-century America, they
often opted for radically different responses. This study will show
that, beginning with their decisions to either accept or reject individual land allotments in 1895, the two tribes often took different approaches to dealing with their subordinate position in

the United States. At times the contrast in tribal attitudes and actions was stark indeed. Often the Southern Utes and their leaders appeared to be distinctly "progressive" in comparison to their seemingly more "conservative" or "traditionalist" counterparts at Ute Mountain. Yet, in reality, the situation was much more complicated; a simple "progressive-conservative" dichotomy has never accurately described the two neighboring Ute tribes. Each tribe has dealt with essentially the same dilemmas, and in the face of overpowering outside forces for change, each has struck a delicate balancing act between resistance and accommodation. Likewise, individual tribal leaders such as Chief Jack House present a multifaceted picture. Even though Jack House was frequently scorned by federal officials as an obstructionist, on many occasions he took the lead in prompting his people to adapt to the modern world. This book will examine the common dilemma faced by the Southern Utes and Ute Mountain Utes as each tribe struggled to find its place in modern American society. As this story unfolds, it will become clear that the courses followed by the two tribes have been clearly divergent in some respects but also marked by major underlying commonalities.

This volume presents a broad perspective on the history of the Southern Ute and Ute Mountain Ute tribes during the twentieth century. Chapter 1 provides the background to the story of the modern Ute Indians of Colorado. It spans several centuries of Ute history, ranging from the pre-European period to the establishment and subsequent division of the Southern Ute Reservation at the close of the nineteenth century. Chapter 2 examines the experiences of the Southern Utes and Ute Mountain Utes on their respective reservations during the opening decades of the twentieth century. Chapter 3 then presents a portrait of life on both Ute reservations during the 1930s, and Chapter 4 chronicles the onset of fundamental political and economic change as both tribes took initial steps toward self-determination under the Indian Reorganization Act. The accelerated pace of change during the 1950s, as a result of newly acquired tribal wealth, is explored in Chapter 5. Each of the next three chapters addresses a different aspect of the Southern Ute and Ute Mountain Ute experiences after 1960: tribal economics (Chapter 6), tribal politics (Chapter 7), and tribal society and culture (Chapter 8). This study then closes with some concluding thoughts.

1

THE SOUTHERN UTES
AND UTE MOUNTAIN UTES
PRIOR TO 1900

The Utes are a Great Basin people linguistically related to their neighbors to the southwest, the Southern Paiutes. Both tribes speak the Ute language, a part of the Southern Numic branch of the Uto-Aztecan language family.[1] At the time of earliest European contact, the Utes, the oldest continuous residents of the state of Colorado, occupied a vast domain of mountain, mesa, desert, and high plains that stretched from the Great Basin across the Rocky Mountains to the western fringes of the Great Plains. The Utes, or Yutas as they were called by the Spanish, regularly ranged over most of present-day Colorado as well as parts of Utah, Arizona, and New Mexico. Even though their territorial range was immense, the Utes have never been very large in population. The total population of all Ute bands at the opening of the nineteenth century is estimated at around 8,000, declining to just over 6,000 people by 1873.[2]

Although some cultural differences emerged—especially following contact with Europeans—between the Utes of Colorado and those living west of the Green and Colorado Rivers in Utah, all Utes spoke the same language and shared an essentially com-

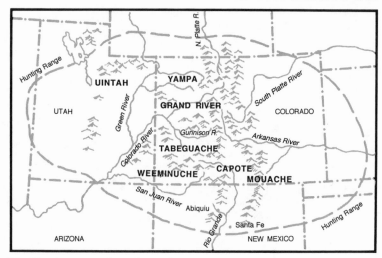

The Ute domain in the eighteenth century, showing approximate locations of the seven bands and their collective hunting range.

mon culture. The Utes, who refer to themselves as Nuche, meaning "the People," have also been distinguished by physical similarities: they are characterized by a short and stocky build, and their dark complexion led other tribes, such as the Cheyenne, to refer to them as the "Black People."[3] In comparison with the typical Ute physique, the people of the Navajo tribe are considerably taller and thinner, absurdly so in the eyes of the Utes. The Ute word for "cattails" was sometimes used as a nickname for their neighbors to the south.[4]

The Utes have never been a unified tribe. Instead, their existence prior to the reservation period revolved around seven loosely constituted bands, defined largely by geographical range: the Uintah band occupied the Uintah Basin of Utah; the Yampa band, later known together with the Parianuc Utes as the White River band, lived in the vicinity of the Yampa River in northwestern Colorado; the Parianuc, or Grand River, band resided along the Colorado River (formerly called the Grand River) in Colorado and Utah; the Tabeguache, later known as Uncompahgre, band inhabited the valleys of the Gunnison and Uncompahgre Rivers in western Colorado; the Weeminuche band roamed throughout the San Juan River drainage in the Four Corners area; the Capote band occupied the San Luis valley and the surrounding San Juan and Sangre de Cristo ranges; and the Mouache band ranged across southern Colorado and northern New Mexico from the Sangre de Cristo Mountains east out onto the plains.[5]

Prior to the reservation period and the removal of the Yampa, Parianuc, and Tabeguache bands from Colorado, an east-west cultural division was evident among the various Ute bands. The culture of the Western Utes—the Uintah band and other Utes living west of the Green and Colorado Rivers in Utah—was distinct from that of the six bands residing in eastern Utah and Colorado, collectively referred to as the Eastern Utes.[6] The environmental contrast between the arid west and the mountainous east led to dietary differences between the Western and Eastern bands. The latter group was blessed with a more bountiful supply of land mammals, while the Western Utes relied more heavily on plants, fish, and insects.[7] The Western Ute diet included a number of items typically not consumed by the relatively game-rich Eastern Utes, including piñon nuts, snakes and lizards, and even ants. Comparative abundance of mammal life also gave rise to a noticeable difference in clothing among the Utes. Eastern bands had more deer skins and were generally better dressed, whereas their Western counterparts had much less buckskin clothing.[8] This Eastern-Western cultural divergence was greatly accentuated by the arrival of Europeans. The Eastern bands were influenced by more frequent contact with the Spanish, and their way of life was more substantially impacted by the acquisition of the horse. This latter development brought a greater infusion of Plains cultural elements to the Eastern Utes than to the Western Utes. The Weeminuche Utes, although considered an Eastern band, actually represented a cultural midpoint between the Eastern and

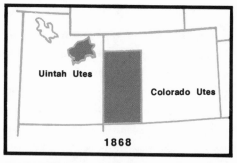

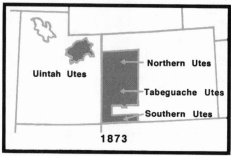

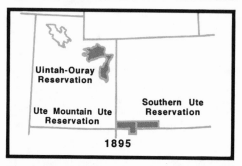

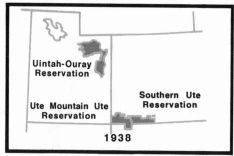

Ute reservations since 1868.

Western Utes.[9] Since the Weeminuches' domain included the desert lands of the Four Corners country, the band shared many cultural elements with its Uintah kin to the northwest.

Events in the late nineteenth century resulted in a Northern-Southern division among the seven Ute bands that superseded the earlier distinction between Eastern and Western groups. The term *Northern* Utes—which today is applied to the Utes residing on the Uintah-Ouray Reservation in Utah—originally referred to those bands living north of the Gunnison River in Colorado, whereas those living south of this river, the Weeminuche, Capote, and Mouache, were considered to be "Southern Utes." Prior to 1880, both of these groups would have been considered Eastern Utes. No special cultural bond united the three Southern Ute bands; rather, they were bound merely by geography and occasional intermarriage. Even in the pre-European period, however, geography exerted a differential impact on the three Southern Ute bands: the two eastern groups, the Mouache and Capote, lived in closer proximity and thus tended toward greater inter-band unity than either band shared with its more isolated Weeminuche cousins to the west.[10] Nevertheless, events often reinforced the common identification as Southern Utes, and up until 1895 the three bands were jointly identified by this name. It was only then that one of the three bands would come to be known as Ute Mountain Utes, while the other two retained the appellation *Southern Ute*.

THE PRE-EUROPEAN PERIOD

With no single "Ute Tribe" in existence, the largest organized unit in the Ute world prior to European contact was the band, and these groups existed in only the loosest sense. Bands were led by headmen with only limited, noncoercive authority, and even this minimal power operated only during the brief periods when bands were assembled together. Families were free to leave bands,

and an individual's band membership was easily changed.[11] The
extended family held the greatest social and political significance
in the lives of the Ute people.

The Weeminuche, Capote, and Mouache lived a nomadic existence, as staying too long in one place meant starvation. Living
in family groups, the Utes spent the summer scattered throughout the mountains, where game was abundant and the prospect
of attack by Plains Indians least likely. In autumn they emerged
from the mountains, moving south to the plateau country, where
they gathered piñon nuts and hunted before heading for winter
campsites in lower foothills and valleys. Here they hunted an-
telope and other game.[12] These hunter-gatherers generally es-
chewed farming but occasionally traded with neighboring tribes
for corn, beans, or squash. Families typically followed an established migrational circuit, returning to the same hunting camps
in the high country each summer. They rarely came into contact
with others of their band, and it was only in the spring when the
Utes congregated for the annual Bear Dance that social contact
outside the family group took place. This was often the only opportunity for dancing, courtship, and other social interactions
given the difficult struggle for existence that normally kept the
Utes on the move. Life was fraught with uncertainty: summers
brought the danger of enemy raids, and winters were characterized by a desperate search for food.[13]

SPANISH CONTACT AND THE HORSE

Life became much less harsh and uncertain after the arrival of the
Spaniards in New Mexico. Spanish contact was to influence the
Ute people in many ways, but one Spanish contribution stands
out in its impact on Ute life. The Utes were probably one of the
first tribes north of Mexico to acquire the horse, although no one
is certain as to the date when the Ute people first obtained these
animals from the Spaniards.[14] Estimates range from as early as

1600 to 1680 and later, but in any case the Utes had clearly become equestrians by the close of the seventeenth century.[15] The
introduction of the horse spurred a dramatic transformation of
Ute culture. Whereas established migrational patterns and food
preferences remained largely intact, the increased range and efficiency of Ute hunters brought forth substantial changes in Ute
society and culture.[16] The band, which had previously played
only a minor role in Ute life, now assumed much greater func-
tional importance. With increased mobility and the ability to
transport food over greater distances, previously dispersed family
groups now concentrated in large band camps. Hunters ventured
far out onto the plains and hunted buffalo much more frequently
than in the past; food became more plentiful and hunger less of
a concern. The Utes also became much more warlike than in
their preequestrian days, as mounted Utes proved a formidable
fighting force in encounters with neighboring peoples. Accordingly, a new type of leadership arose in the band camps. Family elders retained much of their traditional authority, but the camps
increasingly came to be dominated by powerful war leaders.[17]

During the seventeenth century, the previously peaceful Utes
often waged war on their neighbors. They fought at times with
the Spanish, but more often their foes were other Indians, the
Comanche in particular. The Comanches, living as they did on
the vast open plains, underwent an even more dramatic transformation on acquiring horses than did the Utes. The Comanches
quickly adopted a highly mobile lifestyle, one that the Utes could
never match given their differentiated environment, marked by
mountain, plateau, basin, and canyon.[18] Nevertheless, mounted
Ute bands began to venture outside their mountain strongholds
with greater frequency, often sending hunting or raiding parties
out onto the plains. The mountain warriors began to win the
grudging respect of their enemies that roamed the plains. "The
Utes are the Switzers of America," Colonel Richard Irving Dodge
of the U.S. Army reported in the 1880s, "and though the whole

force of mountain bands numbers but little over four hundred men, all the powerful Plains tribes, though holding them in utter contempt on the Plains have an absolute terror of them in the mountains."[19] As a result of their forays out onto the plains, the Eastern Ute bands soon adopted cultural elements from the Plains tribes: tipis began to replace traditional conical brush shelters, buffalo hunts became the primary source of food, and raiding became commonplace.

Yet despite this material evidence of a transformation to the lifestyle of the Plains peoples, in spirit the Utes remained primarily a Shoshonean people with many cultural ties to the Great Basin.[20] Ute warfare, for example, was notably distinct from that of the Plains Indians. Whereas warriors from the latter group were in large part motivated by the desire to count coup and win praise for feats of bravery, Ute raiders sought only to obtain loot and safely bring it home.[21]

The impact of the Spanish presence, however, went far beyond merely serving as the source of the Utes' horses. The settlement of Santa Fe by the Spaniards in 1609, ushering in the establishment of the frontier colony of New Mexico, brought the borderlands of the Spanish Empire to the fringes of the Ute domain. Although the Spaniards were unable to conquer or displace the Utes from their mountains, basins, and plateaus, they did introduce significant changes to the Ute world. Zebulon Pike noted the effect of Spanish contact on the Utes when he encountered these Indians on his 1805–1807 expedition. He observed that the Utes "are armed in the same manner and pursue the same game as the Kyoways. They are, however, a little more civilized, from having more connections with the Spanish."[22]

Ute culture was most profoundly affected by the Spaniards chiefly through trade. Ute Indians frequently visited Hispanic settlements in northern New Mexico beginning in the early eighteenth century, and they developed a symbiotic relationship with the residents of this frontier area.[23] A lucrative trade, largely unsanctioned by Spanish authorities in Santa Fe, sprang up between nomadic Utes and their Hispanic neighbors in towns such as Abiquiu. The Utes traded hides for horses or knives, and they exchanged deer or buffalo meat for corn or flour. Often, however, this trade revolved around human captives. Ute traders would offer Indian women or children, obtained through raids on other tribes, in exchange for horses. Hispanic settlers who purchased the captives in this illegal but popular form of trade would then either resell the captives or raise them in their own households. In times of scarcity, some Utes even traded their own children in order to obtain horses.[24]

Ute-Hispanic trade in northern New Mexico was mutually beneficial, and the two groups developed close ties free of dominance by either side.[25] A measure of the cultural interchange occurring between these two peoples is the large number of Spanish-speaking Utes found on the Southern Ute Reservation during its early years. The close ties between the Southern Utes and their Hispanic neighbors did not end with the onset of U.S. control or even with Ute removal from New Mexico to the reservation in Colorado. Many of the Utes' Hispanic acquaintances would eventually follow the Utes to the reservation, thus continuing their social and economic relationship. Of the three Southern Ute bands, trade with Hispanic settlers exerted the greatest impact on the Capote and the Mouache since geographical isolation blunted the impact of the Spanish presence on the Weeminuche.[26]

Interaction with Hispanic trading partners and growing reliance on European goods were not the only forms of Spanish influence on the Southern Ute bands. The Spanish settlement of New Mexico initiated a state of endemic warfare in the region that persisted through the late eighteenth century.[27] Nomadic Indians frequently raided Spanish settlements or pueblos in New Mexico, and the Spaniards retaliated with counterraids. In an attempt to protect settlements and contain their nomadic neighbors, Spanish officials forged alliances with various tribes, including the Utes. Thus, the Ute bands often fought against their Indian enemies as allies of the Spanish.[28]

Spanish influence was thus substantial, but neither Spain nor Mexico was ever able to dominate the Utes or seize their lands. Geography was the key to the persistence of Ute independence from Spanish control. Both the rugged basin-and-range terrain of the Ute domain and its location on the periphery of the Spanish colony served to insulate the Ute bands from the levels of disruption experienced by both the Pueblo peoples in the heart of New Mexico and the Comanches who roamed the nearby open plains.[29]

The eighteenth century was the apogee of Ute power. The Ute bands had expanded their territorial domain and were enjoying a new material prosperity and enhanced security against enemy intrusions. They occasionally felt pressure from the Spaniards to the south, but the Utes had not been forced to yield territory.

The glory days of the Southern Utes and their northern kin did not last long. Whereas the Spanish—and later, Mexican—presence had been only minimally disruptive, a far more dangerous force was approaching from the east. Zebulon Pike and his men were but a puny vanguard of the immense Anglo-American invasion that would soon explode across the land. The United States—stronger, wealthier, and more populous than either New Spain or Mexico—posed a much greater threat.[30] The Utes would find this influx much more destructive of their established way of life than the earlier intrusion from the south. From their eighteenth-century pinnacle, the Southern Utes were about to descend into a century of defeat and decline.

TREATIES AND RESERVATIONS

With the end of the Mexican War and the signing of the Treaty of Guadalupe-Hidalgo in 1848, the Ute domain became U.S. territory. Soon thereafter, the U.S. government negotiated the first of its many treaties with the Ute Indians. The Calhoun Treaty, also called the Treaty of Abiquiu, was signed by Mouache and Capote leaders in 1849 and ratified by the U.S. Senate the following year. This treaty recognized U.S. jurisdiction over the Ute lands and permitted the federal government to establish military posts and Indian agencies on these lands.[31] Nevertheless, Ute raiding, directed mainly toward Anglo wagon trains and military installations, continued sporadically into the 1850s; and a brief war broke out in 1854 when the Mouache responded to the intrusions of white settlers by conducting raids on various ranches and settlements. The offending Utes were defeated by a military force from New Mexico, and a treaty signed on September 1, 1855, ended the fighting but was never ratified by the U.S. Senate.[32] Never again did any of the three Southern Ute bands engage in warfare with the United States.

A more controversial treaty was negotiated in 1863 at the Ute agency in Conejos, and it was signed by President Abraham Lincoln in late 1864 and subsequently ratified. Many Utes were angered by this treaty because, while it relinquished claim to one-quarter of the Ute domain—land occupied by several bands—only one band, the Tabeguache, had signed the agreement. The Capote and Mouache representatives refused to sign; the Weeminuche declined to even send a representative to the conference.[33] This Treaty of Conejos, also called the Tabeguache Treaty, was favored by the leaders of this band because, while relinquishing the hunting grounds of other Ute bands, it maintained Ute title to the land of the Tabeguache band.[34]

An important actor at these negotiations was Ouray, a chief of the Tabeguache band. Son of a Jicarilla Apache father and a Tabeguache mother, Ouray had followed the normal custom of becoming a member of his mother's people, whom he joined in 1850 after spending his early years as a sheepherder in New Mexico.[35] Ouray's mixed ancestry was not unusual since many Utes from northern New Mexico had allied themselves and intermarried with branches of the Jicarilla Apache tribe.[36] At the 1863 talks, the U.S. government began to recognize the cooperative and influential Ouray as head chief of all the Utes, when in fact he held no such position. The Tabeguache leader had never been selected by his fellow Utes to play such a preeminent role, nor was he considered by most Utes to be a particularly powerful chief. Furthermore, the various Ute bands had never before acknowledged the existence of a head chief over all the bands. Many of the Southern Utes, led by Chief Ignacio of the Weeminuche, did not support Ouray's leadership.[37] Although his leadership of all Utes was thus of questionable legitimacy, Ouray did prove to be an effective advocate for his own band. The favorable treatment he obtained for himself and his Tabeguache people between 1863 and 1880, as in the Treaty of Conejos, greatly exceeded that accorded any other Great Basin Indian group except the Eastern Shoshone under Chief Washakie.[38]

Given the lack of tribal support for the 1863 agreement, a new treaty was negotiated in 1868. A Ute delegation, including Ouray as the government-recognized chief spokesman for the tribe, went to Washington and proceeded to sign away one-third of the tribe's land base. The Utes lost the portion of their domain lying east of the Continental Divide, retaining only the western slope of Colorado—that part of the state lying west of the Divide. The treaty also provided for the establishment of two agencies on the Ute reservation to serve the bands' needs—one in the north along the White River, the other in the south on the Los Pinos River.[39] But the Southern Ute bands, which were supposed to be served by the Los Pinos Agency, refused to leave their current domain, which lay mostly in northern New Mexico. Thus began the long battle among the Southern Utes, the U.S. government, and a variety of interested residents and officials—hailing from several western territories and states—over what should be done with the Southern Ute Indians.

The initial fight was over the government's plan to move the remaining Mouaches, Capotes, and Weeminuches in New Mexico out of that territory and into Colorado, where their reservation was actually located. Both the 1868 treaty and the Brunot Agreement of 1874 called for the establishment of a "Southern Ute Agency" to be located on the southern part of the large Ute reservation; the three Southern Ute bands were then to be relocated to this site.[40] The Brunot Agreement's primary purpose, however, was the acquisition by the United States of another piece of Ute territory, the rich San Juan mining district, which was being overrun, illegally, by prospectors following the discovery of gold and silver. By virtue of this agreement, the Utes ceded this large rectangular area—right in the middle of their reservation—to the United States in exchange for annuities to be provided by the federal government. Thus, even before the Southern Utes had agreed to locate on their reservation, it was again reduced in size.

The Ute bands in New Mexico were reluctant to move, and the new Southern Ute Agency failed to materialize. In the meantime, these bands continued to be issued supplies at temporary agencies at Abiquiu and Cimarron in New Mexico. This was not an ideal situation, as the agents in charge regularly reported. S. A. Russell lamented the state of affairs at Abiquiu in his 1876 report regarding the Utes in his charge: "Their moral condition is worse than a year ago, and will continue to grow worse as long as the agency is continued at this place, where they can easily obtain, through the Mexicans, all the whiskey they want."[41] And once again the location of the Weeminuche domain had placed the members of this band largely beyond the reach of outside influence. Agent Russell stated in 1877 that, whereas the Capote Utes typically stayed close to the agency, the Weeminuche Utes, who lived 50 to 150 miles away, seldom appeared at all.[42]

Finally, the impasse ended when Congress passed an appropriation bill in 1877 providing for establishment of the new agency.

On June 7, 1878, Agent Francis Weaver stood along the banks of the Rio de los Pinos (the Pine River) at a central location in the southern portion of the Ute reservation.[43] Here, in a fertile valley stretching south from the foothills of the San Juan Mountains and surrounded by dry mesas dotted with sagebrush, piñon, and juniper, he began the construction of facilities for the long-sought agency.

The battle over the fate of the Southern Utes was far from over, however. The Indians themselves were not happy with the site. When Weaver encountered the Weeminuche leader Ignacio en route to the Los Pinos River site, the chief demanded that the agency be established to the east on the Navajo River. The same complaint was voiced by Utes still in New Mexico who felt that they were being pushed too far to the west and forced to surrender more land.[44]

After the New Mexico agencies were closed and a troop escort provided, the reluctant Indians finally headed north, and they began to filter into the Los Pinos River Agency, site of the future town of Ignacio, late in 1878. The issue was still far from settled, however, for at the same time that Agent Weaver was having temporary buildings constructed at the new agency, Congress was considering a bill for the removal of the Utes from Colorado. Soon after the buildings were completed, the agent received a letter from the commissioner of Indian affairs directing him to suspend further construction.[45] Thus, the battle over what to do with the Southern Utes began anew. Many land-hungry Coloradans—including William N. Byers, who had acquired land at Hot Sulphur Springs and whose *Rocky Mountain News* editorialized that "The Utes Must Go!"—wanted all the state's Utes removed to Indian Territory.[46] Others sought to consolidate the Utes at the White River Agency, and a bill to this effect passed Congress in 1878. The Southern Utes rejected this arrangement as they did not want to leave their traditional home in the south, nor were they interested in living with the Northern Utes at

White River. They did agree to relinquish their present reservation in exchange for a new one to the east, but Congress refused to accept this alternative.[47] Having just completed one relocation, the Southern Utes were not particularly eager to move again, but many of them saw the proposed reservation to the east, located as it was on mountainous terrain, as a means of thwarting the government's plans for making farmers of them. In fact, as the Ute removal struggle lingered on through the following decade, many Southern Utes continued to express support for relocation proposals not because they wanted to leave the Los Pinos River area but because they hoped to avoid the prospect of being forced to till the soil and of having their land allotted in severalty.[48] Allotment of reservation land involved the division of tribal land into small sections, typically 160 acres each, for the use and eventual ownership of individual tribal members.

AN UNCERTAIN FUTURE

While the Southern Utes were settling uneasily in their new homeland in southwestern Colorado, two of the Northern Ute bands were even more distressed at the state of affairs on their reservation in the northwestern portion of the state. Referred to now as the White River Utes, after the agency that had been established to serve them, the people of the Yampa and Parianuc bands were headed for a violent confrontation with the agent in charge at White River. Assigned to White River in 1879, Agent N. C. Meeker was determined to implement the federal government's Indian policies, which called for transforming the Utes into farmers and ranchers. Amid growing conflict with his Ute charges, Meeker's decision to plow up a Ute racetrack in 1879 led to an ugly confrontation with leaders of the White River Utes. Agent Meeker then panicked and called for military protection. The sudden arrival of a U.S. Cavalry detachment frightened the Utes, and violence quickly exploded across the reservation. Ute warriors engaged the cavalry troops in a battle at Milk Creek, and thirty-seven Utes and twelve soldiers were killed in several days of fighting. Meanwhile, a party of White River Indians attacked the agency, massacring Meeker and seven male agency employees and kidnapping the three women present at the agency. The fighting failed to spread to either the Tabeguache band or to the Southern Utes, and the White River Utes soon agreed to release their captives and cease fighting.[49]

The "Meeker Massacre," as it was quickly labeled, sparked increasingly strident demands from many white Coloradans that all of the Utes—not just the White River Utes involved in the fighting—be removed from the state. Colorado governor Frederick Pitkin stated his position to the press, revealing the underlying motive of many Indian-hating Coloradans: "My idea is that, unless removed by the government, they must necessarily be exterminated. I could raise 25,000 men to protect the settlers in 24 hours. The state would be willing to settle the Indian trouble at its own expense. The advantages that would accrue from the throwing open of 12,000,000 acres of land to miners and settlers would more than compensate all expenses incurred."[50]

In the aftermath of the violence at White River, Southern Ute leaders Ignacio, Buckskin Charlie, Severo, and Ojo Blanco traveled to Washington, where they agreed to the relocation of their bands. Approval by three-quarters of the adult male Southern Utes was required for the agreement to go into effect, and in this endeavor the government was counting on Ouray's assistance. The gravely ill chief died, however, while on a visit to the Southern Ute Agency, before all the necessary signatures could be obtained. Shortly before his death, Ouray selected Buckskin Charlie, a Mouache chief, to be chief of the Southern Utes. When Ouray died, Charlie and several other Utes buried the chief's body in a rock crevice not far from the agency, where it would remain hidden until 1925.[51]

Despite initial protests by the Southern Ute people, especially among the Weeminuche, tribal members eventually approved the relocation agreement. However, as with most agreements concluded between these bands and the U.S. Government, the terms were not carried out as planned. By the end of 1882, all of the Northern Utes—both the White River Utes and the Tabeguache (Uncompahgre) band—had in fact been removed to Ute reservations in Utah, as called for in the agreement. The former group was sent to the Uintah Reservation, while the latter band was relocated to the new Ouray Reservation adjacent to the existing Utah reservation. Plans to locate the Southern Utes on allotments along the La Plata River, however, were derailed by the discovery that the dusty land there was incapable of supporting the farming activities of 1,200 Indians.[52] Thus, the Southern Utes were not relocated. They continued to live on their southwestern Colorado reservation, but their future was still uncertain. Efforts to relocate the three remaining Ute bands of Colorado would persist for the next twelve years before the issue was finally resolved.

Life on their reservation was made more difficult for the Southern Utes by the growing presence of Anglo Americans in the area. In 1881 the Denver and Rio Grande Railroad constructed a line across the eastern section of the reservation, and more and more ranchers were settling in close proximity to Ute land. Relations between the Utes and their neighbors were frequently tense. Although Anglo-American settlers often complained loudly of problems caused by the Indians, the Utes were generally guilty of nothing more than begging meals from neighboring ranches—a totally peaceful activity but one that ranchers bitterly resented.[53] Substantially greater trespasses were visited on the Utes by whites. In 1878 the Southern Ute agent reported thousands of head of cattle and sheep illegally grazing on reservation land, driving off wild game on which the Utes still depended for subsistence. As cattle operations continued to trespass on Ute land, particularly in the western section of the reservation, conflicts between In-

dians and cowboys became more prevalent. In 1884 some cowboys from a large cattle company were killed in a clash with Utes.
The following year, in an apparent revenge killing, a family of six
sleeping Utes was murdered in its tent. Agent Christian Stollsteimer later reported of the murderers, "Even if they were known,
I doubt whether the State authorities would take steps to arrest
and punish them. An Indian is hardly considered a human being
by a certain class of whites."[54]

Frustrated by increasing encroachment on the reservation by
railroads and ranchers, and not enthusiastic about the prospect of
becoming farmers, the Ute people began in the mid 1880s to call
for a move to southeastern Utah. Buckskin Charlie and Ignacio
both testified before a U.S. Senate committee in 1886 in support
of this proposal. Their testimony identified many of the problems
posed by their current situation in southwestern Colorado. Buckskin Charlie stated through an interpreter that he wanted to move
"because of the encroachments of white men." He further explained: "We come here to see if we cannot exchange our reservation for another. . . . We want to go west of the present reservation. . . . We want to go west and get grass land and raise stock.
Where we are we do not live comfortably." When asked about
his interest in having a boarding school on the new reservation,
Charlie responded affirmatively—with one stipulation: "We are
willing to send our children to school; but not away from home,
because when they go away they die, and we cannot account
for it."[55]

Ignacio's testimony, again through an interpreter, is similarly
revealing of life on the reservation in the 1880s:

Q: Do you agree with Chief Charlie in what he has said?
A: Yes, that is all right. Whatever Charlie has said is straight.
Q: Have you got any stock?
A: I have got some sheep.
Q: How many sheep?
A: Very few.

Q: How many?

A: About a hundred.

Q: What do you do with the wool?

A: I sell it.

Q: What do you do with the money when you get it?

A: I have got a mouth. I buy things to eat.

Q: What do you do in the summer?

A: I worked all summer in a ditch, but the water did not run
    through it.

Q: Have you got any children?

A: No, they died last summer.

Q: Do all of the Indians of your tribe want to move west?

A: Yes.[56]

Ignacio's last surviving child had been one of twelve Southern
Ute children to fall victim to disease at the Albuquerque Indian
School between 1883 and 1885. Nearly one-half of the twenty-
seven Ute children sent to the school during this time died.[57]
Given this disastrous experience, Buckskin Charlie's objection
to off-reservation boarding schools is hardly surprising. Furthermore, Ignacio's experience with the waterless ditch is indicative
of the problems plaguing early agricultural efforts on the Southern Ute Reservation.

Congress passed a Ute removal bill in 1888, and the requisite
three-quarters of adult male tribal members subsequently approved
the tribe's relocation to a new reservation in southeastern Utah,
but follow-up legislation died in the House, and the move never
took place.[58] The political squabble over where to put the Southern Utes continued. Coloradans, eager to seize Ute land for their
own use, called loudly for the removal of the Utes to Utah; meanwhile, residents of the latter territory, along with Eastern reformers who felt that the arid isolation of Utah was not conducive to
"civilizing" the Utes, actively opposed any such move and were
able to quash numerous removal bills in Congress. Agents at the
Southern Ute Agency often joined the fray on one side or the

other depending on how their personal financial interests would be affected by removal of the Indians in their charge.[59]

The stalemate over Ute removal was finally broken with the introduction of an alternative solution: the Southern Utes would remain on their present reservation, but they would be placed on individual allotments of 160 acres each. The Hunter Act, passed by Congress early in 1895, applied the concept of allotment in severalty of tribal lands to the Southern Ute Reservation. The initial Ute removal bill of 1880 had called for allotment of the reservation, and allotment of tribal land was subsequently made official U.S. policy with the passage of the Dawes Severalty Act in 1887. Allotment in severalty involved subdividing commonly held tribal land into 160-acre plots for assignment to individual tribal members. These individuals would have full use of their allotments for the duration of a twenty-five-year period in which the land was to be held in trust by the U.S. government. At the conclusion of this period, the allottees would gain full title to their land.

To reformers and government officials such as Senator Henry Dawes of Massachusetts, the elimination of communal ownership of land was the key to "civilizing" the Indians. Before sponsoring the Allotment Act, Dawes had visited the lands of the Five Civilized Tribes (Cherokee, Creek, Choctaw, Chickasaw, and Seminole) in Indian Territory. He admired the tangible achievements of these people, but this did not offset what he saw as the single biggest blight among these tribes: "Yet the defect of the system was apparent. They have not got as far as they can go because they own their land in common, and under that [system] there is no enterprise to make your home any better than that of your neighbors. There is no selfishness, which is at the bottom of civilization."[60] With the passage of the Dawes Act in 1887, it became the official policy of the U.S. government to introduce "selfishness" into tribal societies through the allotment of tribal lands.

To Colorado residents disappointed by the fact their Indian neighbors would not be leaving after all, the Hunter Bill offered at least some consolation: after the allotment process was completed, the remainder of the reservation, so-called surplus land, would be opened to white settlement. The Hunter Bill also provided another option to the members of the three bands: those who elected not to accept allotments could continue to live on tribal land "in the West forty miles of the present reservation."[61]

Not only did passage of the Hunter Bill end a long period of uncertainty and frustration for the Weeminuche, Capote, and Mouache bands; it also presented them with a stark choice of lifestyle. Although none of the Southern Ute bands had ever shared the Indian Service's enthusiasm for agriculture, by 1895 differences were emerging among the bands concerning the willingness of tribal members to begin farming. Most of the Mouache and Capote Utes agreed to accept individual allotments, but the Weeminuche Utes, perhaps as a result of their relatively infrequent contact with Europeans, almost unanimously rejected severalty and the accompanying expectations of an agricultural lifestyle.

A key factor in these divergent responses to the Hunter Bill was the role of tribal leaders. Forty-five-year-old Buckskin Charlie, son of a Ute father and an Apache mother, had been the preeminent chief of the Mouache band since around 1870. Buckskin Charlie, also known in later years as Charles Buck, was part Capote as well as Mouache and so became a leader of this band as well.[62] Following Ouray's death in 1880, and at the request of the dying Tabeguache leader, Charlie became principal chief of the Southern Utes, although his authority never actually extended to the Weeminuche band.[63] Charlie exerted considerable influence over both the Mouache and Capote peoples at a time when the Ute way of life was increasingly coming under assault. With hunting becoming less productive because of diminishing game populations and with the tribe's land base about to be reduced once again, Charlie realized that the traditional hunting-gathering economy was no longer a viable option. The Mouache chief was one of the first Southern Utes to settle down and begin farming. Largely through his example and influence, the Mouache and Capote people became interested in education and farming.[64] Even so, there was considerable hesitation among the people of these two bands. When the proposal for allotment was put before the 301 eligible male voters among the Mouache and Capote, 153 voted in favor, while 148 voiced opposition to allotment of the reservation. Although this vote was certainly not a resounding expression of Ute support, the secretary of the interior seized on the narrow victory as evidence of tribal endorsement of allotment.[65]

The Weeminuche chief, Ignacio, exhibited a different response to the Southern Ute predicament in the 1890s. Ignacio was by no means totally opposed to accommodation with Anglo-American ways. Although not always supportive of Indian boarding schools, he did not reject the idea of education; he had, after all, sent his own children to boarding schools—with fatal results. He lived for a time in an adobe house provided to him by the government, and he had also served as captain of the Indian Police on the reservation.[66] But Ignacio was not eager to take up his own piece of land and till the soil, nor did he want to endure any longer the encroachments of white neighbors.

Following passage of the Utah removal bill in 1888, Ignacio and his Weeminuche people had eagerly headed west toward the new reservation. When that plan was abandoned by the government, Ignacio and his frustrated Weeminuche followers had for the most part remained in the barren western portion of the existing reservation, where they established a camp far from the Los Pinos River Agency. As of October 1894, the Weeminuche ceased coming to the agency.[67] Unlike Buckskin Charlie, who reacted to the changed environment by opting for an agricultural existence—at least to a limited extent—Ignacio's resentment of U.S. government control and of white ways, and his bitterness over the impending shrinkage of tribal lands, prompted him to lead his band to the isolated west end of the reservation, where they would suffer less outside interference.[68] Although he would subsequently accept an allotment for himself, one that he would settle on much later, Ignacio in 1895 led the Weeminuche people in refusing allotments.[69]

By April 14, 1896, 371 Mouache and Capote Utes had accepted allotments—typically 160-acre plots for each family head and 80 acres apiece for minors—covering a total of 72,811.15 acres. Most of these allotments were located along the Los Pinos River, with a few along the Animas and La Plata Rivers. Allotments along the Los Pinos were contiguous in order to keep out whites, particularly potential "bootleggers."[70] Meanwhile, the Weeminuche settled to the west on land in common—land that would remain under tribal, rather than individual, ownership. To meet the needs of the Weeminuche Utes, the Navajo Springs Subagency, located in the shadow of Sleeping Ute Mountain along Navajo Wash, was established in 1896.

On May 4, 1899, many neighboring non-Indians finally got their wish when the remaining unallotted portions of the reservation were opened to settlement. A total of 523,079 acres in the eastern portion of the reservation became available to non-Indian settlers for $1.25 per acre. Eager would-be farmers and ranchers lined up in anticipation, and as clocks struck noon, bells were rung and whistles blown, signaling the opening of the long-awaited land rush.[71] The bulk of the eastern portion of the reservation was thus taken from Ute ownership, and the tracts still under Indian control as individual allotments were often bounded by newly acquired non-Indian landholdings. No longer did the tribe possess a contiguous block of land. The unallotted Weeminuche, however, did retain a contiguous reserve at the west end of the old reservation.

The Southern Ute Tribe, which had never truly existed as a unified entity, had split. The allotted Mouache and Capote Utes

living on the eastern section of the old reservation would continue to be known as the Southern Utes, whereas the unallotted
Weeminuche band, living on land in common in the relatively
isolated western end of the old reservation, would come to be
known as the Ute Mountain Utes. Now two distinct peoples living on separate reservations, the newly divided tribes would pursue starkly divergent paths in their respective homelands.

Ute delegation members and government officials in Washington, 1880. *From left to right:* Ignacio, Secretary of the Interior Carl Schurz, Woretsiz, Ouray, General Charles Adams, and Ouray's wife, Chipeta. This Ute delegation went to Washington in the aftermath of the 1879 Meeker Massacre and negotiated an agreement whereby the Northern Utes of Colorado were relocated to Utah. The three Southern Ute bands were never relocated as called for in the agreement. Ouray, recognized by the U.S. government as the principal chief of the Utes, died soon afterward while attempting to win Southern Ute acceptance of this agreement. (Courtesy, Colorado Historical Society, F7100.)

Ignacio, the Weeminuche leader who became the first chief of the Ute Mountain Ute Tribe. Ignacio led his people in rejecting allotment in severalty in 1895, preferring instead to settle on commonly held land in the western end of the reservation. This William Henry Jackson photograph shows the chief wearing his tribal police badge. (Courtesy, Colorado Historical Society, 5720.)

Buckskin Charlie (also called Charles Buck), the Mouache leader who served as chief of the Southern Ute Tribe from the time of Ouray's death in 1880 until his own passing in 1936. Charlie was one of the first of his people to begin farming, and he was instrumental in convincing most Mouache and Capote Utes to accept allotment in 1895–1896. He was also, to the consternation of Indian Service officials, an active participant in the peyote rites of the Native American Church. (Courtesy, Denver Public Library, Western History Department, F2797.)

Southern Ute Indians attending the city of Boulder's semicentennial celebration in November 1909. Chief Buckskin Charlie is standing at center; his son Antonio Buck is standing third from the left, and his wife, Emma Buck, is seated third from the left. The traditional dress worn by these tribal members, as well as the tipi in back, reveals the extent to which the Utes adopted elements of Plains Indians culture following acquisition of the horse. (Courtesy, Colorado Historical Society, F3617.)

The Navajo Springs Subagency, established in the Montezuma Valley in 1896 to serve the Weeminuche Utes who had recently settled in the isolated western end of the reservation. After some twenty years at Navajo Springs, the agency was relocated a few miles to the northwest, closer to Sleeping Ute Mountain (seen here in the background), at a place called Towaoc. (Courtesy, Colorado Historical Society, F30234, Charles Goodman photograph.)

Ute Mountain Ute students posing with their teacher S. F. Stacher and his family at Navajo Springs in 1906. Stacher, who would later become superintendent of the Consolidated Ute Agency, established the first school on the Ute Mountain Reservation here in 1906. (Courtesy, Colorado Historical Society, F25131.)

A 1924 visit to Ouray's original burial place, the location of which remained a closely guarded secret until that year. Buckskin Charlie, at left in the foreground, displays bones retrieved from the crevice in which Ouray's remains had been buried nearly forty-five years previously. (Courtesy, Colorado Historical Society, F1412.)

Ute tribal leaders posing on horseback in front of the Consolidated Ute Agency in Ignacio on the occasion of Ouray's reburial, May 24, 1925. The four men on the left were pallbearers at the original burial of Ouray's remains in 1880; they were, from left to right: George Norris, Joseph Price, Colorow, and Buckskin Charlie. (Courtesy, Denver Public Library, Western History Department, F6377, George L. Beau photograph.)

The reburial of Ouray, May 24, 1925. A lengthy funeral procession, with Ouray's remains transported in the brush-covered pickup truck shown here, proceeded to the Tabeguache chief's final resting place in the Southern Ute tribal cemetery. (Courtesy, Colorado Historical Society, F28259.)

Edwin Cloud, in a 1932 photograph. Cloud belonged to a family that was very active in the political, cultural, and spiritual affairs of the Southern Ute Tribe. A subchief under Buckskin Charlie, Cloud was also his tribe's Sun Dance chief and one of the last medicine men among his people. Like most Southern Ute shamans, but unlike their counterparts at Ute Mountain, Edwin Cloud strongly opposed peyotism. (Courtesy, Colorado Historical Society, F41910, Leroy Hafen photograph.)

Herding sheep in the lower reaches of Mancos Canyon, 1933. Stock raising, centering first around sheep and later cattle, was for years the predominant economic activity on the Ute Mountain Reservation. (Courtesy, Colorado Historical Society.)

A women's sewing meeting at a camp near Towaoc, 1934. Throughout the first half of the twentieth century, most Ute Mountain Utes lived in tents such as the one pictured here. (Courtesy, Colorado Historical Society, F34247.)

The Ute Mountain Boarding School girls basketball team in 1935. In this year, the boarding school in Towaoc was closed and a day school opened in its place. Several years later, the Ute Mountain School was closed completely, leaving the people at Ute Mountain with no school on their reservation. (Courtesy, Colorado Historical Society, F7149.)

The campus of the Southern Ute Boarding School, located just north of Ignacio adjacent to the Consolidated Ute Agency. Education, through boarding schools such as this one, was long regarded by the Indian Service as the cornerstone of the government's assimilation policy. The building at far right is the Edward T. Taylor Hospital, which opened in 1933. The hospital closed in 1955, and the Southern Ute Tribe established its tribal offices in this building in 1959. (Courtesy, Colorado Historical Society, F1612).

2

TWO TRIBES
IN A NEW CENTURY

As the Southern Ute people stood on the threshold of the twentieth century, the uncertainty surrounding the fate of their reservation was finally behind them. Unlike their cousins in the Tabeguache, Yampa, and Parianuc bands, the people of the Weeminuche, Capote, and Mouache bands had been able to retain at least a small corner of their original domain in Colorado; and after enduring nearly two decades under the constant threat of removal, these Utes now seemed securely established on their two reservations in the southwestern corner of the state.

The Ute people still faced a tremendously difficult situation, however. They were still confronted with the assimilationist policies of the U.S. Indian Office, which sought to impose a new way of life on them. Such government policies were even more frustrating for the Utes since they were administered by an ever-changing parade of Indian Service officials, many of whom were corrupt or incompetent. The Southern Ute people also faced the challenge of adapting their cultural heritage to the alien socioeconomic system of twentieth-century America. As the people of the Weeminuche, Capote, and Mouache bands sought to make this painful transition, they did so in often distinct ways on their two separate reservations. The "allotted Utes" of the latter two bands and the "unallotted Utes" of the former band both faced a common dilemma, and yet their respective problems and responses were often quite unique.

THE ALLOTTED UTES

The Mouache and Capote people were not prepared to embark on successful farming careers as they took up their allotments in 1896. For seventeen years, the Southern Ute Agency had existed on a year-to-year basis, its future fate far from certain. As a result, little had been done to prepare for agricultural development of the reservation. And the Utes were anything but enthusiastic, at least initially, about adopting this way of life. Indian Service personnel regularly commented on the Utes' disdain for labor. Agent Henry Page's 1879 report indicated that these Indians were a far cry from becoming the "civilized" farmers of Indian Office dreams: "The Southern Ute Indians are wholly uncivilized . . . and as a class they are opposed to labor in any form, considering the same degrading, and only to be performed by whites and 'squaws.'"[1] The situation looked no brighter the following year; the Utes still lived in tents and brush shelters, moving frequently across the reservation. None spoke English, none had attempted any farming, and they still preferred their traditional medicine men to non-Indian physicians.[2]

The Indian Office enlisted the services of two key reservation officials—the agency farmer and the field matron—to help its Indian wards become self-sufficient agrarians. Agency farmers were charged with providing Indian men with agricultural instruction and encouraging them to begin farming on their allotments. The agency farmer's female counterpart, the field matron, was given the job of working with Indian women, teaching them the woman's role in maintaining an agrarian home. Thus, the field matron at the Southern Ute Agency instructed Ute women in such domestic arts as food storage, cooking, sewing, cleaning, and gardening.[3]

Slowly the Ute people, particularly those of the Mouache and Capote bands who would subsequently accept allotment, began to adjust to the new reality of life on their reservation, and the government's assimilation policies started to yield some minor successes. Although the Utes still spoke virtually no English in 1885 and continued to "tenaciously adhere to their blankets" rather than adopting the desired "citizen's garb," as government officials referred to the clothing worn by white Americans, the Southern Ute agent noted approvingly that many Indians were herding sheep and several industrious individuals were engaged in farming. Most of the farming on Ute allotments, however, was being done by non-Indians, particularly local Mexican-American settlers. Beginning in the late 1880s, Mouache and Capote allottees arranged shares agreements whereby tenants farmed their land and remitted one-half the harvest to the Ute landholder. Many allotted Utes may have been spurred to enter farm shares agreements by the need to supplement the meager quantity of supplies issued to them by the agency. In 1885 the Southern Ute agent reported that the rations provided to the Utes were "not enough to keep them from starving."[4] In any case, thirty-one of the thirty-two Ute farms in 1887 were being worked by Hispanic farmers under such shares agreements.[5]

This was just one example of the steadily growing interaction between Southern Utes and their Hispanic neighbors. The association between these two groups was actually a continuation of the symbiotic relationship that the Utes and Hispanic settlers had forged in northern New Mexico beginning in the seventeenth century. Many of these Mexican Americans came to the newly established Southern Ute Reservation on the invitation of the Utes themselves. At a time when their Anglo neighbors were encroaching on reservation lands and actively working to secure

their removal, the Ute people found these New Mexican trans-
plants to be "useful and entertaining neighbors," as one scholar
has put it.[6] For their part, the Mexican-American neighbors
clearly benefited economically from their renewed association
with the Utes. They were allowed to graze stock on the tribal
range. They found employment clearing land and digging irrigation ditches for Ute farms, which they themselves often ended up
farming. Hispanic workers also built houses for thirty-two tribal
members and then were able to live in these homes themselves
since the intended occupants disdained living in such structures.
Some of the local Mexican Americans, to the disgust of many an
agency superintendent, sold liquor to the Utes and profited from
gambling with them.[7]

A significant amount of cultural adaptation took place between
the two neighboring groups, and as a result of the steady contact
between Mexican Americans and Utes, Spanish became the lin-
gua franca of the Southern Ute Agency and the reservation community.[8] In general, a mutually beneficial relationship between
Ute and Hispanic neighbors served the tribal members as a buffer
against Indian Office domination and the intolerance of Anglo
neighbors.[9] For example, it was one of the Utes' Mexican-American neighbors, Jose Blas Lucero, who served as a spokesman for
disgruntled Southern Ute leaders in 1925 and 1926 when they
stepped forward to protest U.S. government policies and actions
of the superintendent.

By the opening of the twentieth century, the allotted Utes had
begun to make some strides toward acculturation. While the superintendent penned a less than encouraging report on the condition of the unallotted Weeminuche in 1900, he expressed opti-
mism with regard to developments in the eastern section of the
reservation. The Indians there were said to be rapidly developing
their allotments into "fine farms," which yielded revenue to their
owners. Furthermore, nearly two-thirds of the total population
was at this time wearing at least some element of "citizen's dress,"

with most of these individuals belonging to the ranks of the allotted Utes.[10]

One problem resulting from the long battle over relocation was
the lack of schools in the eastern section of the reservation. A
day school, attended by twelve to fourteen Ute children, had been
established near the agency in 1886. Attendance dropped, however, after the facility was converted to a boarding school. By
1890, amid all the uncertainty over the continued existence of
the reservation, the building had deteriorated, and the school
was closed after only a few years of operation.[11] Fort Lewis near
Hesperus was converted from a military post to a boarding school
in 1891, but this was located far from the Los Pinos River valley,
and enrollment was meager.[12] Only twenty-five Utes attended
school there in 1900, and of this number one died and several
others ran away.[13] Not surprisingly, the Southern Utes disdained
boarding schools after the deadly experience of Ute pupils at
the Albuquerque Indian School in 1885. Between 1885 and 1913,
very few Ute children were willingly sent to distant boarding
schools.[14] It was not until 1902, with the establishment of the
Southern Ute Boarding School adjacent to the agency, that a
school opened in the Los Pinos area. From this date forward, attendance increased steadily both at this school and at the Allen
Day School, which opened further up the valley in 1909. Tribal
members apparently accepted having their children attend these
schools as agency superintendents often complained that they
lacked sufficient capacity to accommodate all the pupils. In 1920
the boarding school was closed, and Ute children began to be enrolled in local public schools.[15]

Despite such instances of Ute adjustment to Anglo-American
society, problems persisted on the reservation. Many pertained
to the allotments. The existence of multiple heirs to individual
allotments, the growing numbers of tribal members born since
allotment, and the practice of allotments being sold through
arrangements made by agency superintendents all combined to

create a growing class of landless Southern Utes. To protect Indians such as the Utes from losing their land to predatory non-Indian buyers, the U.S. government was obligated under the 1887 Dawes Severalty Act to hold all Indian allotments in trust for a period of twenty-five years. As the years passed, however, the federal government proved increasingly lax in its trusteeship. One means by which trust protection was ended for individual Indian allottees was for the government to declare them "competent"; they were then granted patents for their land and were thus able to sell it. Additionally, agency superintendents were empowered to sell those allotments belonging to individuals who were deemed "incompetent" to run their own affairs or those claimed by multiple heirs. Commissioner of Indian Affairs Cato Sells was an ardent advocate of "freeing" Indians from federal protection, and between 1913 and 1921 he presided over the sale of more than 1 million acres of trust land nationwide.[16]

This general trend in U.S. Indian policy was certainly evident on the Southern Ute Reservation. Superintendent Charles Werner proudly reported to Washington that during 1911 he had sold 1,040 acres of inherited land and 1,400 acres of incompetent land.[17] Nor was this an isolated case for the Southern Utes. By 1934, 33,500 acres of land that had been allotted to the Mouache and Capote in 1896—46 percent of their total allotted land—had been sold to non-Indians.[18] Thus, during the early decades of the twentieth century, many Southern Utes were becoming landless or left with only small allotments, reduced in size through the division of inheritances or agency-sponsored sale of land.

Many of those who did own allotments lacked the water needed to irrigate their land. Access to water has long been a problem for many tribes with reservations in the arid West. This has been the case in spite of a 1908 U.S. Supreme Court decision asserting the priority of Indian water rights over the claims of most non-Indian parties. Western states allocate water according to the doctrine of prior appropriation, under which the earliest user of water has highest priority. The Winters doctrine, which arose out of the 1908 *Winters* v. *U.S.* case, holds that a tribe's priority date for water is the date of establishment of its reservation—even if the tribe did not use the water at that time. The Winters doctrine, in theory, guarantees most tribes preeminent rights to the water flowing through their reservations. In reality, however, state and federal governments have typically ignored the Winters doctrine, and Indian water has been appropriated for the use of non-Indians—often through water projects built by the federal government.[19]

The Southern Utes and Ute Mountain Utes, like most western tribes, have lost water as a result of the federal government's failure to uphold their water rights. In the case of the Mouache and Capote Utes, very few individuals were able to obtain the water needed to irrigate their allotments. In the early years of the reservation, water legally belonging to the Utes was continually taken for use by non-Indians. Ditches were built across the reservation, with or without government approval, from which the Utes derived little, if any, benefit. After a 1913 drought, the agency farmer predicted that if the following year was equally dry, "the Mexican, the Whiteman, and Government employees will get what water they can out of the Pine River and the Indians will get what is left provided their head-gates and ditches are in shape to handle even that little."[20] As late as 1908, many allotments were not reached by irrigation ditches, and the Utes were not getting the water they needed. In that year an assistant engineer at the agency urged the government to build a reservoir on the Los Pinos River to assure adequate supply for meeting Ute water needs.[21] The federal government took no action, and it was not until the early 1940s that Vallecito Reservoir was built upstream.

Those Southern Utes with land and water and the inclination to farm faced an additional problem—lack of adequate farming equipment. U.S. Indian policy throughout the first half century of the Southern Ute Reservation centered on turning Indians into farmers, and yet the Mouache and Capote allottees were continually denied access to the tools and machinery needed to successfully bring about this transformation. The federal government often balked at making the capital expenditures, such as investments in draft animals, irrigation ditches, and modern machinery, needed to support Ute agricultural operations. Adding to government stinginess was the problem posed by the Indian Office's emphasis on hand labor at a time when neighboring non-Indian farmers were generally working the land in a mechanized fashion. For example, an 1884 request by the Southern Ute agent for authority to purchase a reaper was denied with the explanation that the secretary of the interior "refuses to sanction the purchase of labor-saving machinery at Indian Agencies."[22]

The biggest problem of all on the Southern Ute Reservation— at least in the eyes of Indian Service officials—was the failure of the Utes to become self-supporting. The Ute people continued to rely for their subsistence on rations and annual cash payments, or annuities, which they had been promised in various treaties with the U.S. government. Government officials, however, regarded these treaty obligations instead as "dole"—handouts that were counterproductive to the Indian Service's efforts to ensure that all Indians engaged in productive work.

The Indian Service periodically instituted new policies on the Southern Ute Reservation intended to push all tribal members to support themselves. These efforts accelerated in the first two decades of the new century. In 1913 a new policy of requiring labor in exchange for receiving rations was implemented, as was the new "reimbursable system," which required individual tribal members to reimburse the Indian Service for farm supplies purchased by the agency with tribal funds, with the tribal fund then replenished by payments from those receiving supplies. The new policies were a total failure: the Utes balked at having to work for rations that they insisted were owed to them by the government in exchange for past land cessions, and since their farm supplies

were purchased with tribal funds, they saw the reimbursable system as an attempt to charge them twice for needed supplies. They
were also bitter over the curtailment of cash annuity payments
after 1910. These annual payments to tribal members, guaranteed by various treaties and agreements between the Utes and
the U.S. government, were terminated following a multi-million-
dollar land claims judgment in favor of the Confederated Bands
of the Utes by the U.S. Court of Claims in 1910. In place of annuities from the federal government as called for in the treaties,
individual Utes would now receive per capita payments issued
from the interest on the judgment fund. Yet even these payments,
coming from the Ute bands' own land claims money, generally
never reached individual Utes in the form of cash. Instead, such
per capita payments were typically deposited directly into Individual Indian Accounts, to which tribal members could gain
access only with the superintendent's permission. Between 1913
and 1926, only a few of the many Utes with such bank accounts,
those deemed "competent Indians," were permitted to withdraw
substantial sums for use for their own "betterment."[23]

Though such policies did little to promote self-support, they
brought severe economic hardship to the Utes of the Los Pinos
River valley. Coming at a time when more and more allotted
Utes were becoming landless, reductions in rations and elimination of annuity payments placed many tribal members in a difficult economic squeeze. Superintendent Walter Runke bleakly
described the typical Southern Ute of 1914 as "a disgruntled,
half-starved Ute with a few decrepit head of horses or ponies to
help in his farm work . . . discouraged because his thin winter diet
has sapped the foundation of any ambition."[24]

By the mid 1920s, government efforts to assimilate the allotted
Utes had produced mixed results. These Indians, sometimes referred to as the "Ignacio Utes" following the 1909 founding of
the town of Ignacio 1 mile south of their agency,[25] had adopted
many of the trappings of modern Anglo-American life: they sent

their children to school, spoke some English, and engaged in some farming. Many lived in houses. Beneath the surface, however, they remained, in the words of agency personnel, "irritatingly, stubbornly and obnoxiously Ute."[26]

THE UNALLOTTED UTES

"We, the Weeminuche, balked, and refused to accept allotments. We did not want to become farmers, and left the fertile valley and established our own holdings in the shadow of our beloved mountain, the Sleeping Ute. We face barren hills and frowning cliffs— and love every inch of our home."[27] Thus did the Ute Mountain Tribal Council recall in 1970 the circumstances by which their ancestors had come to settle in the forbidding landscape of the Ute Mountain Reservation. High and dry mesas, dotted with piñon and juniper trees and deeply cut by rugged canyons, characterize most of the eastern section of the unallotted reservation. To the west of the mesas lies the grassy expanse of Montezuma Valley, drained by the usually waterless Navajo Wash. Sleeping Ute Mountain rises steeply on the west side of Montezuma Valley, and to the south and west of the Sleeping Ute stretches a vast expanse of barren land covered only by sparse desert grasses. Water is a rare commodity throughout this area of the San Juan Basin, with the Mancos River the only substantial watercourse on the reservation.

Despite such bleakness, the Weeminuche of both 1895 and 1970 were strongly attached to their small corner of Colorado, particularly to its most prominent landmark, Sleeping Ute Mountain. Long ago this mountain gave rise to a legend among the Ute people. It was said that once a Great Warrior God had come to fight against Evil Ones who were causing much trouble, and a tremendous battle ensued. After being wounded in this battle, the Great Warrior God lay down to rest and soon fell asleep. The blood flowing from his wound turned into water for all living creatures to drink. The Utes believed that when clouds gather around the peak—as they often do—the Warrior God is pleased with his people and is letting rain clouds slip from his pockets to provide them with water. They also believed that the Great Warrior God would one day rise again to help the Ute people fight their enemies.[28] From various vantage points in the Montezuma Valley to the east of Sleeping Ute Mountain, the long series of peaks does indeed resemble the figure of a reclining warrior. His head lies at the northern end of the mountain and his feet to the south; his arms are crossed over his chest, forming the highest point, Ute Peak, at an elevation of 9,977 feet. The town of Towaoc sits a couple miles to the east of the sleeping warrior's "East Toe." The Sleeping Ute towers over the reservation and is visible from far beyond its boundaries.

"The lands are very good, but we have no water. Washington said we would have water." Thus did Chief Ignacio describe the lands to which he and his people had moved in 1895. Their land was ruggedly beautiful and blessed with impressive landmarks: the towering presence of Sleeping Ute Mountain, the high green tableland of Mesa Verde, and the long serpentine chasm of Mancos Canyon. It was magnificent country, but most of it was bone dry. Without the water that the government had promised to provide back in 1895, the land was largely worthless. By 1899 Ignacio had tired of the steady stream of unfulfilled promises and bureaucratic obstacles emanating from "Washitone," as he called the nation's capital: "Washitone-Washitone-Washitone-talk-talk-talk. No bueno. . . . Washitone—all time Washitone—no bueno. Papers-more papers-manyana-manyana."[29]

Here the Weeminuche lived in a manner radically different from that of their allotted cousins to the east. There were no individual allotments or houses or farms. The unallotted Utes perpetuated an existence that more closely resembled prereservation Ute life: they roamed with the changing seasons up and down the canyons and across the high desert of their communal reserve. There were some notable departures from the past, of course. Tipis were still to be seen—especially in the vicinity of the Navajo Springs Subagency—but the people increasingly adopted army-style tents, which were more easily transported. And even though hunting and gathering continued much as in the past, the seasonal movements of the Weeminuche were now dictated largely by the need to find grazing for their livestock—mostly sheep, some cattle, and also horses.[30] Many members of the band engaged in stock raising.

The contrast between Southern Ute and Ute Mountain Ute modes of existence may be partially explained by the bands' respective histories up to 1895. The Weeminuche Utes had been less exposed, by virtue of their relative geographical isolation, to contact with Spanish and Anglo-American neighbors. Thus, although all three bands shared a common cultural heritage, differences were apparent by the early years of the reservation period. An agent made the observation in 1885, for example, that the Weeminuche Utes were "the least civilized and most warlike of the entire Ute nation."[31] Differences between this band and the other two Southern Ute bands were magnified tremendously in the aftermath of the events of 1895. In addition to the impact of leaders such as Ignacio, the key factor after division of the reservation into allotted and unallotted halves was the nature of the land in each section. While the allotted Utes settled on fertile land with at least some capacity for irrigation, the Weeminuche Utes took refuge on some of the least productive land in the state of Colorado. Here, in relative isolation and without the water they had been promised, their hostility toward outsiders and white ways grew.[32]

In the early years of the twentieth century, most of the unallotted Utes gathered twice each month at Navajo Springs to receive their rations. Approximately twelve to fifteen head of cattle were turned over to the Indians at the beginning of the month. The Weeminuche Utes butchered the animals and distributed the meat, along with flour, baking powder, sugar, salt, and soap. On the midmonth ration day, salt pork and beans were substituted for the beef. Tribal members regularly supplemented their rations through hunting and through gathering of berries and through purchase of canned fruit and vegetables, coffee, and other items from reservation trading posts. After rations were issued, the people usually lingered for feasting and entertainment, particularly horse racing and gambling. Their races pitted two riders against each other on a straight three-quarter-mile racetrack located just south of the agency.[33] Like the allotted Southern Utes, the Weeminuche people at Ute Mountain were avid equestrians and inveterate gamblers.

For the first ten years after moving west, the unallotted Indians had no school near their agency, being served only by the Fort Lewis boarding school, located some 65 miles distant. Given the Utes' stated aversion to distantly located boarding schools, few Weeminuche children received any schooling before 1906. In that year a day school opened at Navajo Springs, and twenty-two children from the tribe were enrolled. Attendance was irregular, however, because of the opposition of a tribal faction led by Chiefs Mariano and Redrock.[34] At this time, the Navajo Springs Subagency was administered by the superintendent of the Fort Lewis School, and the only Indian Service official at Navajo Springs was a financial clerk.[35]

Both the administrative and educational arrangements at Navajo Springs soon changed, however. First the site was granted its own superintendency; then in 1918 the entire agency was relocated a few miles to the northwest, closer to the base of Sleeping Ute Mountain; and finally a new and much larger school, the Ute Mountain Boarding School, opened there in 1919.[36] A hospital was also constructed near the site of the new agency, which was called Towaoc, a Ute word meaning "all right."[37] In 1923 the administrative situation changed once again when the Ute Mountain Agency in Towaoc was placed under the jurisdiction of the

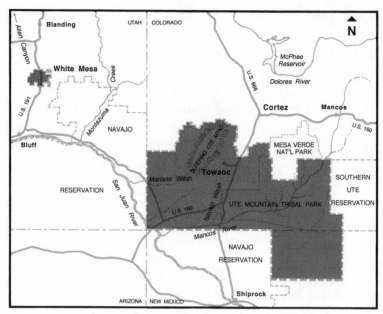

The Ute Mountain Ute Reservation at the close of the twentieth century. The boundaries of the reservation are indicated by bold broken lines.

Consolidated Ute Agency, which replaced the former Southern Ute Agency located outside the town of Ignacio.[38] Both the Southern Utes and the Ute Mountain Utes would be served by this Ignacio agency for the next forty-five years.

Another band of Indians, residing outside the reservation in southeastern Utah, was also to be provided with rations and other government services first by the agency at Navajo Springs and then by the new agency in Towaoc. A few groups of Weeminuche Utes, particularly those under the leadership of Johnny Benow (also called Green Ute), Mancos Jim, and Old Polk, had settled to the west of the reservation in San Juan County, Utah. Here, in the western reaches of the traditional Weeminuche domain, they lived apart from the rest of their band and often intermarried with Paiutes.[39] These Indians settled principally along Monte-

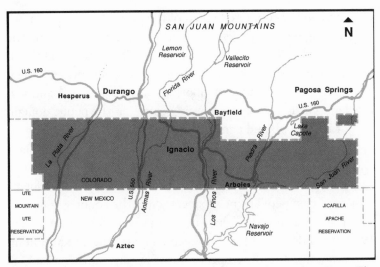

The Southern Ute Reservation at the close of the twentieth century. The boundaries of the reservation are indicated by bold broken lines.

zuma Creek and in Allen Canyon. The location of Weeminuche-Paiute camps along the latter drainage, on the southern flank of the Abajo Mountains (also referred to as the Blue Mountains) west of the town of Blanding, led to the designation of these off-reservation Indians as "Allen Canyon Utes." Some of these Indians took advantage of homestead laws to file on lands in the area, and Mancos Jim's group began to farm on homesteads in Allen Canyon.[40] Most of the Allen Canyon and Montezuma Creek Utes, however, simply continued to live along the various river bottoms of San Juan County without the benefit of any legal title to the land. Old Polk and Johnny Benow were the leaders of the Montezuma Creek band, while the Allen Canyon contingent was often led by the Paiute headman Posey.[41] Many of these Indians were related to families living on the Ute Mountain Reservation.[42] Nevertheless, they expressed some fear of the latter band and resisted government entreaties to relocate on the reservation.[43]

During the later part of the nineteenth century, the Allen

Canyon band encountered much of the same conflict with non-Indian neighbors experienced by their Colorado kin, but the Utah Utes, lacking the protection of a reservation, found themselves much more vulnerable to the trespasses of white cattlemen who coveted their land. Neighboring Mormon ranchers and several large cattle companies running cattle on the public domain sought the use of land occupied by the Utes. Such conflict over land use led to several violent confrontations between Indians and whites during the 1880s.[44]

Pressures came to a head again in 1915 with a series of incidents that were trumpeted by newspapers across the country as constituting an "Indian war." Tsenegat, son of Old Polk, was accused in 1914 of murdering a Mexican sheepherder on the Ute Mountain Reservation. After the suspect refused to turn himself in, a U.S. marshal recruited a posse of twenty-six Colorado cowboys to ride to Utah and retrieve the fugitive Ute. The posse, with many cowboys likely drunk, surrounded the camp of Polk and Tsenegat one night and, with no announcement or warning, began shooting into the camp. Posey and some of his men, who had been camping nearby, came to the aid of the besieged Indians and fired back at the posse. By the time the shooting stopped, people on both sides had been killed, Tsenegat and the rest of the Ute camp had fled, and rumors of an Indian war were in the air. Before Tsenegat, Polk, Posey, and the other escapees were induced to surrender, most of the Allen Canyon Utes had been intimidated by white cattlemen into abandoning their lands. Eventually all charges were dropped against the fugitive Indians except for the murder charge against Tsenegat, who was quickly acquitted at a trial in Denver. The acquittal, however, was small consolation to the Indians of southeastern Utah who had been driven off their land by opportunistic white neighbors. One hundred sixty Indians were removed from Utah during the crisis and sent to the Ute Mountain Reservation. Not until 1920 did some of the Utes straggle back to Allen Canyon and Montezuma Creek.[45]

Violence again erupted in 1923 in an incident sometimes referred to as "Posey's War." It began with the robbery of a sheep camp by two young Ute boys. After turning themselves in to the sheriff in Blanding, the youths later fled. Townspeople then set out in pursuit not only of the two boys but also of Posey, who was assumed to be behind the escape. The Allen Canyon leader had long been perceived by Blanding residents as the chief instigator of Indian-white troubles. The ensuing manhunt set off a mass exodus of Utes and Paiutes reminiscent of the 1915 "Ute War." Described by the Consolidated Ute superintendent as an "uprising," what actually occurred was a mass roundup by local Mormons of Utes living in the Blanding area, seventy-nine of whom were placed in a barbed-wire enclosure in Blanding. Posey, who was shot while attempting to evade capture, rode off but died of his wounds a month later. The Ute captives, who once again lost most of their livestock and other property, were held prisoner in Blanding until Posey's death had been confirmed by the discovery of his body. In response to this latest disturbance, the U.S. government determined that the largely landless Utes should be placed on allotments granted from the public domain. Thus, remnants of Posey's band returned to Allen Canyon and Polk's band to Montezuma Creek to settle on 160-acre allotments.[46]

In the aftermath of the Posey War, the Indian Office and the Consolidated Ute Agency finally acknowledged the presence of nonreservation Utes in the Blanding area, and for the first time ever, the Indian Office took steps to provide on-site services to the Allen Canyon Utes. This seemed particularly necessary to agency officials given the unacculturated condition of these Indians, whom a later superintendent would describe in 1930 as being "the most primitive and backward band of Indians" he had ever encountered.[47] The following year the same superintendent asserted that these Indians were "at least 40 years behind the Southern Utes [in their progress toward civilization]."[48] Throughout the 1920s, for example, none of these Utes lived in houses, residing instead in tents or earthen hogans.[49] In addition to being granted land allotments, these Utes were soon being attended to by their own Indian Service official. Agency stockman E. Z. Black arrived in Blanding in 1925 to begin assisting the Allen Canyon people in their agricultural development. Although Black reported that the Utes knew very little about farming, they were eager for his assistance and soon began planting crops in Allen Canyon. By 1927 Black was reporting that 132 acres of crops—beans, squash, melons, and potatoes, plus a number of grains—had been planted.[50]

Nevertheless, Black and the Utes faced an uphill battle, as the Allen Canyon site presented a number of problems. It was isolated, plagued by bad road access, and rugged: of the 2,600 acres allotted in the canyon, fewer than 200 were suitable for cultivation.[51] And the distance separating these allotments from the reservation was still a problem. Prior to 1931, Ute children in San Juan County had to travel over 100 miles from home to get an education at the Ute Mountain Boarding School in Towaoc. Allen Canyon families were often unenthusiastic about sending their children away to school. Stockman Black reported spending a great deal of time tracking down children who had run away from school.[52] Likewise, a school census report from the late 1920s showed over one-half of all Ute children from San Juan County failing to attend school. Various reasons were given for nonattendance: "Mother says it is too far," "Excused to take care of Mother's sheep," "Grandmother objects," "Father says they let his other girl die," or, simply, "Don't want to go."[53]

Because of these problems, the Indian Office was soon pushing the Utes to abandon their homes in Allen Canyon in favor of moving to the Ute Mountain Reservation. Despite the difficulties posed by their isolated location, however, the Utes were adamant about staying put in their own familiar piece of Utah canyon country. Superintendent E. J. Peacore worried in 1930: "They will never consent, without a fight to be taken back on the Ute Mountain Reservation. . . . At any rate if these people are moved away, a number of them will have to be moved in coffins."[54]

Although not faced with the violent confrontations and uncertainty experienced by the Utes of southeastern Utah, the Weeminuche people residing on the reservation in Colorado did confront outside forces intent on changing their way of life. The Indian Office campaign for Indian acculturation encountered greater obstacles in dealing with the unallotted Mountain Utes than with their Southern Ute neighbors to the east. Despite the opening of the large new Ute Mountain Boarding School adjacent to the Towaoc agency, only 41 Ute children were attending this school, which had a capacity of 150 students, in 1921.[55] The seminomadic ways of the unallotted Utes made school attendance problematic and stymied the agency's attempts to influence tribal members toward assimilation. Traditional beliefs—derided by non-Indians as "superstition"—continued to hold sway. Very few tribal members spoke any English. Combined with the harsh, arid environment, the Utes' failure to follow efficient grazing practices often derailed the government's attempts to expand stock raising on the reservation. Early in the 1910s, for example, four thousand head of Hereford cattle had been bought with tribal funds and distributed by the agency. Overgrazing of particular ranges caused the death by starvation of more than one-half of these animals. The bulk of the surviving cattle were seized by the superintendent and sold to prevent them from suffering a similar fate; only those Indians who kept their cattle where feed was available were permitted to retain their stock.[56]

HEALTH, MEDICINE MEN, AND SPIRITUALITY

In the fifty years following the establishment of the Southern Ute Agency, the Weeminuche, Mouache, and Capote Utes suffered a dramatic decline in population. Not only was the adjustment to a new way of life on the reservation an exasperating experience; it was also often a fatal one. The tribe's early encounters with boarding schools are a case in point: an 1894 report by the Southern Ute agent revealed that one-half the Ute students attending boarding school in Albuquerque died and that one-fourth of the Ute children sent to the Fort Lewis School contracted trachoma, a disease that left them blind.[57] Throughout the first half century on the reservation, the combination of a radical change in lifestyle and diet, poor housing and sanitation, and unsafe drinking water left the Southern Utes and Ute Mountain Utes ravaged by disease. Tuberculosis was endemic, and the Utes were also struck down by venereal diseases and flu epidemics. Many were blinded by trachoma, which afflicted hundreds of tribal members in almost any given year.

In 1880 the Southern Ute agent counted 1,330 members of the three bands at the agency on the Los Pinos River.[58] By 1900 the combined Southern Ute and Ute Mountain Ute population had declined to 995, and it continued to fall precipitously over the next twenty-five years. Together both groups numbered only 781 in 1923.[59] The worldwide flu epidemic of 1918, occurring before the completion of the Towaoc hospital, was particularly devastating.[60]

The two Ute tribes did not pull out of this downward population trend at the same time. The Southern Utes rebounded first, hitting a low of 334 people in 1920 and then beginning a slow increase in numbers that has continued ever since. The Ute Mountain Utes, by comparison, continued to shrink in number until 1930, when their population fell to 444.[61]

The longer duration of the downward spiral at Ute Mountain was probably the result of the tribe's isolation and seminomadic lifestyle. Cultural attitudes also played a major role. The Ute Mountain people were much slower to accept modern medical care than were the allotted Utes in Ignacio. Ever since the establishment of the Southern Ute Agency in 1878, agents had reported the existence of an ongoing battle between agency physicians and traditional medicine men for the confidence of sick Indians. Although members of all three bands were initially quite dubious of the value of modern medicine, physicians won converts much more quickly among the Mouache and Capote than among the Weeminuche. Even among the former two bands, there was a particular reluctance among women to accept modern medical care during the early reservation period. When venereal diseases became a problem on the reservation in the 1880s, for example, the men generally accepted medical treatment once their symptoms became apparent, but the women did not. One factor behind the aversion of Southern Ute women to medical treatment in general and gynecological/obstetric care in particular may have been the traditional practice of isolating females during menstruation and childbirth.[62]

The Weeminuche people were generally more skeptical of modern medicine than their neighbors to the east, and they continued to prefer the assistance of traditional healers. Although the Ute Mountain band was the first to be served by its own hospital, this did not lead to an appreciable improvement in the health of tribal members as they seldom took advantage of the hospital's services. More than the Ignacio Utes, they held fast to the traditional Ute aversion to places where people had died, and Ute Mountain men continued to observe the prohibition regarding contact with women who were menstruating or giving birth.[63]

The role of the medicine man, or shaman, slowly diminished in Ute society, especially among the Ignacio Utes following allotment; but the influence of such traditional healers lingered for a long time, contrary to persistent reports of the demise of shamanistic medicine issued by agency physicians. The same could not always be said for individual medicine men, however. There was a high turnover among shamans during the early years of the reservation owing to the fact that the death of a patient was typically regarded as evidence of "bad medicine" on the part of the attending shaman. In such cases, revenge killings of medicine men were not uncommon and were regarded by most Utes as justifiable. One particularly notable instance of revenge killing of a medicine man took place in 1904 after the death of Ignacio's son-in-law following treatment by his own uncle.[64]

In addition to the practices of medicine men, other aspects of Ute culture—some old, some new—persisted through the first quarter of the twentieth century. The Bear Dance, an important spring ritual originated by the Utes and practiced by all bands since before European contact, continued to be held annually both in Ignacio and at Ute Mountain. The Bear Dance was principally a social, rather than a spiritual, dance. Two other rituals that were new to the Utes and primarily spiritual in nature—the Sun Dance and the peyote ritual—were performed by members of both Ute tribes. The Sun Dance, a ceremony originating among the Plains Indians and reinvented in its modern form by Shoshone shamans on the Wind River Reservation in Wyoming during the 1880s, was introduced to the Colorado Utes via the Northern Utes on the Uintah-Ouray Reservation in Utah. A Ute Mountain medicine man named Tonapach, who had learned the ritual from the Northern Utes, was the first to sponsor a Sun Dance among the Weeminuche, and he in turn taught the dance to Southern Ute medicine man Edwin Cloud, who became the first to hold such dances in the Ignacio area. This cultural innovation was initiated on both Colorado reservations around the turn of the century and quickly became accepted among the Ute people as an important focal point of tribal spiritual life.[65]

The peyote ritual, first introduced to the Colorado Utes in the 1910s, was another spiritual innovation borrowed from the Plains peoples, again via the Northern Utes. This new spiritual practice, involving the consumption of hallucinogenic peyote cactus buttons, was brought to the Ignacio Utes by a Sioux named Sam Lone Bear, who proselytized among the Northern Utes for several years before bringing peyotism to the Southern Utes. Peyote rituals were first held in Ignacio in or shortly before 1917. The acceptance of this new spiritual institution was promoted by Chief Buckskin Charlie, who overcame his initial opposition to peyote, and his wife, Emma Buck. Isaac Cloud, brother of shaman Edwin Cloud, was also a prominent early supporter of the new rite. The practice of the peyote ritual was also boosted by a steady stream of Cheyenne peyote missionaries from Oklahoma who visited the Southern Utes throughout the 1920s.[66]

At roughly the same time as the Southern Utes were being exposed to the peyote rite, the new ritual was being introduced to the Ute Mountain Indians by a Northern Ute named Wee'tseets'. Wee'tseets', who probably came to Ute Mountain between 1914 and 1917, taught his hosts the "Old Sioux Way," one form of the peyote rite. Shortly thereafter, but still prior to 1918, a Cheyenne named John Peehart arrived on the first of what would become regular yearly visits to Ute Mountain, and he brought with him the ultimately more popular "Moon Way" form of the peyote ritual. The first Ute Mountain peyote priest, sometimes called a "road chief" or "roadman," was George Mills, who began conducting rituals in 1917 or 1918. By the 1920s, three other Ute Mountain Utes had gone to Oklahoma for training and returned home to become peyote priests.[67]

The peyote ritual was part of a larger institution known as the Native American Church, a pan-Indian religious movement integrating Christian beliefs with Indian rituals, including the consumption of peyote as a sacrament. Once introduced among the two Ute tribes of Colorado, the practice of peyotism followed starkly different paths in Ignacio and Towaoc. Whereas the consumption of peyote for spiritual purposes was quickly embraced by nearly the entire Ute Mountain population, it remained the practice of only a minority of Southern Utes.[68]

The peyote rite of the Native American Church incorporates many Christian elements both in its symbolism and in the prayers uttered throughout the ceremony. This blending of religious traditions came easily to the Utes, who often combined their traditional spiritual beliefs and practices with elements of Christianity picked up from Catholic and Presbyterian missionaries.[69]

Reverend James Russell of the Presbyterian mission in Towaoc commented on the spiritual eclecticism of the Utes in 1929, observing that "it does not seem to occur to the Utes that there is any incompatibility between . . . the Great Spirit and the Christian God. Those who participate in the Sun Dance also attend the mission services."[70] Even though both the peyote rite and the Sun Dance were twentieth-century, postreservation phenomena, these two cultural innovations nevertheless had a conservative dimension as they offered Utes a means of asserting traditional values and identity in the face of a Euro-American cultural onslaught.

TRIBAL POLITICS

The first half century of reservation life was often an exercise in exasperation for the Ute people. Forced to radically change their pattern of living, they were confronted by paternalistic restrictions on their freedom to act either as individuals or as a tribe, by assimilationist policies emanating from Washington, and by an endless procession of agency officials who were frequently incompetent, hostile, corrupt, or some combination of these. Frustrated Utes often attempted to assert some control over their lives through the actions of their leaders and their Tribal Councils.

The U.S. government had frequently engaged in "kingmaking" with respect to the Utes, beginning with its dealings with Ouray. To simplify the government's relationship with the tribe, Indian Service officials would usually select one of several band chiefs to be elevated to the preeminent position of "chief." Thus, among the Southern Utes, Ignacio of the Weeminuche, Buckskin Charlie of the Mouache, and Severo of the Capote were initially recognized by the U.S. government as principal chiefs of their respective bands.[71]

Sometimes the government later came to regret its selection of a tribal leader when a chief proved to be less than accommodating to U.S. interests. Ignacio, for example, was frequently a source of irritation to agency officials. It was Ignacio, after all, who led his people in rejecting the government's allotment policy, with the result that the Weeminuche were able to secure a homeland, albeit mostly barren and dry, which they could retain on a communal basis. Furthermore, Ignacio often acted to derail Indian Office plans to send Ute children to distant boarding schools. In 1892, for example, he was temporarily discharged as captain of the Indian Police force on the reservation as punishment for his leading role in resisting a plan to send more Ute children to the Fort Lewis boarding school.[72] The agency superintendent in 1894 saw the Weeminuche chief as an obstacle to "civilizing" the Utes: "Chief Ignacio is a potent foe of education, and he is not without influence, particularly in the Weeminuche tribe. He is stubborn, practically unsusceptible to reason, and an unyielding stickler for the habits, customs, and methods of his early days."[73] Twelve years later, however, an official at Navajo Springs regarded Ignacio in a much more positive light, seeing him as relatively progressive in comparison to a conservative Weeminuche faction led by Subchiefs Mariano and Redrock. It was the latter group, not the chief, that fought against allowing Ute children to attend the new day school at Navajo Springs. Ignacio, whom Mariano accused of talking "like a white man," was reportedly unable to hold together the two factions in his band.[74] Nevertheless, Ignacio remained chief of the Ute Mountain Utes until a few years before his death in 1913. Ignacio was succeeded as chief by John Miller.[75]

Most influential among the Southern Utes to the east was Buckskin Charlie, who had been selected both by Ouray and the U.S. government to represent the Mouache and Capote bands. From the agency perspective, Buckskin Charlie was a perplexing tribal leader. Charlie was one of the first among his people to settle on a piece of land and build a cabin, and he was one of the first Southern Utes to clear land and begin farming. Like Ouray, he never strayed from maintaining peace between his people and the United States, and he favored the education of his tribe's children. He had no qualms about Indians worshiping as Christians, and he himself attended church services on occasion.[76] Yet despite all of these apparently "progressive" tendencies, Buckskin Charlie could also be—in the eyes of government officials—frustratingly "conservative" or "traditional" in clinging to Indian ways and resisting Indian Office policies.[77] Charlie was one of the prime forces behind bringing the Sun Dance to Ignacio, and he was also an active leader in the introduction of the peyote ritual among the Southern Utes. The Indian Office sought to ban the former and declared the latter to be illegal.

Aside from such instances of cultural traditionalism, Buckskin Charlie's actions as chief did not always serve the interests of the Indian Service. The aging Mouache leader did not simply do the agency's bidding, and he frequently protested government policies that conflicted with past agreements and treaties. As part of a delegation visiting Washington in 1886, Charlie presented federal officials with a list of grievances in support of a request for a new reservation in Utah. One item regarded the failure of the Indian Service to provide annuity goods and farm animals as previously agreed. Charlie firmly declared, "These goods are not given to us for nothing, but come from the sale of our lands."[78] When the chief asserted Ute treaty rights in the face of the government's failure to honor its obligations, he was generally correct in his recollections, and he was occasionally able to win concessions from federal officials. As part of another Ute delegation negotiating with a federal commission regarding relocation of the Colorado Utes to Utah, Buckskin Charlie protested the government's insistence that Indian parents send their children away to school in order to be eligible to receive gratuity payments. Charlie asserted that the only criterion for eligibility was "good conduct," and the commission agreed.[79] The continued authority of Charlie's leadership, and the confidence of his people in his ability to confront federal officials, was indicated by the chief's election to head the 1926 delegation sent to Washington to demand an accounting for the actions of Indian Service officials in both Ignacio and Washington.[80]

Thus, at the opening of the twentieth century, the emerging political systems at both Ignacio and Ute Mountain were characterized by strong chieftaincies. Among the Ute Mountain Indians, Ignacio established the precedent of a single strong chief, and he was succeeded by John Miller, who led his people for more than two decades. Under Miller's successor, Chief Jack House, the strong chieftaincy again thrived and proved quite resilient, lasting until House's death in 1971. Meanwhile in Ignacio, Buckskin Charlie carried on as a principal chief in the manner of Ouray for an incredible period of fifty-six years. He was succeeded after his death by his son Antonio Buck. Thus, among the three Colorado Ute bands that had been accustomed in prereservation times to the informal and fluid leadership of headmen, the new institution of the strong chieftaincy, first established in the early reservation period, became firmly entrenched at the onset of the twentieth century.[81]

Yet the authority of these chiefs was clearly subject to limits. Buckskin Charlie's influence over his people, for example, was not always as extensive as the government might have wished. An official noted in 1917 that, even though the chief still commanded the allegiance of older tribal members, "younger men and women do not give him the same consideration."[82] Ignacio, too, faced challenges from Subchiefs Redrock and Mariano. Even as the new chieftaincies became well established, the power of tribal leaders continued to rest on personal popularity and to be effective only when it was exercised in conformity with the consensus of tribal opinion.[83]

Chiefs were not the only political actors among the Southern Utes and Ute Mountain Utes. The Tribal Council increasingly became an important forum for addressing developments on the reservation and at the agencies. Begun before the reservation era as bodies for negotiating agreements with the U.S. government, the councils continued to function periodically on the reservation, and participation on these once-exclusive bodies became more inclusive as time went on. A council convened in 1896 was particularly significant as it represented the first assertion of tribal interests in opposition to the government.[84] The land claims case initiated at this meeting culminated in a $3,408,611.40 judgment by the U.S. Court of Claims in 1910 in favor of the Confederated Bands of the Utes. This award was based on Ute land claims pertaining to the 1880 Ute removal agreement.[85] Several years later, Tribal Councils were reported to be held regularly in 1911, but a later superintendent, Edward E. McKean, who saw councils as a hindrance, banned such meetings at Ignacio.[86] They continued at Towaoc, much to the annoyance of Superintendent McKean, who decried the Ute Mountain Tribal Council for its unprogressive opposition to "whatever the Government or any outside white man wishes them to do."[87] The five-member Ute Mountain Tribal Council had been something of a hindrance to the agency from its inception, seeking to pressure the government to meet tribal demands, beginning in 1900 with the issue of unfulfilled government promises to supply the Utes with water.[88]

Upset by a long succession of perceived abuses at the hands of agency officials and the Indian Office in Washington, the Utes sent two delegations—the first of the two was not recognized by the government as an official delegation—to Washington in 1925 and 1926. Through testimony in Washington and through letters written on the Utes' behalf by Jose Blas Lucero, a Mexican-American resident of Ignacio who described himself as "a friend of the Utes," the joint Southern Ute–Ute Mountain Ute delegations enumerated a long list of tribal grievances. They complained of corruption at the agency, referring to Superintendent McKean as "the worst enemy of the Utes . . . a man who is seeking the ruination of the Utes for his own financial benefit."[89]

A ten-point letter of March 24, 1926, summarized the tribe's complaints, which included the following: the commissioner of Indian affairs had made mathematical errors that resulted in understatement of the amount of tribal funds remaining on deposit in Washington, and, furthermore, these funds were being used to pay for Indian Office services that the tribe regarded as being "more injurious than beneficial to us"; the reimbursable system was unfair; the superintendent had forced tribal members to sign over their allotments, leaving them landless; and tribal members were not permitted to buy, sell, or trade their own personal property without making arrangements through the superintendent, "which transactions always turn out to our disadvantage." The letter closed by stating, "We have concluded to place our lives in our own hands, hoping that the domestic Bureaucratic Tyranny be forever vanished, and to remain with us only as a hideous dream."[90]

The superintendent denied all of the allegations, and the commissioner responded with a letter refuting each of the tribe's charges. No changes in government policy resulted from this episode, but the two Ute tribes of Colorado were beginning to learn how to speak out on their own behalf. Never hesitant to sound off in opposition to Indian Office policies, the Colorado Utes, beginning in 1896 and again in 1925–1926, acted aggressively to seek political remedies for their grievances. With each encounter, they became more confident in their ability to present their case and to maneuver among the various echelons of the vast and powerful federal government: the agency, the Indian Office, the Department of the Interior, Congress, and the courts. And the Utes often were able to wrest concessions from the government.[91] Interestingly, in the early twentieth century it was the Southern Utes of Ignacio who were the most aggressive and successful of the two Colorado tribes in asserting their rights before the federal government. The Southern Utes, often described by agency officials as much more progressive and cooperative than the supposedly stubborn and hostile Utes of Ute Mountain, actually fought more actively against the workings of U.S. Indian policy to guarantee their rights.

AN ECHO FROM THE PAST

Roughly forty-five years prior to this latest round of exchanges between Ute leaders and the Indian Office in 1925–1926, the Southern Ute people had been presented with an agreement concluded between tribal leaders and the U.S. government. This agreement, negotiated in the aftermath of the 1879 Meeker Massacre at White River, called for the relocation of all six Colorado Ute bands. Ouray, chief of the Tabeguache band and recognized by U.S. officials as principal chief of all Ute bands, had come to the Southern Ute Agency to promote acceptance of this agreement among the Southern Ute people. But before his mission could be completed, the forty-seven-year-old chief became ill, possibly as a result of kidney trouble. The Tabeguache leader died near the agency on the west bank of the Los Pinos River on August 24, 1880, and he was quickly buried in traditional Ute fashion. A party of seven Utes, including Buckskin Charlie, interred the body under a large rock at the head of an arroyo about 2 miles south of the future town site of Ignacio. In accordance with custom, three of Ouray's horses were killed on the spot, and then the burial party quickly departed from the grave site. Also following Ute custom, these Indians refused to reveal the location of Ouray's grave, which would remain a secret for nearly forty-five years. During this time, there was much speculation by residents of the Ignacio area as to the location of the chief's burial site, and it was widely rumored that Ouray's remains were buried in the San Miguel Mountains.[92]

"Me getting old. Me soon lie down and die. Me like see monument for Ouray in Ignacio. Ouray good friend of white man. You know. You say you help get monument Ouray. All right, me tell secret burial place." Thus did Buckskin Charlie reportedly explain to a local white trader in 1924 that he would end the mystery surrounding Ouray's final resting place. Prompted by talk of erecting a monument in Ignacio to the late chief and by the prospect of reburying Ouray's remains alongside those of his wife, Chipeta, who had recently passed away, the aging Southern Ute chieftain led the trader, along with a reporter and a photographer, to the burial site south of Ignacio on August 21, 1924. From the crevice in which Ouray's body had been interred in 1880, a number of human bones were retrieved.[93]

Ouray's bones were reburied the following spring in the tribal cemetery on the east bank of the Los Pinos River. After four days of sacred Ute ceremonies and a concluding Christian service, the great chief's remains were reinterred on May 24, 1925. Four members of the original burial party, Buckskin Charlie, George Norris, Joseph Price, and Colorow, served as pallbearers in this second ceremony, which drew a mixed crowd of both Indians and whites—the largest group ever assembled on the Southern Ute Reservation up to that time.[94] In a striking juxtaposition of old and new, a stream of automobile-borne non-Indians joined a number of traditionally attired Ute Indians on horseback, decked out in ceremonial headdresses, in descending on the Southern Ute Reservation. A lengthy procession made its way to the tribal cemetery, with Ouray's coffin, covered by a pile of brush, transported in the back of a pickup truck.[95]

The proposed side-by-side burial of Ouray and Chipeta never took place, as the remains of "Queen Chipeta" were never moved from a burial site near her former home in Montrose. The plot next to Chief Ouray's grave would eventually be occupied instead by the remains of the Mouache chief whom Ouray had long ago selected to be his successor as leader of the Southern Utes. This would not come to pass any time soon, however. Buckskin Charlie, the octogenarian chief, was not yet finished leading his people.

3

RESERVATION LIFE
IN THE 1930s

The Southern Utes and Ute Mountain Utes of the early
1930s lived an existence far removed from that of the people
who had gathered at the newly established Southern Ute Agency
in 1878. Fifty years of living under Indian Service supervision on
a small part of their former domain—during which time the Utes
had been largely reduced to dependency on rations and annuity
payments, forced to attend the white man's schools, and generally denied the ability to actively control their own destiny—had
wrought fundamental changes in tribal society. The experience
had not, however, transformed the Utes into creatures of modern
Anglo-American society, nor had these Indians passively accepted
their lot. Although unable to independently conduct their own
affairs, the two Ute tribes asserted their interests and often acted
to resist Indian Office policies.

In the late nineteenth century, the Office of Indian Affairs set
out to remake the Utes—and other Native American peoples—
in the white man's image. First, Indians were to be placed on
reservations and no longer permitted to engage in the seasonal
migrations that had characterized their past way of life. Then

they would be educated and Christianized, and each family would be given its own 160-acre tract of land. With Indian Service guidance, the Indians would then become successful farmers and productive members of modern American society. This had not happened, however, to the Utes of southwestern Colorado. Ute society had certainly undergone dramatic change, but this change had come only slowly and fitfully—much to the exasperation of the agents and superintendents whose job it was to shepherd these two tribes along the road to assimilation.[1] The Mouache, Capote, and Weeminuche bands had taken incremental steps along this route, but the government-designated destination was still far over the horizon.

The three bands—newly organized as two tribes—had not traveled at the same pace as they moved down this road. The Mouache and Capote people of the Southern Ute Tribe proceeded more rapidly than their Weeminuche kin at Ute Mountain, who more frequently dug in their heels to resist the forces impelling them down the road. As a result, life on the two adjacent reservations was remarkably dissimilar throughout the 1930s. But for both tribes, reservation life during this period was characterized by a mixture of continuity and change, resulting from an ongoing battle between the Utes' impulses to accommodate the modern, outside world and to maintain tribal identity and traditions.

HOUSING

The Ute Mountain Utes clung tenaciously to a seminomadic style of life throughout the 1930s, and thus permanent housing remained a rarity among these people. Moving with their sheep and horses between winter and summer ranges, the vast majority of tribal members at Ute Mountain still lived in tents, as they had since relocating to the western section of the old reservation in 1895. In 1930 only eight Mountain Ute families lived in permanent dwellings, compared to ninety-seven families living in tents, tipis, or other temporary forms of shelter. On the allotted Southern Ute Reservation, the numbers were reversed: ninety-two families lived in permanent housing and only four in temporary shelters.[2] Superintendent E. J. Peacore explained to a U.S. Senate subcommittee in 1931 that he had begun a housing campaign on the Ute Mountain Reservation two years previously, with four frame houses built for tribal members in 1930 and more dwellings being constructed in response to the tribe's request for eight additional units. Peacore pointed out that the new homes were about the size of a tent "because that is all they are capable of taking care of." He added that these Indians, whom he described as being "very, very primitive," slept on sheep pelts, had few dishes, and wanted no furniture.[3]

A 1934 survey again highlighted the contrasting housing conditions on the two reservations. The housing stock of the Ignacio Utes consisted of 52 adobe homes, 50 frame houses, and 1 log structure; no tents were reported.[4] Yet tents had not fully disappeared from the Ignacio area, despite the relative abundance of permanent houses, built mostly in the years following the 1910 land claims judgment. During the 1920s, the majority of Southern Ute families still resided in canvas tents or brush shelters rather than in their houses—at least during the summer.[5] This housing arrangement continued into the 1930s, when houses and tents could be found side by side in the Ignacio area. Families typically slept outside or under canvas during warmer weather.[6] Houses were still a rare sight at Ute Mountain in 1934. The Ute Mountain Utes of Towaoc had seen only a slight increase in permanent housing since 1930, counting among their homes at this time 1 adobe dwelling, 5 log homes, 8 frame houses, 7 hogans (mud and log structures adopted from the neighboring Navajo people to the south), and 108 tents.[7] Housing in the Allen Canyon district in Utah, whose Utes and Paiutes remained under the jurisdiction of the Towaoc agency, was even less developed. The majority of the Allen Canyon Indians, whom superintendents consistently described as extremely primitive, still lived in either tents or traditional brush shelters in 1935.[8]

Although the radically dissimilar housing situations on the two neighboring reservations were obvious, it is possible to overstate the progress made by the Southern Utes in this area. All Southern Ute families possessed houses of some sort as early as 1932, but the agency's categorization of "permanent homes" provides little clue to the nature or quality of tribal housing. At the close of the decade, the Southern Ute Tribal Council prefaced a resolution calling for housing improvement with the observation that "the housing situation on this reservation is in a deplorable condition, and sometimes as many as ten persons occupy a two-room shack. . . . Stoves, furniture, and bedding are lacking in our homes."[9] Council members continued to complain of inadequate tar-paper-shack homes into the early 1950s. The mere existence of permanent houses—of whatever quality—did not necessarily imply full tribal acceptance of Anglo-American–style residential living; a 1935 visitor to Buckskin Charlie's allotment observed that the elderly chief, one of the first of his people to adopt permanent residency and a house, was living on his allotment in a tipi.[10]

THE RESERVATION ECONOMY

It is hardly surprising that the Ignacio Utes, living on allotments in a farm-based economy, chose permanent housing more readily than did the seminomadic herders of Ute Mountain. As the decade began, however, even the settled Indians of the former group had been unable to achieve economic self-sufficiency. The Consolidated Ute Agency reported in 1930 that no Utes on either reservation were "entirely self-supporting from their own industry and thrift."[11] Even the more industrious Indians, be they farmers, stock raisers, or wage workers, continued to rely on rations provided by the agency and per capita payments out of tribal funds. Government officials had long lamented the antimotivational effects of these distributions; one agency farmer in 1913 had been so frustrated by the resulting lack of farm productivity that he submitted a request for his transfer to a reservation "where no rations had ever been issued."[12] Annual payments of as much as $200 per capita had been issued in the past out of the tribal fund, which had been enriched significantly by the 1910 land claims award; but the payment amounts declined over the years as the tribal fund steadily diminished. Tribal members did not receive these payments in cash; instead, they were deposited into Individual Indian Accounts. Access to these accounts was strictly controlled—to the frustration of Indians seeking the use of their money—by the agency superintendent, and money was typically siphoned out of these accounts to pay tribal members' reimbursable debts or debts owed to licensed traders.[13] The per capita distribution dropped to $50 in 1931, and in 1933 such payments ceased altogether, as did the ration system.[14] Despite the protests of older Utes who insisted that the government was obligated to provide tribal members with gratuities as guaranteed in past treaties, no more money or food was forthcoming.[15] Economically, the people were now on their own.

The Southern Utes provided for themselves through farming, stock raising, wage work, and leasing of allotments to non-Indian farmers and ranchers. In 1931 the tribe boasted eighty farmers, seventy-three stock raisers, and thirty-six members who worked for wages.[16] Ute farmers harvested alfalfa, wheat, oats, and hay; but even though they had come a long way as farmers since accepting allotments in 1896, problems persisted. Ute farmers faced a host of disadvantages—small acreages, inadequate farm machinery, lack of water for irrigation—in comparison to neighboring non-Indian farmers. Agency farmer (later superintendent) Elbert J. Floyd reported to a U.S. Senate subcommittee in 1931 that, whereas white farmers could make a living farming in the reservation area, the Indians could not. Whereas the former group regularly produced 30 bushels of grain per acre, the latter were capable of harvesting only 18–20 bushels. Nevertheless, he saw signs of progress, noting that Ute farmers had doubled their production in the previous two years.[17]

The Utes of Ignacio also raised livestock, primarily sheep. Their stock consisted in 1933 of 5,389 sheep, 247 goats, 369 horses, 79 dairy cows, and 31 beef cattle.[18] Sheep raising began in Ignacio in 1928 when the superintendent convinced the Indians to accept 5 sheep per person, purchased on the reimbursable plan.[19] Since then the sheep had shown a steady increase, but so had the reimbursable debt loads of many tribal members. An additional obstacle to both farming and stock raising was the fact that as of 1933 nearly one-half of the tribe's members held no land.[20] Through the sale of Southern Ute allotments and the division through inheritance of many remaining allotments, individual holdings in the form of allotted land had been cut nearly in half since 1896. At this point, the Southern Utes, unlike the Ute Mountain Utes, had no tribally held acreage.

The Ute Mountain Indians had a head start in the sheep business over their neighbors to the east. They had been raising large numbers of sheep and goats since around 1920, with many herds in existence before this date. In 1933 tribal members possessed 11,015 sheep and 82 goats, roughly twice the number held by the Southern Utes. The Mountain Utes also had 520 horses and 91 beef cattle.[21] At the close of 1932, however, the agency stockman reported that the number of sheep had been decreasing over the previous six years as a result, at least in part, of the tribal members' practice of handing over their possessions to medicine men to procure assistance in healing sick family members.[22] The lack of water on the reservation and the failure of Ute herders to move their animals off overgrazed areas also limited stock-raising activity. Nevertheless, at mid-decade sheep remained the cornerstone of the Ute Mountain economy, with 90 percent of tribal members owning sheep.[23]

Wage work assumed increasing importance at Ute Mountain

as the decade wore on and the country sank deeper into the Great Depression. The New Deal, in the form of the Civilian Conservation Corps–Indian Division, came to both reservations to provide jobs for unemployed Indians, and a total of $558,000 in CCC-ID funds was expended between 1933 and 1942 for the construction of fences, roads, wells, and reservoirs on the Colorado reservations.[24] The Indian CCC, established following passage of the Emergency Conservation Work Act in 1933, proved an economic boon to Indians throughout the West. Over 25,000 Indians were recruited to work in nearly seventy-five camps located throughout fifteen western states to help improve reservation lands.[25] Work with the CCC provided Indians $30 per month in wages and yielded important educational experience and on-the-job training. Employment with the Indian CCC often gave tribal members their first encounter with a wage economy and put cash in their hands, possibly for the first time.[26] Both Colorado tribes benefited from this employment, but it was particularly important to the Towaoc Utes. As many as seventy-five Ute Mountain Indians at a time were often employed in this program.[27] This yielded substantial income to tribal members but also led the agency farmer, who described the Mountain Utes in 1940 as being "wage-minded," to worry about what would happen when this relief work disappeared.[28] Indian CCC projects also brought about a substantial influx of Navajo workers onto the Ute Mountain Reservation. CCC payrolls show two to three times as many Navajos as Utes working on many Ute reservation projects.[29]

In 1937 farm agent Elbert J. Floyd issued a glowing report of economic conditions on the Southern Ute Reservation. He stated that cash income per family in the Los Pinos River valley had reached $514, a substantial increase over the $200 income earned five years earlier, making these Indians "almost self-supporting."[30] Given the sometimes questionable accuracy of agency reports— past superintendents had been accused both by tribal members and by agency employees of falsifying data to overstate progress on the reservation—it is difficult to evaluate the truthfulness of this rosy assessment of the Utes' standard of living in Ignacio.[31] Only two months before Floyd's statement appeared, a far different picture had been painted by Marvin K. Opler, an anthropologist who had recently completed four months of fieldwork on the two reservations. His comments, focusing primarily on the Weeminuche at Ute Mountain, emphasized the despair of a people wracked by disease and poverty.[32]

Opler also asserted that these poor Indians were constantly victimized by the profiteering of government-licensed traders who sold goods on the reservation. The trading post was an important institution during the early reservation period (and into the mid-twentieth century) on Indian reservations throughout the West. Traders played an important economic, social, and even political role on reservations; they were much more than mere grocers. Traders functioned variously as translators, spokesmen, counselors, buyers, bankers, and bartenders. Many factors—geographic isolation, lack of transportation, lack of cash, inability to speak English—made Indians dependent on government-licensed Indian traders for the purchase and sale of goods. The limited number of traders on a given reservation added to the monopolistic nature of trading posts. Accordingly, the potential for abuse of Indian customers was great, especially since Indians typically purchased goods on credit and were therefore often in debt to traders.[33] Profiteering by traders at times plagued the Ute reservations in Colorado. In the early part of the century, there were instances in which agency superintendents established improper business ties with licensed traders. One trader in particular, Hans Aspaas, was accused by a superintendent of colluding with agency personnel to provide underweight and defective animals for Indian rations.[34]

Traders continued to play a key role, especially on the more isolated Ute Mountain Reservation, later in the century. Sometimes this was a positive role, as in the case of trader Frank Pyle. In addition to owning and managing the Towaoc trading post, Pyle was for many decades a trusted interpreter and adviser for the tribe.[35] Relations between tribal members and Pyle's son Byron, who took over the post at midcentury, however, were much more controversial. In addition to operating the reservation's only trading post, Byron Pyle was also U.S. postmaster for Towaoc beginning in 1948. In 1977 tribal members angrily accused Pyle of having withheld or cashed customers' checks mailed to the Towaoc Post Office so that he could collect on their debts at the trading post.[36]

EDUCATION

School attendance by Ute children continued to increase during the 1930s. The school situation in Ignacio had changed during the 1920s with the closure of the Southern Ute Boarding School in 1920 and its subsequent reopening to serve Navajo students in 1924. The nearby Allen Day School also closed in 1927. These school closures were part of the new policy of enrolling Southern Ute children in local public schools. A small number of Ute students once again began attending the boarding school, located near the agency just north of Ignacio, after the facilities there were enlarged in 1930 to accommodate a capacity of 200 students. This school offered instruction through the eighth grade.[37] The majority of Southern Ute students, however, were served by the public schools. In 1933, 52 children attended such schools, while 28 attended the Southern Ute Boarding School and 14 others attended off-reservation boarding schools.[38] Even though the Ignacio public schools and those in nearby Bayfield had decidedly heterogeneous student bodies, the Ignacio Utes did not necessarily experience desegregated schooling; they, along with Hispanic children, were typically separated from whites because of a lack of English skills.[39] Most tribal members spoke at least some

English: in 1931 the agency reported that 275 of 369 Southern Utes were able to speak English.[40] Apparently tribal members did not always appreciate the job being done by the public schools; a number of Utes at a 1937 meeting expressed the opinion that their children should be taken out of the public school and placed in the boarding school.[41] Nothing came of this matter.

School attendance at Ute Mountain was higher than in previous years but continued to pose more of a problem than in Ignacio. Whereas a 1934 survey showed only 10 out of 106 Southern Utes between the ages of six and sixteen not attending school, 34 of 110 Ute Mountain Ute children were not in school at this time. An additional disparity lay in the fact that, unlike students on the reservation to the east, Ute Mountain children experienced a totally segregated education: in 1933, 71 children attended reservation boarding schools—most attended the Ute Mountain Boarding School, with a much smaller number being served by the boarding school in Ignacio—while 4 others attended off-reservation boarding schools; only 1 child was educated that year in a public school.[42] These statistics are not surprising given the nature of the Ute Mountain Reservation and the way of life led by its inhabitants. Geographic isolation—and suspicion of outsiders—precluded public school education, and the seasonal movements of many stock-raising families at Ute Mountain made regular school attendance problematic.

In fall 1935, the Ute Mountain Boarding School, which previously had housed both Navajos and Utes in its dormitories, was converted to a day school for Ute students only. However, this new arrangement failed to meet the educational needs of a tribe whose members were scattered widely over a vast reservation. Superintendent S. F. Stacher reported in 1938 that only ten students lived within walking distance of the school. Like most of his predecessors and some of his successors, the superintendent was certain these Indians would be better off if they sent their children to the boarding school in Ignacio, but he reported that repeated attempts to win their assent to this arrangement had failed owing to the persistence of animosity between the Southern Utes and Mountain Utes.[43] Though the school situation at Towaoc was clearly fraught with difficulty, the people there looked on education in an increasingly positive light. An Indian Office school official stated in 1938 that one of the major tribal objections to a proposed relocation of Ute camps for the purpose of alleviating overgrazing was that people in the new camps—located away from the school bus routes—would not be able to send their children to school.[44] Despite this support for educating their children, there could be no denying the lack of educational achievement among the population as a whole. Following fieldwork on the reservation in the late 1930s, Marvin Opler observed that out of a total of 450 tribal members, only "half a dozen" spoke English. Fewer still had obtained a high school education.[45]

DISEASE AND DOCTORS

Though Utes increasingly utilized modern medical care during the 1930s, disease continued to take a heavy toll on the people, especially those at Ute Mountain. In 1930 deaths outnumbered births on both reservations, resulting in a 1931 population of 369 Southern Utes and 438 Ute Mountain Utes.[46] This represented the nadir of Southern Ute population, which subsequently increased fairly steadily for every year but one (1935) through the rest of the decade, closing with a population of 423. The record was much more bleak at Towaoc, where the Mountain Utes continued to decline in number until reaching an all-time low of 436 in 1933. The Weeminuche population subsequently climbed, very slowly, to a total of 459 at the end of 1939—but not before the tribe experienced two more deadly years in which deaths outpaced births.[47]

The high death rate of Ute Mountain Ute males during the 1930s is particularly striking. Whereas the ratio of males to females among the Southern Utes increased slightly over the course of the decade, the sex ratio at Ute Mountain took a distinctly different turn, falling from roughly 1.25 males per female in 1930 to less than 0.99 in 1940.[48] During these years, tribal members fell victim to the same diseases that had ravaged the tribe in preceding decades. Tuberculosis and venereal disease continued to be ever present—the latter increasingly prevalent as the decade wore on—while measles and flu epidemics often paid deadly visits to the reservations. Treatments for trachoma were still a common occurrence, so much so that in 1931 the Ute Mountain School was designated as a "trachoma school," reserved solely for students afflicted with this eye disease.[49]

Disease, and resulting death, struck with greater frequency in Towaoc than in Ignacio. This is evident from a survey revealing the number of Indians afflicted with various illnesses at each jurisdiction in 1934: tuberculosis, 30 Southern Utes and 50 Mountain Utes; trachoma, 195 Southern Utes and 250 Mountain Utes; and venereal disease, 156 Southern Utes and 200 Mountain Utes.[50] The Southern Utes were aided in their battle against disease by the February 1933 opening of the Edward T. Taylor Hospital in Ignacio, but this gave them no particular advantage over their neighbors to the west since the Ute Mountain Hospital had been in operation since 1920. Of more significance was the better housing in the Ignacio area and the "much better sense of sanitation" that Superintendent D. H. Wattson attributed to the Ignacio Utes in 1935. In the same report, Wattson identified another key factor in the differential incidence of disease and death: "The medicine man is with us in Ignacio, but [he] does not seem much in vogue." This was not the case in Towaoc, where, "slowly the Indians are coming to use the hospital, but it is an uphill grind, because the medicine men, of whom there are several in that district, are extremely active and endeavor to influence the Indians not to use the hospital." Largely as a result of the medicine man's continued popularity in Towaoc, "these Indians are still skeptical of a doctor."[51]

John Miller, chief of the Ute Mountain Utes, sadly described the health situation on his reservation to a U.S. Senate subcommittee in 1931 by saying of his people: "They all have sickness among them. They have been decreasing." He then tried to explain why his people preferred traditional medicine men to white doctors. An interpreter spoke for the chief:

> He says we have Indian medicine men and the doctors will work on them and they will die just the same, and if we take any person that is sick and take up to the hospital he die, too. He says, you take it among the Utes over there, there are a lot of Utes who do not understand English. They may be sick or something else and the doctor might give them different medicines than what the sickness is. He says you people are white people, you make your own medicines; you understand for what purposes you take it, and my Indian doctors they know something about this sickness this fellow got and they might help him out in case he is sick.[52]

The medicine men in Ignacio did not enjoy this same degree of devotion, and they found themselves playing an increasingly marginal role in Southern Ute society. One Ignacio healer sadly explained the decline of *pö' rat* (the Ute term for medicine man or shaman) to Opler in the late 1930s: "Today, the Indian doctors are not so good because they live in houses. They forget the old ways. The young people go to the White hospital, thinking that the White doctor can cure Indian sickness. In the old days everyone knew the Indian doctor alone could cure Indian sickness and they believed in him. They helped singing in his tipi when the pö' rat sang his strongest songs. They took him in a serious way. Today they laugh when they see him. . . . The pö' rat forgets."[53]

Not only did the people at Ute Mountain retain faith in the medicine man to a greater extent than did those in Ignacio; they also held fast to Ute taboos dating from the prehorse aboriginal period. For example, when an elderly pneumonia patient in the Ute Mountain Hospital heard that a newborn baby was in the building, he jumped through a window and ran off; he was simply following the traditional prohibition on a man being in close proximity to the birthing process.[54] Such incidents no longer oc-curred in Ignacio, and soon after the opening of the new hospi-tal in 1933, it was "usually filled to the limit."[55]

CULTURE

Clearly, more elements of traditional Ute culture had survived among the Ute Mountain Utes, but more of their people were dying as a result. The cultural status of the two Ute tribes of southwestern Colorado during the 1930s represented a mixture of continuity and change, a result of the interplay of accultura-tion and conservatism. Both of these opposing forces acted on each of the tribes, but the net impact differed greatly as cultural conservatism proved much stronger among the Mountain Utes.

In addition to the factors already identified—past as well as present geographical isolation, arid and unproductive land, his-torical lack of contact with European Americans, bitterness over unfulfilled government promises, and conservative leadership over time—an additional condition reinforcing Ute Mountain Ute conservatism throughout the reservation period was the extremely high proportion of full-blood tribal members. In 1930 only 5 peo-ple out of a total membership of 444 Mountain Utes were of mixed Indian and non-Indian ancestry. The situation among the Southern Utes for the same year reveals a much higher incidence of mixed ancestry: 50 out of 369 tribal members were mixed-bloods.[56] This same contrast remained in place in 1935: the Moun-tain Utes included 442 full-bloods and only nine mixed-bloods; the Southern Utes counted 317 full-blood members and 67 mixed-bloods.[57]

It is not surprising that intermarriage was more common among the Ignacio Utes, living as they did in close proximity to both Hispanic and Anglo neighbors. This situation arose from the 1896 allotment of their reservation, followed by white homesteading on the so-called surplus land. The resulting checkerboard pattern of Indian and non-Indian landholdings was accentuated even further in subsequent years with the sale of allotments to white buyers. Intermarriage was fostered in the Ignacio area by the close ties that developed between Southern Utes and their Mexican-American neighbors. Furthermore, a handful of Ute children who had been raised in Hispanic homes tended to marry Hispanic spouses.[58] The incorporation of non-Indian spouses into Southern Ute society inevitably provided a boost to the forces of acculturation.

Many traditional Ute social conventions that predated European contact continued to function in the Ute society of the 1930s. One feature of tribal society, decried by agency officials ever since the establishment of the Southern Ute Agency, was the comparatively casual nature of marriage among the Utes. In the 1930s, as in earlier decades, many Utes neglected to procure legal marriages, preferring to form and dissolve unions as they saw fit without any legal impediments to the free change of marital status. The Presbyterian missionary at Towaoc lamented this aspect of Ute culture in 1931: "It is a very simple matter with the Indians with their own form of practices to take up a young man with a girl and it is just as simple for them to separate again and take up with someone else."[59] Opler observed that "brittle marriages" and a high frequency of divorce still characterized family relationships among both tribes in the late 1930s.[60] Also common throughout this decade was the practice of Ute children being raised by their grandparents. This arrangement harks back to the prereservation migrational pattern of existence, which required that young parents be freed of the constraints of child-raising to preserve their mobility and ability to gather food for the extended family.[61]

Old fears and taboos and accompanying practices also persisted. The fear of ghosts led many Utes to forsake places where people had died and even to destroy the property of deceased Indians. Property was no longer destroyed in Ignacio, although some older tribal members still shunned buildings in which people had died or avoided speaking the names of the dead. Traditional fears and taboos surrounding death were more widely heeded in Towaoc.[62] Related to this fear of ghosts was a long-standing fear of witchcraft and evil medicine. Again, this cultural trait was more commonly retained among the Mountain Utes and the Allen Canyon Utes of southeastern Utah. The superintendent reported in 1938 that the latter band had for over twenty-five years lived in fear of both the Mountain Utes and the Southern Utes. These Utah Utes were afraid that the other two tribes, especially the Ignacio Utes, possessed the power to cause sickness and death in others.[63] And within each tribe accusations of sorcery resulting in death continued to surface throughout the decade.[64]

Many popular pastimes during the 1930s were continuations of long-established elements of Ute culture. The Utes had always loved to gamble, and people on both reservations made wagers on any number of games and events. The traditional Ute hand game had been a popular source of entertainment and gambling since long before European contact. This was a team contest in which players from one team attempted to guess which of an opponent player's hands held a die or other such object. This often spirited game, which is still popular among Utes today, would continue for a long time as wagers and guesses were made back and forth by both teams. Horse racing was another favorite pastime, one that had been the focus of wagering ever since Ute acquisition of the horse. More recently, the Utes had taken up card playing as a new vehicle for gambling. "Monte," a Mexican card game, was a particular favorite among both men and women.[65]

The Bear Dance was another traditional activity that continued to be held each year throughout the 1930s. Probably the oldest of Ute dances, the Bear Dance was a festive, social dance that had always been held in the spring before winter camps disbanded and family groups went their separate ways in search of food. According to Ute legend, this springtime ritual was taught to the Utes long ago by a bear. The story tells of a man who, following instructions received in a dream, journeyed to a certain spot in the mountains where he encountered a bear just awakening from his winter hibernation. The bear was shuffling forward and backward in a dance that he proceeded to teach to the Ute man. He then told the man to return to his people and teach them to perform the Bear Dance.[66] Soon Ute people of all bands were gathering each spring in large circular Bear Dance corrals, constructed of juniper boughs especially for this important social event, and shuffling forward and backward as the bear had taught them. The dance would begin with women selecting partners with a flip of their shawl in the direction of their desired partner. Then, to the accompaniment of singing and a rumbling musical sound produced by rubbing wooden rasps (called "moraches") on a metal resonance chamber, the partners faced each in two long lines—one of men, one of women. After shuffling forward and backward in these lines, a dance leader called a "cat man" would break up the two lines into individual pairs of partners, who then danced forward and backward on their own. The Bear Dance typically lasted for three days, though in recent years it has sometimes been held over a four-day period.[67]

Twentieth-century constraints sometimes led to changes in how this traditional dance was carried on or when it was scheduled. This was more true of Ignacio Bear Dances than of those held at Towaoc, which tended to remain closer in form to the original pattern.[68] The agriculturally bound Southern Utes, for example, altered the traditional date of the dance so as not to interfere with spring planting.[69]

Traditional Ute craftwork also survived more intact at this time in Towaoc than in Ignacio. Superintendent Stacher noted in 1939 that the Southern Utes engaged in no beadwork for commercial purposes and in no basketry at all. He further observed that their arts and crafts could not be compared with those produced by the people at Ute Mountain, "where the Indians have always devoted more of their time to basketry and beadwork."[70]

Like most aspects of tribal life, the practice of religion in the 1930s was characterized by both continuity and change, as both Christianity and more traditional forms of spirituality figured in Ute religious life. Missionaries first spread their faiths among the Southern Utes in Ignacio, but by the beginning of the 1930s the focus of missionary activity had shifted to Towaoc, where two missionaries—one Presbyterian and one Catholic—sought converts among the Ute Mountain people. Although no longer visited by missionaries, the Utes of Ignacio were able to attend both Catholic and Protestant churches in Ignacio. Competition for Indian converts sometimes gave rise to tension between the two rival missions in Towaoc. In 1925, for example, the superintendent reported attempts by "outside missionaries to create an unpleasant feeling" between the Catholic priest and the Presbyterian missionary then working on the reservation.[71] In 1930 a total of 195 Utes—out of a combined population of 813 on the two reservations—were reported attending church services: 123 frequented Catholic services, and 72 attended Protestant services.[72] Given the spiritual eclecticism of the Ute people, however, participation by tribal members in the activities of Christian churches did not necessarily imply abandonment of traditional Ute spirituality. As the Presbyterian missionary in Towaoc explained in 1929, the Ute people saw no contradiction in worshiping both the Great Spirit and the Christian God.

Both the Sun Dance and the Native American Church played important parts in Ute spiritual life during the 1930s, although not to the same extent among both tribes. The Sun Dance, which was a relatively recent innovation in Ute culture, had by this time become firmly established as a tribal institution. Originating among the Plains tribes possibly as early as 1700, the Sun Dance was transformed by Shoshone shamans in the late nineteenth century into a ritual more attuned to the hardship and disillusionment of the early reservation period. As a reflection of the new realities and changing concerns of reservation life, elements relating to war and bison hunting were dropped from the dance. At the same time, Christian features were added to the ritual.[73] This new Sun Dance, the one adopted shortly after the turn of the century by the Utes of Colorado, was a dance born of poverty and oppression. It was a ceremony that sought relief from the illness, death, and factionalism that afflicted Indian reservations; and it was a redemptive movement that enabled participants to reaffirm their integrity and identity as Indians in a world that was markedly hostile to the Native American.[74]

By the end of the 1930s, it had become clear that this ceremony was much more solidly entrenched in Towaoc than in Ignacio. At this time, with only five dancers participating in the annual rite in Ignacio and the Sun Dance chief there announcing his retirement, the future of the dance among the Southern Utes looked bleak. It looked much more promising in Towaoc, however, where more than three times as many dancers turned out, community response was greater, and observance of the rite was more traditionally accurate.[75]

An even more striking divergence between the two tribes was evident with respect to their acceptance of another spiritual practice—the peyote ritual. This ceremony, having been adopted by the Colorado Utes only in the 1910s, was something of a cultural innovation. Yet since it constituted an Indian form of spirituality, as opposed to the government-endorsed religion of Christianity, the peyote ritual in a way represented the continuation of traditional religion. In actuality, however, the peyote rite of the Native American Church embraced a syncretistic spirituality that had strong Christian overtones. A prayer heard by anthropologist Omer C. Stewart at a 1938 Ute Mountain peyote ceremony reveals the Christian underpinnings of peyotism as well as the saviorlike role played by the peyote cactus, which is consumed as a sacrament: "God, Jesus, Mother Mary, Peyote, we beg you this morning to bless each and every one of us. God, we thank you for this good thing you have given us, this peyote you have created for the Indians. . . . Bless us that through the use of it we will have health, strength, ambition, prosperity, and energy every day of our lives."[76]

The Indian Office continually sought to quash Indian use of the hallucinogenic cactus, and this was clearly the case at the Consolidated Ute Agency, where Superintendent E. E. McKean actively campaigned during the 1920s to suppress peyotism on the Ute reservations, with some success among the Ignacio Utes.[77] Peyote use was also controversial among the Utes themselves. Some Southern Utes objected to the high cost of peyote as well as of the food contributions required of ceremony participants. Other Ignacio Utes were bothered by the hallucinogenic effects of peyote on those who consumed it. "They stay up all night and act like drunks," complained one Southern Ute critic of the night-long rituals. "They do anything they want to girls then. They throw up sick."[78] Others, however, contended that peyote had much the opposite effect. A Ute Mountain Indian policeman asserted in the mid 1930s: "Four or five years ago, we people used to have trouble with whiskey. Peyote was just getting a foothold then. Now we have peyote and it helps the people go straight."[79] Peyotists often cited their rituals as an effective weapon against alcohol abuse, as is evident from this 1938 peyote ceremony prayer: "Help us to go straight, to live the right way. Especially make us strong to resist temptation when someone offers us whiskey. We know that all liquor is bad; but we are weak. Make us strong. Help us to become clean and pure through the use of peyote. Clean out from our bodies all poison and sickness."[80]

The responses of the two tribes to the introduction of peyote could hardly have been more contrasting. Whereas peyotism rapidly caught on among the Mountain Utes so that by the end of the 1930s roughly 90 percent of tribal members participated in peyote ceremonies, in Ignacio 90 percent rejected the practice, and only 10 percent of the people engaged in peyote rituals.[81] The latter situation developed despite the active sponsorship of the peyote ritual by Chief Buckskin Charlie. Interestingly enough, the small group of peyotists at Ignacio included many of the most educated, most independent, and seemingly most progressive members of the tribe. This fact undermines the obvious explanation that peyotism failed to thrive in Ignacio on account of the greater degree of acculturation among the Southern Utes. Many Ignacio Utes, most significantly Edwin Cloud and other tribal medicine men, stridently opposed the use of peyote. The sharp disagreement between Edwin Cloud and his brother Isaac Cloud, an ardent peyotist, is symptomatic of the dissension this issue caused among the Southern Ute people.[82]

The relationship between peyotism and shamanism at Ute Mountain was quite different, and this may explain the almost universal acceptance of the Native American Church here at the same time as it was nearly forced underground at Ignacio. Here there was no conflict between medicine men and peyote road chiefs; in fact, most Ute Mountain medicine men eventually became peyote priests themselves. The peyote ritual and the "sucking cure"—an important shamanistic healing procedure in which illness was literally sucked out of the patient's body—were regarded as highly compatible and could even be performed together.[83] In addition to shamanistic support, the widespread acceptance of peyotism at Ute Mountain was also spurred by the active support of political leaders such as Jack House, subchief of the tribe at the beginning of the decade and soon to become the tribe's overall chief.[84]

As with peyote rite acceptance or rejection, the role of tribal leaders in steering their people in the direction of either acculturation or continuity of traditional values could be decisive. The example that Buckskin Charlie provided for his people lay somewhere between the two extremes. Charlie, like many Indian leaders, could not be neatly categorized as either "progressive" or "traditional." To outside observers, his actions sometimes seemed to constitute an endorsement of accommodation with white ways; at other times, however, he appeared to embrace traditional values and practices. The Southern Ute chief had, of course, been instrumental in winning early Mouache and Capote support for accepting allotments, engaging in farming, and sending children to school. The plaque that honors Charlie on the tribe's monument to its great chiefs of the past acknowledges this contribution, remembering him as a "champion for agricultural advancement of his people—a Friend to All."[85] Yet Buckskin Charlie was clearly not an advocate of complete assimilation. He spoke Ute rather than English, he encouraged the continuation of traditional ceremonies, and he often lived in a tipi rather than his house.

Chief John Miller of the Ute Mountain Utes, by contrast, was a consistent proponent of traditional Ute ways and a tireless foe of cultural change imposed by outsiders. One 1935 observer noted the difficulty that the chief posed for the agency superintendent: "Mr. Wattson's problem in dealing with John Miller cannot be over-emphasized. His fanatical opposition to the white man's plans regardless of their effect on the tribe, is an almost insurmountable obstacle."[86] Miller's hostility to Anglo-American ideas was all encompassing. It even extended to home economics projects undertaken at the Towaoc boarding school. The chief undermined a community garden and canning project by persuading five of the twelve participants to drop out; and the project was further derailed by the nighttime destruction of much of the garden crop, "presumably by the older women who are systematically opposing white influence."[87] Cultural conservatism was firmly entrenched among the chief, the older women, and most members of the Ute Mountain Ute Tribe.

TRIBAL CONCERNS

In May 1931 a subcommittee of the U.S. Senate Committee on Indian Affairs visited Ignacio as part of a larger attempt to investigate conditions facing Indians throughout the United States. Senators Lynn J. Frazier and Burton K. Wheeler, along with the assistant commissioner of Indian affairs, held a hearing in Ignacio for the purpose of gathering information from both agency personnel and members of the two Ute tribes. The ensuing testimony by tribal leaders and other tribal members is very revealing of Ute attitudes and concerns on the eve of the Indian Reorganization Act.

Six Indians appeared before the panel, four Southern Utes and two members of the Ute Mountain Ute Tribe. Five of the six men spoke through an interpreter, and all five exhibited considerable irritation regarding government Indian policies and were particularly upset about recent changes in these policies. These men felt that the difficulties faced by their people were the result of the government's failure to live up to its treaty obligations. The abundance of treaties and agreements negotiated between the Ute Indians and the U.S. government from 1849 on, many of which were never ratified or never implemented, bred much confusion over the years; yet the Utes appear to have remembered the terms of every treaty they had signed. Tribal leaders were not always sure, however, which treaty was operative or in which treaty a particular government obligation was established.[88] As a result, the tribal members testifying at this hearing were unable to provide the senators with details regarding the origin of specific government commitments. The interpreter for Nicholas Eaton, for example, related that "he understands the Government owes his people some money. It is way back, at the time when George Washington made a treaty with his people." When the senators dutifully pointed out Eaton's error and suggested that the treaty to which he was referring might actually have been concluded during Abraham Lincoln's presidency, Eaton responded sharply: "Well . . . what did they do with the treaty? Did they bury Mr. Lincoln with the treaties that this tribe make?"[89] All that was important to these Ute men was the fact that their tribe had given up its ancestral lands and way of life in exchange for the promise of rations and annuities and other forms of support from the government. The Ute people had lived up to their part of the bargain, but the U.S. government had not.

Buckskin Charlie, who said that he understood "a little bit" of English but who spoke at this hearing through an interpreter, made similar references to government treaty obligations and to the all-important issue of money. "We have a treaty with the Government to pay to these people as long as they live, [but] they have been telling us we have not been getting any of it," the chief said. He also asserted that "the tribal funds will be there forever that belongs to these people and it will be paid as long as you Indians are living." The senators then asked the chief who had conveyed such guarantees to him concerning the tribal fund—which in actuality was rapidly being depleted—and Charlie replied that he thought it had been the commissioner. Like his fellow tribesmen at the hearing, the Mouache chief was certain that the tribe was owed sufficient money to provide for its future survival, but he was unable to offer any details surrounding this government obligation.

The aging Indian of some ninety years was even more irritated by the workings of the reimbursable system under which farm supplies and other goods were purchased out of tribal funds, with the money later repaid by the individuals who received the items from the agency. Buckskin Charlie had assumed the sheep provided to his people three years previously had been purchased by the government, when in reality, as he found out at this hearing, these animals had been purchased reimbursably out of the tribal fund. Charlie had not been fully aware of this arrangement, and in a question that must have sent shivers down the spines of the self-support–minded assimilationists in the Indian Office, the chief asked: "Why does the Government just want to spend that money buying the sheep for us? Why not pay out to the people cash?"[90] The chief was exasperated by the tribe's inability to make its own economic decisions and the government's refusal to allow tribal members to decide for themselves how to use their own resources.

Buckskin Charlie was very concerned about the tribal fund and about how this money, belonging to the tribe but over which the tribe exerted no control, was being spent. The senators informed him that $268,000 remained in the fund and that only a portion of agency salaries was being paid out of this money. "Well, that might be, he says," the interpreter replied for the frustrated chief, "because he don't know how to read, but we made a treaty with the Government." Charlie stated that in the future "he would like to have a good understanding" of such matters as the reimbursable system and expenditures out of the tribal fund.[91] The old chief, who understood little English, could not read, and had no say in the utilization of his tribe's money, was clearly annoyed by his lack of information regarding current policies and his inability to control matters affecting the destiny of his people.

John Miller, chief of the Ute Mountain Utes, echoed a complaint made three decades earlier by his predecessor, Ignacio: "We have a reservation over there but we have not got any water on the reservation." He cited the injustice that had occurred in the 1890s when his people had been given the most arid land while neighboring non-Indians ended up with much more productive lands: "But where they give us the reservation we have not got no water, but outside the rivers run through there and lots of white people live there that has land they got, but they give us reservation down there where there is no water."[92] Displaying the strong advocacy of tribal interests that would later lead an observer to characterize the chief as "an insurmountable obstacle,"

John Miller adamantly asserted the existence of treaty obligations. With the phasing out of rations and per capita payments
that was already under way, these obligations were increasingly
being ignored by the government: "When the Government made
a treaty with those people they agreed to pay these people so
much, and as long as any Ute Indians live and also they made a
treaty with them that they have rations. . . . That has been kind
of cut out, they have not been getting what is coming to them. . . .
After the Government made the agreement to pay the people so
much they have not received none of that money."[93]

One Southern Ute farmer appearing before the panel, Julian
Baker, provided a stark contrast to the other five Utes who testified that day. Unlike his fellow tribesmen, Baker spoke English
without the aid of an interpreter and made no mention of past
treaties. The thirty-seven-year-old farmer was much more interested in the problems that he confronted on his farm. Julian
Baker was more or less presented as a model farmer, and the superintendent eagerly pointed out that Baker's son was perform-
ing well in the public high school and would be graduating the
following year. Baker responded to the senators' queries about his
farming and livestock operations, and in his statement he raised
the issue of a labor shortage growing out of the agency's policy of
encouraging the Indians to raise sheep. He pointed out that since
the men were busy farming and the children were in school, this
left the wives to take care of the sheepherding. After initially
protesting this delegation of work to the women, the senators accepted Baker's explanation that this was not being done because
the Ute men were lazy but because they were already busy with
farming duties. In response to the senators' push for expanded
sheep-raising operations, the Ute farmer replied that he had no
desire for more sheep since this would require him to purchase
additional hay, his own hay crop already being insufficient. Baker
also told the panel that he understood the workings of the reimbursable system.[94]

The senators and the assistant commissioner, often vexed by the testimony of the other five Utes, were clearly encouraged by what Julian Baker had to say. Whereas the others had been interested primarily in obtaining continued government support, here was a hard-working, English-speaking Indian farmer who appeared to constitute the Indian Office ideal. Thus, this hearing, by highlighting the varied nature of the Ute response to a half century of Indian Service supervision, yielded something of a mixed verdict on the assimilationist Indian policies pursued by the U.S. government at the Southern Ute–Consolidated Ute Agency. Many Utes, particularly those of the older generation, continued to cling to nineteenth-century treaties and resist government entreaties to assimilate, but some younger tribal members, at least among the Ignacio Utes, were beginning to make some accommodations to the modern American society that surrounded them.

4

THE INDIAN
REORGANIZATION ACT
AND PURSUIT OF
SELF-DETERMINATION

On May 9, 1936, Buckskin Charlie died at the age of ninety-six in the tipi that stood on his allotment 2.5 miles north of Ignacio.[1] Here, on a section of the Los Pinos River valley where he had for years planted crops and tended livestock, he ended his long reign as chief of the Southern Utes. Born in 1840, before the Anglo-American onslaught had reached the Ute domain, the Mouache headman had been the principal chief of both his own band and the Capote Utes for fifty-six years. As a leader, Buckskin Charlie championed not only adjustment to an agricultural economy but also maintenance of traditional cultural institutions. A measure of his success as a leader lies in the fact that after more than a half century of enduring assimilative forces and government control on a small and noncontinuous reservation, the Southern Utes still existed as a distinct community.[2] Unlike their neighbors to the west, the Southern Ute Tribe at this time observed a hereditary chieftainship. Accordingly, Charlie was succeeded as chief by his eldest son, Antonio Buck Sr.

During this same year, John Miller, chief of the Ute Mountain Utes since the death of Ignacio in 1913, also passed away. Like Buckskin Charlie, John Miller had been an influential leader among his people, with outside observers concluding that the tribe was "dominated" by the strong-willed chief.[3] Unlike the Southern Ute leader, however, Miller had been a staunch opponent of virtually all government policies. His demands for continued government support of his people, in the form of rations and annuity payments, had been unrelenting—but ultimately fruitless. This was the legacy of conservative resistance to the Indian Office that was bequeathed to Jack House, the tribal subchief whom Miller selected as his successor shortly before his death.

Thus, 1936 marked the end of an era for both the Ute Mountain Ute and Southern Ute Tribes. Both tribes lost leaders to whom they had become well accustomed, chiefs who had instituted well-established patterns of response to the ever-present intrusions of the U.S. government. This changing of the guard occurred at the same time as the two Ute tribes were responding to a fundamental shift in the U.S. government's policy toward its Indian wards. The Indian Reorganization Act, an innovation emanating from the Indian Office and made law by Congress in 1934, was being implemented on the two neighboring reservations; and at the time of Buckskin Charlie's death, younger leaders of the Southern Ute Tribe were in the process of adopting a new tribal constitution in accordance with provisions of the act. Several years later, after a slower and more grudging start, the Ute Mountain Tribe would follow suit with a new constitution of its own. Thus, in the late 1930s both tribes were about to embark, under newly designated chiefs, on the task of forming new tribal governments. Both in their subsequent responses to the IRA and in the roles that they would define for their new chiefs, the tribes would prove, once again, to be strikingly different in their approaches. Jack House and Antonio Buck Sr. would both be the last chiefs of their respective tribes; but whereas one would wield immense political power until his death many years later, the other would soon fade into the shadows of another institution of more recent origin, retaining only a symbolic role for himself as chief.

THE INDIAN REORGANIZATION ACT

The advent of fundamental change—as opposed to the sporadic incremental change that had been the norm on both Ute reservations since 1895—began with the Indian Reorganization Act, which became law on June 18, 1934. Initially introduced as the Wheeler-Howard bill after its two principal sponsors, Representative Edgar Howard of Nebraska and Senator Burton K. Wheeler of Montana, this legislation was the brainchild of John Collier, Franklin D. Roosevelt's commissioner of Indian affairs. Collier sought to reverse the course of U.S. Indian policy, which for nearly half a century had endeavored to assimilate Native Americans through allotment of Indian lands, erosion of tribal sovereignty, and destruction of native cultures. Although Collier's program did not necessarily renounce the ultimate goal of assimilation, it did entail the abandonment of allotment in severalty and of the federal assault on traditional cultures; and it also called for a new emphasis on tribal self-government. Collier's proposal ran into congressional opposition, prompting the commissioner to seek President Roosevelt's aid in winning additional support. The president responded with a letter to Congress in which he decried the current policy of "autocratic rule by a Federal department over the lives of more than 200,000 citizens of this Nation [which] is incompatible with American ideals of liberty." Roosevelt urged passage of the Wheeler-Howard bill, which he described as "a measure of justice that is long overdue."[4] A reform bill was subsequently passed by Congress, but the resulting Indian Reorganization Act was watered down considerably and was far less ambitious than the original Wheeler-Howard bill.

Nevertheless, the IRA represented a substantial reform of U.S. Indian policy. It called for the political reorganization of tribes through the creation of elected Tribal Councils that would manage tribal affairs in accordance with new tribal constitutions. Economic reorganization of tribes would be achieved through the granting of corporate charters. The IRA also sought to promote economic development on reservations through the establishment of a $10 million revolving credit fund. Perhaps most significant of all was a package of reforms designed to protect and increase Indian landholdings. The IRA ended the allotment policy that had been so devastating to tribal land bases. Between 1887 and 1933, Indians lost over 87 million acres of land under the Dawes Severalty Act. In addition to prohibiting future land allotment, the IRA indefinitely extended federal trust restrictions on Indian land; it permitted the voluntary exchange of allotments and heirship land, thus enabling tribes to consolidate checkerboard reservations; it restored to tribal ownership remaining surplus land that had been taken as part of the initial allotment process; and it authorized the annual appropriation of federal funds for the purchase of new tribal lands.[5]

Even before Congress voted the Indian Reorganization Act into law, the Indian Office had begun promoting the new policy among the two Ute tribes of Colorado. The initial response from the Utes was not encouraging. After two weeks of informal discussions following receipt of a letter from Commissioner Collier, the Southern Utes held a general meeting, on February 10, 1934, to consider the issue of tribal reorganization. The result was a letter to the commissioner that politely declined his invitation to participate in the new program. The letter revealed a rather conservative sentiment on the part of the tribe's membership: although they welcomed the idea of self-government, they were not at all eager to tamper with the status quo. As the assembled Utes considered the various economic and political arrangements currently in place on the reservation, they consistently concluded in every case that current institutions and policies should be continued. The major pieces of the Southern Ute–Indian Service network—the familiar allotment system, the existing tribal government composed of two hereditary chiefs (one chief and one subchief) and an elected tribal council, the current system of administering the tribal fund—were to be maintained without any significant alteration. The letter, signed by Buckskin Charlie and four members of the Tribal Council, expressed the tribe's belief that "a charter for self-government is unnecessary since by the treaty of 1868 it is guaranteed certain rights and privileges, which are sufficient for its needs." The letter concluded with the following remark: "The tribe appreciates this opportunity of considering its problems, but believes its members are not ready for the opportunities presented."[6]

Given this rather unenthusiastic response from the normally cooperative Southern Utes, the ensuing clear rebuff from the Indians at Ute Mountain probably came as no surprise to Superintendent D. H. Wattson. Chief John Miller, still smarting from the government's decision of the previous year to eliminate per capita payments and rations, was unimpressed with Wattson's explanation of the commissioner's new policy:

> The Commissioner talks two ways. Long time ago he said we should have rations and clothes as long as we lived. Now he takes our rations from us. We are contented as we are. We do not want roads built on the reservation. We have always got along without them and if they are built now the white men will come in and take our reservation. We do not want you to work on our springs. If you do the water will stop running. We do not want jobs for our young men for if they learn to work you will say that they can earn their own living and we shall then never get rations. The President talks straight. George Washington told us we were to have an agent and an agency to look after us and that is what we want. . . . It is not right that we are not given rations and annuities.

The chief refused to even accept the circular from the commissioner when Wattson attempted to hand it to him. Miller's position was simple and unyielding: he did not want jobs or development of the reservation, and he did not want anything that would result in greater intrusion by whites on the tribe's reservation. He simply wanted the government to provide for his people's needs as promised in past treaties, and that was all. Wattson lamented the domination of the tribe by its "retrogressive" chief and Tribal Council, whose authority prevented the "younger progressive element" from taking advantage of opportunities for their own betterment.

Initial rejection by both tribes did not put an end to Indian Office efforts to sell the IRA to Ute leaders. John Collier believed passionately in his reform program, and he was determined to convince—and even at times to coerce—tribes to ratify the IRA and thereby agree to participate in tribal reorganization.[8]

Over time and in the face of relentless campaigning by Superintendent Wattson, the Southern Utes eventually accepted the Indian Reorganization Act. The superintendent was aided in this endeavor by Buckskin Charlie's support of the reorganization program.[9] On June 10, 1935, 95 of the tribe's 188 eligible adult voters took part in a referendum and approved participation in the IRA by an 85 to 10 vote.[10] The Ute Mountain Indians, however, did not prove to be as receptive to the superintendent's campaign. Wattson reported being met at Ute Mountain "by a wall of stoical apathy" and by derision of the more accommodating Ignacio Utes. "They profess to look with scorn upon their neighbors and relatives at Southern Ute," the superintendent related, "though I suspect their attitude is not unmixed with envy of the self-reliance and independence of the latter."[11]

Despite the continued resistance, Wattson proceeded to schedule a referendum on IRA participation for June 12, 1935. John Miller and his subchief Jack House, the latter being referred to by Superintendent Wattson as one of the chief's "henchmen," were largely successful in derailing the election by sitting at the polling place all day and directing tribal members not to vote. Wattson even enlisted the assistance of Southern Ute Tribal Council chairman John Burch in a last-ditch attempt to change the chief's mind or convince younger tribal members to ignore their leader, but it was to no avail. Jack House steadfastly reasserted his opposition, which evidently grew out of a combination of confusion and distrust: "There is one reason we won't vote. If we vote we don't know we will get the annuity back. This bill may not amount to anything. How do we know we will get anything? . . . There may be something behind this bill. I think there is something behind it which we don't understand. Something so the Indians will be worked. They have to work, work, and never get a payroll. . . . The Indians here . . . can't write, they can't read, they don't understand what is behind it." John Miller repeated his previously stated objections to the reorganization program, adding a new complaint regarding the recent closure of the Ute Mountain Boarding School in preparation for its conversion to a day school: "It isn't right to vote. My people are not going to vote. Long time ago they told us we would always have a boarding school, and now it is closed. They are taking it away from us. We don't understand this, and it isn't right to vote. It is just the same as stealing from the tribe for an Indian to vote."[12] Thus, in John Miller's mind, voting in the IRA election was akin to a nineteenth-century Indian signing a treaty that handed over all of his tribe's land to the government.

The reluctance of Ute Indians to vote, as indicated by the vocal opposition of Ute Mountain tribal leaders and by the low voter turnout (barely over 50 percent) in the Southern Ute IRA referendum, is indicative of Native American skepticism at this time regarding participation in federally sponsored referenda. Participation in the electoral process did not come naturally to the members of many tribes that had traditionally governed themselves through consensus. A Tribal Council member of the Onondaga Tribe recalled of his people's narrow rejection of the IRA: "The reason why it was so close was because people did not believe in voting."[13]

After Miller and House left the polling site, 12 tribal members did step forward to cast their votes, resulting in a tally of 9 to 3 in favor of IRA participation. In many referendum elections, including all subsequent Ute Mountain tribal elections, such a low voter turnout—only 12 out of 225 eligible adult voters—would constitute rejection of the issue in question, but not in the case of the IRA. Although the Indian Reorganization Act stipulated that a referendum had to be held before any tribe could be reorganized under the new program, the act was written in such a way that the deck was definitely stacked in favor of reorganization: a tribe would be excluded from participation under the act only if a majority of adult members voted against tribal reorganization.[14] Thus, the fact that only 12 voters materialized in Towaoc in June 1935 guaranteed the Ute Mountain Tribe's enrollment in the reorganization program—in spite of the outspoken opposition of the tribal leadership and the lack of response from the vast majority of tribal members. The voting response, or lack of it, of the Ute Mountain people was not particularly unusual in terms of the nationwide Indian response to the IRA, although the typical tribal election results actually lay somewhere in between the two extremes represented by the two neighboring Ute tribes of Colorado. Of the approximately 97,000 Native Americans eligible to vote in IRA referendums, only 38,000 actually voted in favor of reorganization, the remainder either abstaining or voting against participation under the act. Even with these unimpressive numbers, however, the net result of the referendum process was that 174 of the 252 tribes and bands holding referenda voted in favor of the act.[15]

TRIBAL REORGANIZATION

The two Ute tribes of Colorado—one largely by choice, the other by default—now faced the task of reorganizing themselves under the provisions of the IRA. The first step involved the political reorganization of the tribe through the adoption of a tribal constitution that would establish a new tribal government. The Southern Utes were fairly quick to initiate this process by calling a General Council meeting (an assembly of adult tribal members) in November 1935 at which tribal members selected a ten-member committee to draft a constitution for the tribe. The resulting document was drawn up with the assistance of the agency superintendent and the Indian Reorganization Unit, but as one of the unit's field representatives appreciatively noted in a memo to a colleague, the Ute committee did play an important role in the constitution's creation: "Though full of imperfections which will give our lawyers the jitters, this Constitution was a joy to read, because it shows every evidence of expressing the Indians' wishes. May we have more of this kind!"[16]

The Southern Utes thus were able to have some input in the formulation of what would become their governing document, but the resulting constitution—and undoubtedly most other tribal constitutions dating from the same period—certainly bore the heavy imprint of government officials. Like the Indian Reorganization Act itself, the IRA constitutions tended to be largely the creations of non-Indians. As the Indian Reorganization Unit field agents visited IRA tribes, they brought with them model constitutions that had been drawn up by the Indian Office. Many tribes throughout the country felt that they had little choice but to accept these plans as their own governing document. Not surprisingly, most tribal constitutions adopted under the IRA were thus quite similar.[17] Longtime Southern Ute superintendent Ray deKay indicated in 1972 that the Southern Ute Constitution of 1936 had been one of these generic tribal constitutions. DeKay characterized the 1936 document as "the BIA's Constitution," an "old BIA draft" that had been adopted by fifty to one hundred tribes.[18] Some Indian Reorganization field workers worried that this "incredibly high degree of standardization" among tribal constitutions would undermine the success of these governing documents by giving the impression that these federally designed constitutions were "nothing more than new Indian Office regulations."[19]

The proposed Southern Ute constitution was presented to the General Council for approval in January 1936. The plan was received without any protest and approved with a few abstentions but no dissenting votes.[20] The constitution was then submitted to the Indian Office, which soon returned the draft to the tribe with suggested revisions. These were made by the constitution committee, and on September 12 an election was held in which 69 of 129 eligible tribal voters were present to decide whether the final draft should be adopted. By a vote of 61 to 8, the Constitution and Bylaws of the Southern Ute Tribe was accepted, and it went into effect on approval by the secretary of the interior on November 7, 1936.[21]

This constitution established a new tribal government, replacing the previous arrangement consisting of a hereditary chief and an elected council. The government created by the Southern Ute Constitution, which became effective just six months after the death of Buckskin Charlie, did not provide any political role for the chief. It replaced the old five-member council with a new six-member Tribal Council, and it delineated the powers that this body would exercise. In addition, it stipulated criteria for tribal membership, set forth procedures for holding elections and for amending the constitution, and terminated the allotment of tribal land. Henceforth, all unallotted tribal land was to remain tribal property, although it could be assigned by the Tribal Council for the private use of individual members.

Thus, the Southern Ute Tribe, consistent with its history of considering federal policies and accepting those perceived as beneficial to Ute interests, moved relatively smoothly along the IRA track, much as John Collier had hoped all tribes would do. Much to the frustration of government officials, however, the Ute Mountain Utes remained true to their tradition—one decidedly less accommodating to overtures from the government. Jack House, who became chief on the death of John Miller in 1936, continued to pursue the leadership agenda of his predecessor, one that he had helped shape as tribal subchief. At the core of this agenda was a conservative preference for the status quo, a deeply held suspicion of any outside influence, and an undying distrust of the U.S. government. Given this isolationist tradition—its roots stretching back to such earlier Weeminuche leaders as Ignacio, Mariano, and Red Rock—and also given the tribe's unenthusiastic initial response to the Indian Reorganization Act, it is hardly surprising that the Ute Mountain Tribe did not eagerly embrace the prospect of adopting a tribal constitution.

Not until February 11, 1938, some two and a half years after inclusion in the reorganization program, did the Ute Mountain Utes petition the commissioner of Indian affairs to call a special referendum on the question of adopting a tribal constitution. This request was signed by Chief Jack House; by Anson Whyte, leader of the Allen Canyon band; and by Tribal Council member Isaac Peabody. All three leaders marked the document with their thumbprints since they, like almost all members of their tribe at this time, could neither read nor write.[22] The petition was approved at a February 11 joint meeting with the Southern Ute Tribal Council held in Towaoc. Superintendent S. F. Stacher was encouraged by this favorable response from a people who "in the past have been very difficult to approach and have shown only passive interest in their affairs."[23]

Old habits proved hard to break, however, for the Ute Mountain and Allen Canyon Utes soon had second thoughts. At a joint meeting with council members from both the Southern Ute and Uintah and Ouray Reservations, held in Moab, Utah, on May 10, 1938, Anson Whyte interrupted a discussion of Confederated Ute land claims to explain to his fellow Ute leaders his tribe's position on the adoption of a tribal constitution: "Now about us Ute Mountain Utes. Our children are not educated enough to handle our problems, as well as you people. We were going to adopt the Constitution and By laws but after thinking it over we changed our minds and thought it best to remain as we are. My friends, I am telling you because I'm sure you would like to know why we refused to adopt it." Whyte also took advantage of this opportunity to complain about Superintendent Stacher, who was continually urging Whyte's people to move from the Allen Canyon area of Utah to reservation lands near Ignacio, where they could become farmers. "But we do not like to do that because we like our place regardless how hopeless it is and we aim to remain there."[24]

More than a year after this meeting, the pendulum had swung back in favor of adoption of a constitution as members of the Ute Mountain Tribal Council met with their counterparts from Ignacio in an August 16, 1939, joint meeting. By this time, the Ute Mountain Tribe had already approved a constitutional draft, which the superintendent returned to the council at this meeting along with suggested changes made by the secretary of the interior. Several of the Southern Ute councilmen cited the benefits of their own constitution and urged their Ute Mountain neighbors to approve the document. Isaac Cloud strongly endorsed such a move:

> With our people we feel this Constitution has helped us very much, I feel as a member of the Tribal Council, what we say is set. If we do not understand a certain thing or problem facing us with the help of our Superintendent we find the light in solving our problems, we see it our problems and duty to find out all we can be-

fore we send in a signed Resolution. And I am sure that if you adopt this Constitution you will benefit by it as we have, but it takes time before very much can be done. It will also help you hold your land for you, for we do not know what the future has for us and this Constitution has it [sic] promising act of holding our land and property for us.

Jack House, then chairman of the Ute Mountain Tribal Council as well as the tribe's chief, agreed: "I feel it is all right for us to adopt this Constitution." All four of his fellow council members then voted for the constitution with the suggested revisions.[25]

In a referendum held on May 8, 1940, tribal members approved the constitution and bylaws by a 91 to 12 vote. The Ute Mountain Tribe's long and fitful campaign for adoption of a tribal constitution finally reached fruition with the Interior Department's approval of this governing document on June 6, 1940.[26] Given the illiteracy of tribal leaders, this tribal blueprint could hardly have been anything other than an Indian Office document, and it was almost identical in form and content to the Southern Ute Constitution. Like the Southern Ute plan, this constitution established a new Ute Mountain tribal council as the tribe's governing body. Like its counterpart in Ignacio, this body would consist of members elected for three-year terms, with two members elected by the adult tribal members each year. In addition to the six council members elected from Towaoc, the Ute Mountain Tribal Council was to include one member elected annually by the Allen Canyon group in Utah. Again like the Southern Ute Constitution, there was no mention anywhere in this document of a tribal chief. But whereas this lack of constitutional legitimacy gave rise to a chieftaincy of increasingly diminished importance in Ignacio, it would have no effect on the continuation of chiefly authority exercised by Jack House in Towaoc.

With constitutions in place, each tribe set about forming its new Tribal Council. On November 7, 1936, within days of the secretary of the interior's approval of the governing document, the Southern Utes elected six members to serve on the new Tribal Council. Included among the council's first members were Julian Baker, the model farmer lauded by federal officials in the 1931 Senate committee hearings; Julius Cloud; Antonio Buck Sr., the tribe's chief; and John Burch. Burch, who had been chairman of the preconstitution Tribal Council, was elected by his fellow councilmen to serve as the first chairman of the new council.[27] Burch was soon succeeded by Antonio Buck Sr., who thus came to hold both the title of chief, which no longer conveyed any political power, and that of council chairman, which would soon become the most powerful government position in the tribe. This continuation of the Buck family's leadership eased the transition from the traditional leadership of chiefs to the new governmental arrangement dominated by the Tribal Council.

Even before the Department of the Interior's approval of the document became official, the newly elected members of the first Ute Mountain Tribal Council to be organized under the tribe's constitution held their initial meeting on May 24, 1940. Among the seven members of this body were Jack House, Anson Whyte, and George Mills. Even though Chief House had been chairman of recent preconstitution Tribal Councils, he never assumed this position in the new council; instead, Mills was elected chairman by his fellow council members, and he held this position without interruption into the 1950s. Also serving on this first Tribal Council were two women, Aileen Hatch and Emma South Beecher.[28] Their presence highlights the active participation of women that characterized the Tribal Councils of both tribes in the years that followed. Female council members were particularly active in Ignacio. Although the Southern Utes did not elect a woman to their Tribal Council until 1948, there was almost always female representation, often more than one member, from that time forward.

Having completed political reorganization under the Indian

Reorganization Act, the Ute Mountain Council members now appeared fairly pleased with the results of this process to which they had initially been so opposed. Responding to an inquiry from the commissioner seeking their reaction to the IRA, council members stated in September 1940 that they were "better satisfied with the way it is now."[29]

The second major step envisioned for tribes under the Indian Reorganization Act—one that many tribes, including the Ute Mountain Utes, did not take at this time—was incorporation under a federal charter. The Southern Utes embarked on this process on April 20, 1938, obtaining the signatures of 57 members on a petition to the secretary of the interior requesting that a charter be granted to the tribe.[30] After initiating this process, however, tribal leaders seemed to lose some of their enthusiasm for incorporation, preferring to postpone consideration of this matter until they had attended to other business items. Superintendent Stacher reported on October 3 that the additional time had enabled him to further acquaint the Utes with the proposed charter. Now that they better understood the proposal, he anticipated that a majority of the tribal members would be in favor of its adoption.[31] Stacher's assessment proved correct when on November 1, 1938, the tribe's membership adopted the corporate charter by a vote of 78 to 3.[32]

The Corporate Charter of the Southern Ute Tribe stated that tribal incorporation was intended to promote the economic development of the tribe; confer corporate rights, powers, and immunities on the tribe; secure the economic independence of the tribe's members; and provide for tribal exercise of functions heretofore carried out by the Department of the Interior. Unlike most charters of incorporation, this one imposed certain limitations on the tribe's authority to purchase and dispose of its assets: the tribe was not permitted to sell any of its land or interests, such as mineral or water rights, associated with the land, nor could the tribe lease its land or related interests to non-Indians without the secretary of the interior's approval. The charter did permit the tribe, subject to some limitations, to engage in one practice that was quite popular with the Southern Ute people, namely, the per capita distribution of profit from tribal corporate enterprises in excess of all expenses and obligations.[33]

THE NEW TRIBAL COUNCILS

Once in place, the tribal governments established under the Indian Reorganization Act often failed to live up to their advance billing as instruments for effective tribal self-government. As the new Tribal Councils conducted business on reservations across the country, there was little change in operations at the agency level; despite the advent of constitutional tribal government, it was largely business as usual. The Indian Office still controlled the agenda and authored most tribal legislation.[34] Furthermore, the new Tribal Councils often functioned as if, in the words of one Tribal Organization Division employee, they were "instrumentalities of the Indian service" rather than bodies representing their own people.[35]

Thus, the newly created Tribal Councils in Towaoc and Ignacio often appeared as if they were not in control of their own affairs during their first years of existence. Although the tribal constitutions had given birth to political institutions designed to achieve self-determination, the continued presence of federal government oversight, in combination with tribal leaders' inexperience and lack of self-confidence (the result of a half century of Indian Service paternalism), made it exceedingly difficult for the Tribal Councils to successfully assert their own interests. Accustomed to being dictated to by Indian Service officials, council members seemed passive in the face of agency personnel or officials from the Indian Office who attended their meetings. The minutes of meetings from both Towaoc and Ignacio reveal that such officials frequently dominated the proceedings, often doing most of the talking; and almost all council resolutions were initiated by the agency rather than by the Utes themselves. At one meeting in 1940 when the superintendent was absent, the members of the Southern Ute Tribal Council seemed lost and uncertain as to what they should do without him, the chairman commenting, "Mr. Stacher is the superintendent and he has to lead us on."[36]

This same dominance of proceedings by the superintendent was the norm at Towaoc as well. Here council members offered little input as the superintendent controlled the agenda and typically presented prewritten resolutions, which were explained to the council and then put up for a vote. The other consistent factor in these meetings was the dominance of Jack House over his fellow council members. Whenever agency personnel were not talking, it was the chief's voice that was most likely to be heard. His stance on matters before the council had an immense influence on other council members.

Discussion of tribal pension money at the April 3, 1941, meeting was typical of the procedure followed at Tribal Council meetings in Towaoc. Superintendent Floyd E. MacSpadden explained the situation and then presented two possible courses of action. Jack House responded that he favored one of the two proposals and then asked his colleagues what they thought. They all agreed with the chief, and the matter was settled.[37] Given the lack of education of most Ute Mountain tribal leaders, the council was still forced to ask the superintendent to prepare any resolutions that it sought to adopt even after it began to initiate more of its own actions later in the decade.

Jack House's preeminent position on the Ute Mountain Tribal Council, like Antonio Buck's assumption of the chairmanship of the Ignacio council, bolstered the legitimacy of the new elective governing body by incorporating the established political authority of the chieftaincy. During the 1940s, Chief House, a middle-aged stock-raiser who had never attended school or learned

English, often expressed the traditional Ute Mountain distrust of
the federal government and conservative resistance to government policies that had characterized John Miller's leadership. In
1941 House echoed the familiar refrain of hostility to outside intrusion when he complained about inroads made on the reservation by the Civilian Conservation Corps:

> When our old chief [John Miller] was still living a CCC man came
> to us and had a talk with us about this CCC. Told us that money
> was being appropriated for such work. That this work was more of
> an aid to those folks who do not receive any income. When set up
> will not affect the agency. The chief told him that it was too good
> to be true, and that there must be a catch to it somewhere. He told
> the white man that when it was set up, it might get us into serious
> trouble. But the CCC man said "No, it won't be that way." Before
> we knew it, the CCC men started to work down here on our reser-
> vation and we did not like it because they went ahead without our
> permission.

House was also irritated with Superintendent MacSpadden, who
had moved the council's office out of the agency building to make
room for the CCC. "He and the CCC seem to be taking over quite
a territory," the chief protested.[38]

The superintendent was certainly not enthusiastic about Jack
House's leadership on the council. MacSpadden complained of
opposition to his proposed 1942 budget by "the reactionary element led by Chief Jack House." In this case, House came up on
the losing side of a close 4 to 3 vote approving the budget.[39] Later
that same year, the superintendent and the chief again clashed
over the issue of tribal loans. MacSpadden submitted to the Indian Office an urgent request for budgetary funding, but he explained to the commissioner that there was no immediate need
to obtain the tribe's pension funds since he was hoping to convince the Utes "that the use of credit is desirable." House disagreed with this policy, as the superintendent related: "Chief Jack

House steadfastly refuses to be a party to any loaning of tribal funds to individuals insisting that tribal money should be allotted as per capita."[40]

Tribal council members on both reservations occupied a difficult position as they sought to define their role and determine the extent of their power. They often found themselves caught in the middle between strong pressure for action from their constituents and constraints on their ability to act imposed by the federal government. This was particularly the case in Ignacio, where the Southern Ute Tribal Council faced a vocal tribal membership but had difficulty achieving the results demanded by the people. Councilmen encountered a number of obstacles, one being their own procedural inexperience. Council members frequently jumped from one matter to the next, making it hard to conclude any business. And efficient work habits, such as punctuality, proved slow to develop. An exasperated Chairman Julius Cloud berated his colleagues for their habitual tardiness in 1941: "How can anything be accomplished when things run like this? You have seen other business meetings, for instance [those of] our white brothers, [where] the members do not hang around outside and wait for someone to come out and get him."[41]

Another obstacle confronting the Tribal Council in Ignacio was its lack of popular support. Tribal members were often highly critical of council decisions. This persistent problem plagued tribal governments across the country. Tribal Councils were subject to criticism from constituents not only for their own actions but also for those of the federal government, as tribal members often failed to properly differentiate between the two. When Native Americans were discontented, the U.S. government, which exercised ultimate control over tribal affairs, presented a more distant and less immediate target than the less powerful but much more visible and accessible Tribal Council.[42]

Criticism of the Southern Ute Tribal Council was often quite intense during the council's early years. At one meeting, for example, a proposal to purchase a truck sparked a bitter attack on what one critic regarded as the council's foolish spending of tribal money. Another person in attendance then jumped into the fray, blasting both the superintendent and the council as "a bunch of know-nothings and false-hood dealers."[43] A persistent source of popular dissatisfaction with the governing body was the widely held perception that the council did not listen to tribal members. One older man expressed his irritation over this issue to council members at a 1940 meeting: "No help has been given me for eleven years, therefore I have no interest in your affairs. I only sit in and listen to what you men have to say. What you discuss is not new to me. I know all about it, but once I tried to help you com-mittee men and you would not listen to me, so I feel more like an outsider."[44] At the same meeting, another elderly Ute man ex-pressed the frustration of tribal elders, whose counsel had been highly valued in the past but who felt ignored under the current system: "We have a right to have a say about our affairs. We like to help the councilmen decide because they are too young to foresee the future of the things presented to them. We older men know these things, therefore, we feel confident that we should be included in their struggles."[45]

Even though the Southern Utes were quick to criticize their Tribal Council, they were not always so quick to participate in the political process. Tribal elections had to be postponed time and again when quorums failed to materialize. This was not a new problem, but as the 1940s wore on, attendance by the general membership at Tribal Council meetings dropped precipitously. This was partly the result of the popular perception that the council was not interested in hearing the people's views and partly the result of Superintendent MacSpadden's highly unpop-ular policy of discouraging comments during meetings from any-one other than council members.

When council members were not suffering the complaints of their constituents, they were frequently being reminded of the institutional limits of their power. The Indian Service largely controlled the agenda, leaving Southern Ute Tribal Council members with the impression they were powerless in the face of this bureaucratic giant. One of a seemingly endless series of outbursts arising out of this sense of frustration occurred in Ignacio on May 15, 1940, when a regional official of the Indian Service requested that the council appropriate money for fire suppression. Fed up with being told what to do by federal officials, Antonio Buck reacted bitterly, fuming that the superintendent was eager to spend the tribe's money but that the council could never get what it wanted. Councilman Isaac Cloud then chimed in, "It seems that our Council has no power, all Resolutions which are presented we sign."[46] But it was Julius Cloud—World War I veteran, member of the council since its inception in 1936, and council chairman for most of the 1940s—who was most vehement and unrelenting in his attacks on government interference with the council's attempts to conduct its own affairs. When the agency farmer, Elbert J. Floyd, who doubled as the chief law enforcement officer for the agency, evicted a troublesome Ute man from the reservation in 1940, Cloud was incensed that the agency could take this action without consulting the council: "What is Mr. Floyd that he should chase [the Ute man] off his reservation? Will he always chase people off the reservation? It isn't fair for Mr. Floyd to do that. [The man] was reported by some one who no one knows. Why don't we know? Don't we Council men have the power to go ahead? The employees at the agency are ahead. Council men do not amount to anything."[47]

Although Julius Cloud continued to launch blistering attacks on the Indian Office—rechristened the Bureau of Indian Affairs in 1947—for the duration of his long council career, meetings did become somewhat less contentious as the decade went by and members of the Southern Ute Tribal Council became more comfortable in their new role. Cloud's outspoken advocacy of his people's interests and his verbal assaults on the federal bureaucracy made him quite popular among tribal members. After serving as chairman from 1939 to 1944, followed by continued service on the council under new chairman Sam Burch, Julius Cloud was overwhelmingly reelected to his council seat in 1947. Council members once again tapped Cloud to be chairman the following year.[48] Meanwhile in Towaoc, George Mills remained chairman of the Ute Mountain Tribal Council throughout this entire period, but he did not play a particularly dominant role in council proceedings. Chief Jack House continued to be the single most influential member.

RESERVATION LIFE AND ECONOMY

Jack House and his fellow council members faced a difficult situation on the Ute Mountain Reservation during the late 1930s and early 1940s. In a petition adopted at a General Council of the tribe's members in 1938, reference was made to the grim conditions facing tribal members at this time: "We have lived many years in improvised shelters, tents, muslin teepees, shacks and a few of us in hogans of the Navajos, all unsuited to our needs. There has been much sickness and many deaths in the past years that has been caused by exposure in severe weather. We are without conveniences and sanitation is certainly bad, and it is our desire to improve our situation as speedily as possible."[49]

Although living conditions were still bleak, the tribe had made some progress, as had the Southern Ute Tribe, in adjusting to the post-ration and postannuity economy of the reservation. In 1932, on the eve of the tribe being cut off from the distribution of food rations and per capita payments from the agency, the sum of all earned income received by members of the Ute Mountain Tribe totaled only $8,000, slightly over one-half of this from livestock operations and the rest from wage work. The Southern Utes, by comparison, collectively earned around $40,000 in the same year—$29,000 in agricultural income and $11,080 in wages.[50] By

1940 both tribes had experienced substantial increases in the individual incomes earned by their members. In that year, the Ute Mountain Indians collectively earned $59,040: $28,989 from agricultural pursuits and $20,665 from wage work (most of it with the Civilian Conservation Corps), plus additional earnings from the sale of firewood and arts and crafts. Southern Ute income in 1940 showed a similar increase to a total of $107,743, which was almost evenly divided between farming and livestock income, on the one hand, and wage income, on the other.[51] Throughout the ensuing decade, the Mountain Utes experienced slow but steady increases in their individual incomes. The Southern Utes, however, showed a substantial drop in their total income during the early to mid 1940s, undoubtedly resulting from the departure of forty-six of their members to serve in the armed forces during World War II. Incomes also declined with the termination of the CCC shortly after the attack on Pearl Harbor. Earnings rose again soon after the war's end, and by 1946 the Ignacio Utes had rebounded to an income level only slightly below their prewar earnings.[52]

Much of the agricultural income of the 1940s came from cattle raising, which had increased dramatically on both reservations over 1930s levels. Whereas the Southern Utes possessed only 110 head of cattle, mostly dairy cows, in 1933, and the Ute Mountain Indians only 91 head, by 1945 these numbers had grown to 717 and 1,447, respectively. The shift to a cattle-based agricultural economy was especially dramatic at Ute Mountain, where the tribe's stock of sheep decreased by nearly one-half as its cattle herds boomed. The Indian Office instigated this substitution of cattle for sheep during the 1930s as part of the federal government's pursuit of soil conservation on western lands, including Indian reservations. In addition to utilizing the CCC for the construction of reservation range improvements such as dams and reservoirs, the Indian Office also fought soil erosion by implementing a program of stock reduction. Sheep in particular were targeted since they were much more destructive to range grasses than cattle. This program, which produced substantial economic distress and provoked loud protests among the people of the Navajo Reservation, was also employed on the adjacent Ute reservations of Colorado. Stock reduction had less of an impact in the Ignacio area, where the size of Southern Ute sheep herds remained fairly stable between 1934 and 1945.[53] During this period, however, Southern Ute cattle herds increased substantially.

An additional source of tribal income assumed increasing importance during the 1940s. Even though government officials and white settlers had successfully conspired to strip western tribes of their best lands during the nineteenth century, usually leaving the Indians with the least productive lands, the newcomers had failed to check beneath the surface for a new source of wealth— fossil fuel deposits. The Southern Utes and Ute Mountain Utes subsequently discovered substantial deposits of oil, natural gas, and coal situated beneath their reservations. Even the barren, dry wastelands of the Ute Mountain Reservation—apparently not so worthless after all—were found to contain large petroleum deposits. As early as 1921, Ute Mountain tribal members had voted to approve the leasing of mineral rights for portions of their reservation. This 1921 lease, prepared by the Indian Office, allowed the Midwest Refining Company to drill for oil on 9,600 acres in the eastern end of the reservation in exchange for cash rental payments plus one-eighth of the oil produced.[54] Such petroleum activity continued over the years, and revenue from oil and gas leases grew to substantial proportions for both tribes during the 1940s. Unlike agricultural earnings, however, most of this oil and gas revenue was tribal, rather than individual, income.

Along with rising income, the two Ute tribes also experienced steady population growth. Following their devastating encounters with disease during the 1930s, the Ute Mountain Utes rebounded during the following decade, reaching a tribal population of 502 in 1945. The Southern Utes numbered 458 in that same year.[55] These tribal members, in their increasing numbers, faced major changes in their social environment. Some changes, such as the establishment of a Boy Scout troop at the Ute Vocational School (formerly the Southern Ute Boarding School) in Ignacio, were relatively small in scope and benign in nature.[56] Others, such as military service by many tribal members during World War II, would have profound impacts on tribal society. The service of Ute veterans during the war resulted not only in initiating short-term socioeconomic change but also, more significantly, in planting the seeds of fundamental social and political transformation by exposing future tribal leaders to the world outside the reservation. A total of ninety-four Indians from the two Ute reservations served during World War II, and many of these individuals would come to play major roles in tribal affairs in subsequent decades.[57]

Other developments, such as the growing incidence of drunkenness and crime, were decidedly negative. Liquor on the reservation was nothing new—nineteenth-century agents had complained about the impact of whiskey provided to the Utes by "Mexicans," and Superintendent Wattson had worried about the "increasing prevalence of drunkenness" on the reservation in 1933.[58] Both liquor and crime, however, were becoming more common in the 1940s. Whereas the agency reported only one criminal act committed on the Southern Ute Reservation in 1938, six arrests were reported among the Ignacio Utes in 1945.[59] The Ute people—like all Native Americans at this time—were still forbidden by law from possessing liquor, so those desiring alcohol relied upon the services of non-Indian bootleggers. This level of alcohol abuse and criminal activity, though certainly troublesome, was minor in comparison to the social devastation that alcohol and crime would wreak in decades to come.

Life at Ute Mountain during the 1940s continued much as it had in previous decades, although the residential pattern was slowly beginning to change. Tribal members were earning more income, and more families were living in permanent homes, increasingly built in the vicinity of Towaoc. Most Mountain Utes, however, continued to live in nonpermanent housing in camps scattered throughout the reservation. Tents were still a common sight, with Navajo-style hogans also widely in use.

The most significant development on the Ute Mountain Reservation during the 1940s actually served to slow the pace of change among this people. The school situation in Towaoc, greatly worsened by the 1935 conversion of the Ute Mountain Boarding School into a day school, which made attendance by the tribe's scattered population difficult, went from bad to worse with the closure of this school in 1942. This left the already undereducated tribe with no school on its reservation, and many Ute Mountain children were thus denied an education. A 1951 letter by BIA area director Eric T. Hagberg recounts the situation surrounding the closure of the school and the subsequent ill effects of this move:

> The school was closed in 1942, by order of Superintendent Mac-Spadden. In subsequent correspondence, three different reasons were successively advanced—a shortage of water, non-attendance of pupils and an inability to secure adequate personnel. Through all the correspondence, there was the argument that the Ute Mountain and Blanding [Allen Canyon] tribes would be better off if they would move onto lands in the Southern Ute area where adequate grazing and agriculture resources were said to exist. The Mountain Utes steadfastly refused any attempt to effect such a move and have likewise opposed the transfer of their children to the Ute Vocational School in Ignacio. Only within the last two years has that ever been reasonably successful. Forty-two children were still not enrolled in any school last year [1950].[60]

But the damage did not stop with many of the tribe's children being deprived of an education. In 1942 the Indian Office closed the entire Towaoc agency and withdrew all agency personnel, excluding a stockman and his assistant; and even these two employees were removed in 1948.[61] Thus, for what would be an eleven-year period, the Towaoc Utes were without a school, a hospital, or an agency, being ostensibly served by the Consolidated Ute Agency located some 85 miles away in Ignacio. This isolated people, already characterized by a very low level of education and adjustment to modern society, were cast adrift, with virtually no services other than those they might obtain by traveling all the way to Ignacio. The Mountain Utes, who had always had a somewhat strained relationship with the federal government, now had the "feeling that the Government has sort of walked off and left them and is no longer interested in their welfare."[62]

Former agency farmer and now Superintendent Elbert J. Floyd reported that at his first meeting as superintendent with the Ute Mountain Tribal Council in May 1950, he had been requested to "exert every effort to have this school reopened."[63] The council further indicated its desire to again have a school in Towaoc by voting to appropriate tribal funds for the purpose of school building maintenance. It was not until 1953 that the agency and school in Towaoc were reopened.[64]

TRIBAL BUSINESS

While conducting tribal business during the late 1930s and 1940s, the Tribal Councils in both Ignacio and Towaoc dealt with a wide spectrum of issues, ranging from the date of the Bear Dance each spring to oil and gas leases worth hundreds of thousands of dollars. Agricultural concerns were frequently addressed, with the Towaoc council trying to further the interests of its stock-raisers, while the council in Ignacio was often involved with irrigation questions and other matters affecting the farming and livestock operations of its people. Both councils passed resolutions to improve housing conditions. And they devoted much attention to the utilization of tribal resources, issuing permits both to tribal members and non-Indians for grazing stock, cutting fence posts, harvesting timber, and extracting mineral or energy resources from tribal land. Later in the 1940s, both bodies became increasingly involved with oil and gas exploration and development on their respective reservations.

The Tribal Councils often addressed the financial needs of their people. They awarded monthly pensions to old or disabled tribal members and frequently considered loan requests from individual members. Another type of council resolution, exceedingly popular among the people, involved the distribution of tribal funds on a per capita basis to all tribal members, both adults and children. Such per capita payments, to be issued only out of tribal revenues in excess of all expenses and obligations, were a rare occurrence in the days when tribal budgets were small. The Southern Ute tribal budget, for example, totaled $80,800 in 1939 before declining in the face of limited revenues to a low of $38,500 in 1945.[65] The Ute Mountain Council faced even leaner financial circumstances, with tribal budgets in the amount of $39,800 in 1939, dropping as low as a meager $17,000 in 1946.[66] Later in the decade, increasingly high revenues from oil and gas leasing improved the financial outlook of the two tribes considerably. The Southern Ute tribal fund increased from a balance of $1,491 in 1940 to over $474,819 in September 1949.[67] This made it possible for both tribes to regularly distribute per capita payments in steadily larger amounts. The Southern Ute Tribal Council authorized payments of $50 in 1948 and $75 in 1949, while the Ute Mountain Tribal Council voted for per capita payments of $50 in 1948, $75 in 1949, and $100 in 1950. With fossil fuel deposits bringing the two tribes increasing revenue as they approached the midcentury mark, individual tribal members were able to share in this wealth.

Another ever-present object of council attention was the status of land within the reservation boundaries. The Ute Mountain Tribal Council sometimes endeavored to purchase adjoining white-owned tracts or additional summer range land, the latter being in extremely short supply on its reservation, but land was more commonly a matter of concern to the council in Ignacio because of the checkerboard nature of Southern Ute landholdings. Following allotment of the Southern Ute Reservation in 1896, unallotted or "surplus" land had been opened to non-Indian settlement. As a result, unlike the continuous block of tribal land that constituted the reservation of the unallotted Mountain Utes, the Southern Ute Reservation was a confusing jumble of allotted land, owned by individual Utes but held in trust by the government; unallotted tribal land, owned collectively by the tribe; and non-Indian landholdings. This situation was far from ideal from the Southern Ute perspective. It was further complicated by a half century of inheritance of Indian allotments, resulting in multiple claims on individual allotments that were often quite small to begin with.

Thus, much of the Ignacio council's time was spent trying to improve the land use and land-ownership situation on the Southern Ute Reservation. Beginning in the late 1930s, the Tribal Council embarked on a "blocking up program" that sought to consolidate tribal landholdings in two ways. First, the program reversed the allotment process and settled inheritance disputes by purchasing allotted lands from their Indian owners. This increased the amount of tribally held land and resolved land use problems associated with small tracts of allotted land jointly owned by a large number of heirs. Second, the tribe corrected some of the most problematic examples of the reservation's checkerboard nature by purchasing non-Indian-owned lands that were wholly or in part surrounded by tribal land.[68] To this end, the council appropriated $30,000 each year throughout most of the 1940s for the purchase of land. In essence, with this program, the tribe was buying back its own land—supposedly "surplus" land that had been withdrawn from the reservation following the 1896 allotment. Once purchased by the tribe, tracts could then be assigned by the council to individual tribal members for their use in farming and grazing or as a residence. Other tribal land, such as the Oxford Tract, was directly administered by the tribe for tribal farming operations. The Ute Mountain Tribe operated a similar tribal enterprise, the 200-acre Mancos Creek Farm, on its reservation. Still other Southern Ute tracts were leased to non-Indian ranchers or farmers for their use. With appraisals, purchases, exchanges, leases, and assignments, the Southern Ute Tribal Council was continually occupied with land matters.

UTE LAND CLAIMS

Tribal purchases were not the only means of adding to the tribes' landholdings. In addition to halting the allotment of Indian lands, the Indian Reorganization Act also authorized the secretary of the interior to restore to tribal ownership any remaining surplus land that had previously been withdrawn from reservations across the country and then offered up for sale by the government. Accordingly, Secretary Harold L. Ickes in 1937 took initial steps toward returning certain unsold lands on Colorado's Western Slope to the Utes. These lands had been ceded by their ancestors to the United States in the 1880 agreement negotiated amid the anti-Ute furor following the Meeker Massacre of 1879.[69] The prospect of returning land to the Utes caused a tremendous uproar among Coloradans, particularly West Slope ranchers. Colorado politicians, led by U.S. senator Alva B. Adams (D), quickly mobilized to quash the restoration of land to the Utes. Adams succeeded in attaching to a minor bill an amendment banning the transfer of most Colorado land to the Utes. When President Roosevelt signed this bill on June 29, 1938, 3.5 million acres of western Colorado were reaffirmed as public lands owned by the federal government.[70] The Adams amendment was not a total defeat, however, for the Ute tribes of Colorado: some 222,016 acres south and east of Ignacio and 30,000 acres in Montezuma County were specifically exempted from the amendment, and in 1938 these two tracts were restored to the Southern Ute and Ute Mountain Reservations, respectively.[71] The 220,000 plus acres returned to the Southern Utes were remnants of the surplus lands that had been withdrawn from the Southern Ute Reservation and opened to white settlement in 1899. They had remained unsold because of their lack of agricultural potential, but these high and dry tracts would yield a surprising bonus to the Southern Ute Tribe in years to come with the subsequent discovery of natural gas reserves underlying the acreage.[72]

The Adams amendment of June 1938 also contained a silver lining that would eventually prove very lucrative for the Utes of both Colorado and Utah: it gave them the right to sue the United States in the U.S. Court of Claims over the issue of tribal land claims, and, additionally, it furnished the legal basis for a judgment in their favor in one of the four suits that they initiated over the following decade.

In the early twentieth century, many Indian tribes advanced claims against the U.S. government regarding past loss of land. Tribes were unable to pursue these claims, however, until the federal government waived its sovereign right not to be sued. Congress accommodated many tribes by passing a series of 133 special acts enabling particular tribes to take their land claims to the U.S. Court of Claims.[73] It was one of these special acts that had permitted the Ute Indians, united as the Confederated Bands of the Utes, to sue the federal government and ultimately win a $3,408,611.40 judgment from the U.S. Court of Claims in 1910. The Adams amendment, which Congress passed in 1938, once again gave the Utes the right to present their land claims before the Court of Claims. While these Ute land cases were being considered, the Indian land claims situation in the United States was greatly simplified by congressional passage of the Indian Claims Commission Act on August 13, 1946. This act, supported in part by legislators who regarded it as a step toward terminating the special protective relationship between the federal government and individual Indian tribes, established a new court to hear claims from any interested tribe. The five-judge U.S. Indian Claims Commission would address only those claims arising prior to the act's 1946 passage and filed within five years. Any claims originating after 1946 would be considered by the Court of Claims. Before the abolition of the Indian Claims Commission in 1978, it awarded approximately $800 million to various tribes in compensation for past loss of land.[74]

Since the 1938 Ute land claims suit was initiated prior to passage of the Indian Claims Commission Act, the suit was presented to the U.S. Court of Claims. This claims action, which ultimately yielded the largest monetary award of any Ute land claim, was initiated by the Northern Utes of Utah and later joined by the two Colorado Ute tribes.[75] The suit revolved around the tribes' contention that the Adams amendment, by declaring surplus land remaining from the 1880 Ute cession to be "the absolute property of the United States," had extinguished the Utes' still valid interest in this land. After all, the 1880 agreement had stipulated that the Utes were to receive payment for this land whenever the U.S. government might sell it. Since their claim to this Western Slope land had been extinguished without compensation by the Adams amendment, it could be argued that the Utes were entitled to payment for this land. The Court of Claims agreed with this line of reasoning on October 4, 1943, and it subsequently decided in favor of the Ute bands in three other suits filed during the 1940s. It would be ten long, frustrating years, however, before the Southern Utes and the Ute Mountain Utes actually received any money resulting from these claims cases.[76]

The Southern Utes and Ute Mountain Utes teamed with their Northern Ute kin from the Uintah and Ouray Reservation in

Utah in 1938 by entering into a contract with Salt Lake City attorney Ernest Wilkinson to pursue the land claims. Neither Wilkinson nor his Ute clients could foresee the long road that lay ahead of them as they embarked on this quest for compensation. Along the way, a number of issues arose that would complicate their efforts. The first and most persistent of these was a dispute among the three Ute tribes over how to divide whatever judgment they might be awarded. This question first arose in 1938 and surfaced again the following year, provoking considerable debate among representatives of the three Ute tribes. The Northern Utes contended that according to the "old treaty" of 1880 they were entitled to two-thirds of the total compensation for the loss of their old homeland in western Colorado; one-third was to be divided among the Southern Utes and Ute Mountain Utes. Representatives of the latter two tribes protested that such a distribution formula was unfair, advocating instead that the funds be distributed among the bands according to population.[77]

Disagreement over this issue persisted and was still evident when Ernest Wilkinson met with representatives of all three Ute tribes in Ignacio in 1946. At this time, Wilkinson advised the tribal leaders to set this troublesome issue aside so that they might concentrate on the more pressing matter of appropriating money for the continued prosecution of the suits. Obviously preoccupied with the distribution question, the Ute representatives found it hard to ignore this topic. Distrust was in the air as the Northern Utes were initially suspicious of a Southern Ute resolution regarding the payment of litigation-related expenses: "If anything is under cover, we would like to have it out."[78] The Colorado Utes' distrust of their Utah relatives, and also of themselves, was still in evidence two months later when a question arose at a Southern Ute Tribal Council meeting about alleged attempts by the Northern Utes to influence the Ute Mountain Indians.[79]

An additional task, and a rather large one, was the necessity of determining the value of the lands in question. After issuing a judgment in favor of the tribes, the Court of Claims ordered each party in the case to make an appraisal of the 4.5 million acres of western Colorado land to which the claims pertained. Wilkinson hired a team of fifteen experts to conduct this immense appraisal in 1946.[80] The following year, Wilkinson reported to a joint council of the Colorado Utes that in addition to this surface appraisal, it would be necessary to appraise the mineral value of this vast area in order to establish the total value of the land. Having already expended $116,000 for the surface appraisal, the Ute tribes were now asked by their attorney for an additional $250,000 to pay for assessment of the land's oil, gas, coal, uranium, and vanadium deposits.

The contrasting reactions of the two Tribal Councils to this request revealed the Ute Mountain and Southern Ute Tribes of 1947 to be worlds apart. The Southern Ute Tribal Council members were not ruffled by this request for a substantial outlay of tribal funds, realizing the necessity of making the additional investment. Julian Baker sought to clarify the matter for his non–English-speaking colleagues from Ute Mountain: "Friends, Mr. Wilkinson is asking for some more money in order to do some work for us. . . . Maybe it may not be very clear to you people from Towaoc. It is hard to interpret and you may not understand very clear what is being said." Jack House's response indicated that Baker had been correct in his assessment of the situation: "It is clear to you, but it is not clear to us. You understand what is being said and we do not understand." Julius Cloud, whose impatience with bureaucratic obstacles to tribal action has already been noted, was the picture of patience as he recounted the situation facing the two tribes, indicating that the Southern Ute council was in favor of drafting the necessary resolution and stating that he hoped the Ute Mountain council would also approve this measure. Jack House was not so patient: "At the meeting last summer, I understood that Mr. Wilkinson was going to look for everything on the land that was taken away from the Utes by the Government. It's been a long time now and we haven't got the money yet. It has taken too long for him to get the money for us. I am getting old and some of the other old Council Members I used to be with are no longer here. Mr. Wilkinson has not gotten any money for us."[81]

Ute Mountain council member Marshall Whyte was similarly skeptical of giving Wilkinson any more money: "It may sound good for the Southern Utes, but as for me it does not sound good. Who is going to benefit from it? Who is going to get the money? We are not getting the money. It will take too long for us to get the money. We may all be dead and the money will not do us any good. Maybe the Attorney is going to get all the money. . . . The money he is asking for should not be given. . . . Of course, I do not understand English very well, but I think he should not get the money he is looking for."

Confused by the litigation process, hamstrung by the language barrier, frustrated by the lack of results nine years after the tribes had initiated their claims action, and distrustful of outsiders as a result of the long history of broken promises made to their people, the Ute Mountain representatives saw no reason to give still more of the tribe's precious money to a white man they hardly knew. As the discussion continued, Jack House's skepticism, and his distrust of Wilkinson, grew: "You Southern Utes understand what is being said and can give them the money. We do not clearly understand why he wants the money. . . . He is going to keep on asking for more money and then our money will be gone. . . . He will soon let us go and he will get some of the money. This is all he wants—money. He has not gotten anything for us. He has a lot of help. We want someone else instead of him because he has taken such a long time and yet we haven't got the money." The meeting concluded with the Southern Ute Council agreeing to pass the resolution requested by their attorney. Jack House said that his council members needed to talk with their people before they would take any action.

The patience of members of both tribes would soon wear thin, for the Utes' wait for their judgment money was far from over. Nevertheless, the two tribes now had well-established Tribal Councils whose members were slowly gaining confidence in their ability to conduct tribal business, although this was more true in Ignacio than Towaoc. The former council jealously guarded its preeminence in Southern Ute tribal politics, as its members demonstrated in 1948 when they were "considerably irked" by the fact that the tribe's dance team had made its own contract with the Durango Fiesta Committee, which had failed to contact the Tribal Council.[82] Self-determination remained elusive, but political reorganization, at least in Ignacio, was becoming a reality.

5

THE 1950s:
NEW WEALTH
AND NEW CHALLENGES

At long last, on July 13, 1950, the U.S. Court of Claims entered its final judgments on four land claims suits filed by the Confederated Bands of Ute Indians. All four cases were decided in favor of the Utes, and the U.S. government was ordered to pay a total of $31,761,206 in compensation for land taken from the bands. When the Ute tribes promptly settled their long-simmering feud over distribution of the claims money, approving a division whereby 60 percent would go to the Northern Utes and 40 percent to the Ute Mountain Utes and Southern Utes, it appeared the two Colorado tribes were about to split a windfall of roughly $12.2 million. But one final hurdle emerged from another segment of the federal government to once again delay payment of the claims. Before Congress would appropriate the judgment money, each tribe had to submit a long-range plan delineating how these funds would be spent. Until the Bureau of Indian Affairs and Congress approved such "rehabilitation plans," each tribe's share of the claims money would remain in the U.S. Treasury.[1] The long wait was not yet over.

Since the two tribes were eager to obtain their money and were faced with this government directive, they had no choice but to produce the plans. Thus, the Utes of Colorado embarked on a process that would lead them to a fundamental reassessment of their situation midway through the twentieth century. In order to formulate the required rehabilitation plans, each tribe's leaders would have to determine tribe goals for the future. Thus, the planning process constituted a defining moment in the modern history of the Ute Indians of Colorado.

ADOPTION OF TRIBAL REHABILITATION PLANS

The planning process began as a joint effort of the two tribes under the guidance of the Consolidated Ute Agency. Southern Ute chairman Julius Cloud and Ute Mountain chief Jack House accompanied Superintendent Elbert J. Floyd to Washington to present their three-page plan to the commissioner of Indian affairs in April 1951. The commissioner rejected the plan because it lacked detail and it was primarily the work of the agency rather than the Utes themselves.[2] Thus began a new stage in the planning process, one that would be dominated by tribal leaders. In this phase, the two tribes worked separately and developed individual plans of their own. In many respects, the two resulting plans were very similar, but the processes by which they were formulated and adopted by each tribe contrasted greatly. The Southern Utes' leaders were far better educated and more adept in negotiating the bureaucratic ways of the BIA. Their counterparts in Towaoc lacked language skills and experience in dealing with the white world. Despite this apparent advantage in "civic talent," the Southern Utes proved the slower of the two in adopting a rehabilitation plan. The Ute Mountain Utes, after some initial protest, settled into the task of planning and emerged with a rehabilitation plan that was approved by Congress nearly a year in advance of the plan emanating from Ignacio.[3] The planning process of the Southern Utes, despite—or perhaps because of—

their relative abundance of talent, would become a much more combative and soul-searching affair. For this reason, the following discussion will focus primarily on developments in Ignacio rather than those in Towaoc.

At a May 8, 1951, General Council meeting, the Southern Utes selected the members of a planning committee to begin drawing up a rehabilitation plan. This was the task that had brought John E. Baker, the young engineering student and World War II veteran, back from his studies in Chicago. This body, with Baker as its chairman, produced a lengthy document that was approved by the Tribal Council for presentation to the people at a General Council meeting. The September 28, 1951, meeting of the Southern Ute people, as described at the outset of this volume, was a lively and contentious affair that demonstrated the strong divergence of opinion within the tribe over the question of what to do with the tribe's land claims windfall. John Baker had led the Planning Committee in devising a plan that distributed only a portion of the total amount to the tribal membership: each member would receive $3,500, of which $3,000 could be spent only with the Tribal Council's approval.

Predictably, many in the audience felt that the entire amount should be distributed among the people, with no strings attached. This reaction was only natural for people who had historically been denied access to their own money. Annuity payments from the government and per capita payments out of the tribal fund had in the past been channeled by the Indian Office into Individual Indian Accounts, which were controlled by the agency. Older tribal members no doubt still recalled bitterly having to appeal to Indian Service officials for permission to tap their own funds and being able to make purchases only when officials in Washington deemed them to be "necessary." The Ute people had not seen any cash as a result of their earlier land claims judgment, awarded in 1910. None of the principal from this judgment fund had been distributed per capita to tribal members, and distributions made out of the interest on this fund were deposited directly in the inaccessible Individual Indian Accounts.[4] Now that the Utes anticipated a truly large financial award over which the tribe, not just the Bureau of Indian Affairs, would exert control, many Ignacio Utes favored being given their full share of this windfall.

A key leader of the opposition to the committee's rehabilitation plan was thirty-four-year-old Sunshine Cloud Smith. Like John Baker, she was a well-educated World War II veteran who had returned to the reservation to serve her tribe. Born at dawn in a three-room adobe house in 1916, Sunshine's father, Edwin Cloud, had chosen his daughter's name after witnessing the bright light of the rising sun at the time of her birth.[5] Sunshine Cloud was born into a family that had long been active in the spiritual, cultural, and political life of the tribe. Edwin Cloud was a medicine man, and in addition to being the Southern Utes' Sun Dance chief, he also participated in tribal leadership as a sub-chief under Buckskin Charlie. As a child, Sunshine Cloud quickly learned about the conduct of tribal affairs as she was often present when her father held meetings with Buckskin Charlie and other tribal leaders.

After two years at Ignacio High School, Sunshine Cloud went to the Haskell Institute in Kansas, where she graduated in 1935. She continued her education at both Haskell and the University of New Mexico, studying first in the health field and then majoring in business. In 1940 she married a non-Indian man, taking the name Sunshine Smith. Moving with her husband to Indiana early during World War II, she worked in a factory producing land mines but soon left this job to enlist in the Women's Army Corps. After serving the rest of the war as a surgical technician in Utica, New York, the young Ute woman was mustered out of the service at the end of 1945. Smith then moved with her husband to Los Angeles, returning briefly to the reservation in 1946 to care for her ailing father, who died late that year. Not until 1950 did

Smith and her husband return once and for all to stay on the reservation where she had spent her youth.[6]

Like John Baker, Sunshine Smith had been called back to Ignacio to help the tribe meet its new challenges. It was not surprising that the tribe would turn to Sunshine Smith for assistance in its governance, given the long record of service by various members of the Cloud family. It seemed only natural for Sunshine Smith to follow in the footsteps of her father, her uncles Antonio Buck Sr. and Isaac Cloud, and her brother Julius Cloud, in assuming a leadership position within the tribal government.

In the first of many battles between these two emerging tribal leaders, Sunshine Smith, who had previously been appointed to the council to complete the term of a deceased councilman, outpolled John Baker at the September 28 General Council meeting to be elected in her own right to the Tribal Council. As the discussion shifted to the proposed rehabilitation plan, it became clear that she held a starkly different conception of what should be done with the claims money. Feeling that $3,500 was not enough to meet the needs of individual tribal members, Smith advocated full distribution of the award, amounting to roughly $8,000 per person. She also disagreed with Baker over the restrictions imposed by the committee's plan on how people could spend their money. "What happens to the people?" she demanded to know. "Why don't they [the Bureau of Indian Affairs] give us a chance? They're trying to hold us back, don't they think that we are intelligent enough to spend our money as we please?"[7]

"You might be intelligent enough," Baker retorted, "but are the majority of people?"

At this point Eddie Box, a tribal member and World War II veteran who would soon be elected to the council, rose to introduce an alternative plan favored by many of the tribe's veterans, a plan that called for the distribution of $8,000 to each tribal member. He called on Sunshine Smith's non-Indian husband to present the plan. After a brief explanation by Thurman Smith, John

Baker responded bitterly, objecting to both the plan and its spokesman: "The only veterans that get ahead are the veterans that are working, and by putting money in his pocket [this] is not going to make a better man of him. It is going to make a man go around with a chip on his shoulder. Any veteran that wants to talk to us does not have to get a man to do his talking for him. We are all Indians and he should come to us man to man. But if you have to get a man to do your talking for you—I'm ashamed of myself, because I'm a veteran, also." After much heated discussion, the tumultuous meeting came to a close with an untallied vote in favor of the alternative plan and without any vote on the much-abused committee plan.

This meeting revealed considerable anger and confusion among the tribal membership surrounding the proposed rehabilitation plan. The people were angry, feeling they had not been consulted, and they understood little about the committee's plan other than what they would—or would not—receive in the way of individual money. More significant was the emergence of strong factional disagreement, which pointed to the existence of a fundamental philosophical dichotomy within the tribal leadership. Baker feared the consequences of simply handing large amounts of money to people; instead, he favored the development of tribal programs to maximize the socioeconomic development of the tribe as a whole. He and his supporters were not eager to abandon the tribe's relationship with the BIA and its agency in Ignacio either. As former council member Graves Kent pointed out at a subsequent meeting, the $8,000 plan was both unrealistic and, to his mind, undesirable: "We asked [Commissioner] Myers for $5,000, and he told us we could not have that much money, so how do you expect that they will let us have $8,000? They [the BIA] won't give you that much money. If you get the $8,000, you will have to live as the whitemen do, on your own without the Agency to help you. Maybe the ones that are asking for the $8,000 are ready to live as the whiteman, but we are not.

That $3,500 is right for us and if we want some more we can ask for some more later."[8]

Sunshine Smith, for her part, sounded quite ready to jettison the Consolidated Ute Agency. She had no interest in continuing the federal government's authority over her people, and she blasted Baker's plan as tantamount to a donation of the tribe's money to the Bureau of Indian Affairs. The former surgical technician also strongly objected to being confronted with an already completed plan that had been adopted without any input from tribal members. She was bitter that the people had had no say in its formulation. Furthermore, she was much more concerned with individual welfare and independence than with the establishment of tribal programs such as those envisioned in the proposed plan. She complained that "nothing has been done for the individual Indian, it has always been for the tribe." For example, she asked, "Why not let the Indians buy their own machinery and clear off their own lands instead of buying machinery for the tribe to subjugate land?"[9]

Such arguments advocating the distribution of tribal resources among the members of the tribe and scorning both federal and tribal supervision of the affairs of individual Indians paralleled a growing sentiment in Congress in favor of "termination." This policy, which rapidly gained momentum in Washington during the 1940s and into the 1950s, represented a revival of the assimilationist program—one that refused to die despite the advent of the Indian Reorganization Act—that had been embodied in the Dawes Severalty Act. The 1887 act had sought to break up tribal landholdings, destroy tribal cultures, and promote assimilation of Native Americans into mainstream American society. The termination movement of the mid-twentieth century no longer sought to transform Indians into farmers, but it did embrace the ultimate goal of the Dawes Act—assimilation of American Indians into mainstream American life. To this end, support was being mobilized in Congress to end the wardship status of Native Americans and to terminate federal supervision of tribes. It was not surprising, perhaps, that an educated World War II veteran such as Sunshine Smith would argue some of the same points made by congressional advocates of termination. After all, despite her background as the daughter of a medicine man and Sun Dance chief, the young tribal leader had clearly learned to function comfortably in non-Indian society.

John Baker's vision for the future prevailed when the Planning Committee's document was again presented to the General Council on December 27, 1951. Discussion at this meeting was again heated but less combative than in September. On this occasion, the people seemed to understand the situation more clearly, resulting in a 74 to 6 vote in favor of the rehabilitation plan.[10] Despite this approval of the committee plan by the tribal membership, Sunshine Smith, Julius Cloud, and Eddie Box continued to press for their $8,000 plan during the following year. A General Council held that year, however, affirmed its support of the Baker plan, although the people voted at this time to increase the distribution amount to $4,000 per member.[11]

As divisive as this debate had been, tribal leaders, including Smith, Cloud, and Box, ultimately united behind implementation of this plan. One factor in this late-blooming support among the former opponents may have been a change in the cultural climate on the Southern Ute Reservation at this time. A revival movement took hold in Ignacio during the 1950s and resurrected a number of traditional practices that had been disappearing from the cultural life of the tribe. At approximately the same time as Eddie Box and Sunshine Smith were actively promoting this return to the tribe's cultural heritage—the Sun Dance, the sweat ceremony, use of the Ute language—these outspoken critics of newly approved rehabilitation plan stopped speaking in language that implied support for termination and became more supportive of the tribal program.[12] Factional disputes, however, continued to surface from time to time. On December 15, 1953, as the three principal critics voiced concerns regarding the plan, a frustrated Baker reached his breaking point and announced his resignation from the Planning Committee. No action was taken by the council on Baker's resignation, however. The crisis passed, and Baker continued his work on behalf of the program.[13]

Amid continual government-imposed delay, final approval of the Southern Ute Rehabilitation Plan did not come until June 28, 1954. The comprehensive document that resulted from this sometimes painful birthing process soon became a source of pride for tribal members. John Baker, who later admitted that he and his fellow planners had been "used as a rubber-stamp" by BIA officials in the formulation of the first plan, which had been rejected in Washington, noted proudly of the second plan, "This was something we devised."[14] In a 1956 update report on the rehabilitation program, the Southern Utes asserted that they were "the only Indian tribe that has written its own rehabilitation plan" rather than accepting "a plan tailor-made in Washington."[15] Regardless of the accuracy of this statement, the BIA did use the Southern Ute plan as a prototype for plans adopted by other tribes awarded claims judgments.[16]

Meanwhile, the Ute Mountain Utes had been proceeding steadily—and more quietly—through the rehabilitation planning process. The Tribal Council unanimously gave its preliminary approval to the work of its Planning Committee on October 3, 1951, and again unanimously approved the forthcoming rehabilitation plan on February 4, 1953.[17] This Ute Mountain plan included the same basic provisions found in the Southern Ute plan, but the Ute Mountain leaders decided not to increase the individual distribution amount to $4,000. Instead, they elected to retain the original figure of $3,500 for each member, adult or child, of the tribe.[18] The eighty-eight-page plan also allocated portions of the claims award for specific tribal programs: since the shortage of grazing land on the reservation placed a severe limit on the tribe's economic potential, $1 million were set aside for land purchases; $1.1 million were designated for a tribal credit program; $321,000 were budgeted for irrigation projects; and $100,000 were earmarked for education, with $10,000 in college scholarship funding planned for each of the next ten years.[19]

The rehabilitation planning process in Towaoc was both less turbulent and less tribally directed than in Ignacio. The prospect of adopting a rehabilitation plan did not spark controversy at Ute Mountain, nor did it arouse much popular interest among the tribal membership. When the tribe's proposed plan was presented to the people at a November 17, 1952, General Council meeting, it failed to provoke any response from the assembled Utes; no questions, suggestions, or objections were forthcoming.[20] If tribal members responded passively to the planning process, so, too, did tribal leaders respond to BIA direction of this process. The Planning Committee and the Tribal Council were both very receptive to input from government officials, and the council accepted every suggestion offered by BIA officials with respect to final changes in the plan.[21] When this plan was sent to Washington for approval, Superintendent Floyd praised the Ute Mountain Tribal Council to the BIA area director, commenting that the members of this body had "been very cooperative and very willing to go along with the suggestions made by this [superintendent's] office, [the] Area Office, and the Indian Office in their Rehabilitation Program."[22] Floyd was concerned that the council members might become discouraged if their plan was not approved; accordingly, he recommended that the commissioner—should he not be able to approve the document as is—suggest changes to be made and approve the plan conditionally rather than simply sending the whole program back. The Ute Mountain Rehabilitation Plan was finalized and then approved by Congress on August 12, 1953.

Shortly before this, on August 1, 1953, Congress officially embraced termination of the special relationship that had for so long existed between the federal government and the Indian tribes of the United States. House Concurrent Resolution 108 finally endorsed what many senators and representatives had long advocated—an end to federal supervision of the country's Native American population. A number of tribes, including the Flathead, the Klamath, the Menominee, the Potawatomie, and the Chippewa, were singled out as the first tribal groups to be "freed from Federal supervision and control and from all disabilities and limitations applicable to Indians."[23] The resolution of Indian claims, such as those that the Ute Indians had pursued since 1938, was a part of this larger termination policy envisioned by congressional leaders. Some legislators felt that resolution of Indian claims against the government would remove a substantial legal impediment to withdrawal of federal supervison of Indian tribes, and this apparently was a major factor behind congressional support for the 1946 Indian Claims Commission Act as well as other land claims bills. Not only would claims awards resolve long-standing federal obligations to various tribes, but they would also provide substantial financial resources to help these tribes embark on the road to economic self-sufficiency.[24]

Despite frequent irritation with the Bureau of Indian Affairs and despite arguments seemingly in support of federal termination policy voiced during the rehabilitation plan battle in Ignacio, the people of both the Southern Ute and Ute Mountain Ute Tribes rejected this latest twist in federal Indian policy. A House committee report in 1954 related that sentiment on both reservations opposed removal of BIA supervision. Ute Mountain tribal leaders reportedly felt that "it would be years hence before they would be able to manage their affairs free of wardship." Nor were the Southern Utes at this time ready for emancipation from federal supervision, although they were described as being more advanced in terms of education and assimilation into the local community than their Ute Mountain neighbors. The report asserted of the Ignacio Utes that "the majority of the adult members of the tribe wish to be released from wardship, gradually."[25]

While relations between the Ute tribes and the Indian Office/Bureau of Indian Affairs had often been tense and frustrating for tribal leaders, it is not surprising that the Colorado Utes declined to endorse the severing of their ties with this familiar federal bureaucracy. For seventy-five years, tribal members had been closely supervised by the BIA and dependent on money and other resources distributed by the BIA, and until recently the bureau had been the sole link between the tribes and the world outside the reservation.[26]

IMPLEMENTATION OF THE
REHABILITATION PLANS

By the end of 1954, both of the Colorado tribes had finally received their portions of the 1950 award, dividing their 40 percent share among themselves according to population. Thus, the Southern Utes received $5,966,117, while some $6.2 million went to the Ute Mountain Tribe.[27] Both tribes put their rehabilitation plans into effect, launching ten-year programs designed to achieve economic and social independence and decrease tribal dependence on the Bureau of Indian Affairs. To this end, the plans did not simply hand over large sums of money for tribal members to spend. Instead, even though each tribal member was entitled to either $3,500 or $4,000 of the claims money (the former amount for Ute Mountain Utes, the latter for Southern Utes), a central component of each plan was control by the tribal government over how $3,000 of this money could be spent. Both tribes required each family to submit a plan to a newly created approval committee before parents could have access to their "family plan" funds—a onetime distribution of $3,000 to each enrolled family member. This money was to be used for investment in items of long-term benefit, such as housing or livestock or farming equipment. A minor's family plan funds could be tapped, if approved by the committee, only for the purchase of items that would be of long-term benefit to the child; otherwise such funds would be invested for the minor's future benefit.[28]

The rehabilitation programs of the two tribes, however, involved more than simply giving out money, albeit with some restrictions. New tribal programs were initiated to promote the achievement of socioeconomic goals. The 110-page Southern Ute Rehabilitation Plan elaborated in great detail fourteen basic goals for the ten-year program. With these goals in mind, the tribe implemented a number of new programs dealing with such issues as credit, land, agriculture, and law and order. Implementation of these new programs required the creation of a vast new tribal bureaucracy, administered by the following committees: Approval, Agriculture, Education, Health, Social, Range, Timber, and Home Improvement.[29] All of these committees were supervised by the rehabilitation director, later referred to as the program director, who was hired by and served at the pleasure of the Tribal Council. A similar bureaucracy was instituted at Towaoc, where in 1953 the Tribal Council created the Approval, Credit, Resource, Land, Education, Health, Social Welfare, and Home Improvement Committees.[30] The operations of these bodies, like those at Ignacio, were coordinated by a rehabilitation director working under the authority of the council.

Both Tribal Councils had a difficult time finding—and retaining—qualified rehabilitation directors. The Southern Ute Tribal Council, which was determined to have a tribal member fill this position, selected John Baker as its first director. Baker's resignation one year into the program created a void that proved hard to fill for some time until the council selected another tribal member, David Box, to head the program. The Ute Mountain Tribal Council, without a similar pool of educated tribal members, was forced to turn to outsiders for the direction of its rehabilitation program, and problems soon surfaced between the Tribal Council and the non-Indian director.

Ute Mountain council members proved reluctant to place

their rehabilitation program in the hands of an outsider, and they jealously guarded the power of the Tribal Council. When John Rainer was tapped to be the tribe's rehabilitation director in 1954, council members had a difficult time defining the scope of his duties and authority. At a meeting convened with BIA officials to address this subject, Jack House expressed his opposition to placing a director, especially a non-Indian one, above the council: "It isn't right for this person to be equal in rank or above the Council. After all, this person is working for the Tribe."[31]

Rainer never was able to develop a workable relationship with the Tribal Council, and he soon announced his resignation. A frustrated Rainer complained about the unbusinesslike way in which the tribe conducted its programs, alleging that certain tribal employees received "preferential treatment." Rainer also expressed concern over the decisionmaking dynamics of the Tribal Council: "Although there are seven members on the council, most decisions result from the expressions of a single individual, who in turn is highly influenced by a close non-Indian associate."[32] This was clearly a reference to Jack House as the dominant decisionmaker on the council and to Frank Pyle, longtime local trader and interpreter, as the chief's influential non-Indian adviser. The outgoing director clearly implied that Frank Pyle had undue influence on Jack House. George Mills questioned Pyle's influence as interpreter during one contentious 1954 meeting, but House defended Pyle's role: "He listens what the people say about the [rehabilitation program's family] plans. People might think what they are going to do with their plans. Our friend is helping us out. He is a White man and he understands. Frank is going to help all the people to take care of things." At this same meeting, held to consider John Rainer's role and the implementation of the rehabilitation plan, several council members expressed impatience over the lack of tangible results from the plan. Harry Wall was irritated that the plan had yet to produce any of its promised benefits, chiefly houses and livestock.[33]

Clearly, implementation of the Ute Mountain Rehabilitation Plan was no easy task. After John Rainer, the council went through two more directors in fairly rapid succession before settling in January 1956 on a white tribal employee, John Kelly, as the new rehabilitation director.[34] Nor was this an isolated case. Given an uneducated and inexperienced population, the Ute Mountain Tribe was forced to rely much more heavily on non-Indians to staff its burgeoning tribal bureaucracy than did the Southern Utes. For example, the Tribal Council stipulated that only one out of a total of three members on the new Credit Committee was required to be a tribal member; the other two were to be "chosen from reliable white people." Furthermore, the council delegated authority to select these committee members to the superintendent.[35] A couple of months later, when considering the question of who would serve as tribal treasurer, council members exhibited little faith in their own ability to direct certain tribal affairs. Even though the tribal constitution provided that one of the council representatives could serve as the tribe's treasurer, the councilmen cited their limited education in explaining that none of them desired to assume responsibility for the tribe's money. Instead, they suggested that perhaps the constitution could be changed to allow the tribe to deposit its funds in a bank and then arrange for the banker to serve as treasurer.[36]

Filling all of the positions in the new tribal bureaucracy proved a major challenge to the Southern Ute leadership as well. As Sunshine Smith, who was involved with appointing Southern Ute tribal members to the new committees, later recalled, many individuals were hesitant about serving on these bodies. A typical response she encountered was, "I never worked before in my life. I don't know how to do this." For that matter, the council members themselves, now in control of millions of dollars in tribal funds, could not always claim much more experience in such matters: "None of our Council [members] had been a businessman or nothing—[they were] just out here being farmers, and all of the sudden they had to do all that."[37]

In addition to the onetime distribution of rehabilitation funds, tribal members enjoyed the regular distribution of increasingly large per capita payments. This money came out of the substantial oil and gas revenues received by each tribe. The Mountain Utes in particular profited from a tremendous infusion of fossil fuel wealth, realizing over $1.9 million in royalty and bonus payments in fiscal year 1956 alone.[38] As a result, the amounts of annual per capita payments, which had been only $50 in 1948, skyrocketed to $500 in 1954 and continued to increase as the decade progressed.[39] Southern Ute tribal members enjoyed a similar increase in the size of their per capita payments, with the annual payment reaching a high of $1,200 per member in 1958. Both tribes sought to protect the financial interests of children under the age of eighteen—for they, too, received per capita money—by establishing trust funds and requiring various portions of each minor's payment to be placed in this fund for their future use. The Ute Mountain council prefaced its trust fund resolution with the recognition "that certain members of the Ute Mountain Tribe must be protected from their own improvidence [or] the exploitation of others."[40] Withholding portions of minors' per capita payments, however, was not usually a popular measure, and at various times the Tribal Councils in both Ignacio and Towaoc elected to forego such deductions in favor of full distribution of minors' shares.

Such payments, as popular as they were among members, became increasingly problematic as the decade wore on. For one thing, the amount of money involved in such distributions was staggering. Southern Ute per capita payments in 1955 totaled $2,422,000 out of a total budget of $2,964,668.[41] By decade's end, over $4 million in per capita payments had pushed total expenditures for the first six years of the program to $7,649,843, an amount that, owing to declining natural gas income, greatly exceeded tribal income. At this rate, the Southern Ute Tribe was headed for bankruptcy. As a result, the tribe was forced to rein in the size of these payments in 1959, instituting a series of $100 reductions each year through 1964.[42]

But there was an additional problem aside from bleak tribal balance sheets. The human impact of per capita money was cause for concern. John Baker grew increasingly worried as he saw the extent to which some members were coming to rely on these payments for their support: "These people who are just sitting back and waiting for the per capita payments should stop doing this, because when the per capita payments are lowered they will not have a way to make a living."[43] Southern Ute tribal member Leonard Burch was similarly concerned by this situation when he returned to the reservation after several years in the air force. He found on his return that fewer of his people were now farming or raising livestock and that many of them "just sit and wait for their per capita payments."[44]

Per capita payments represented unearned income in that they were automatically received by all individuals listed on the tribal rolls. Some tribal leaders, such as John Baker and the young Leonard Burch, and most federal officials strongly objected to the reliance of some tribal members on unearned income for their support. But many Utes regarded such "unearned income" in a different light. Historical factors led many tribal members to believe they were entitled to any and all per capita payments they might be able to obtain. From the mid-nineteenth century on, their ancestors had assented to a succession of treaties and agreements that obligated the federal government to provide annual distributions of money and food to the tribal members and their descendants. This was not an act of charity, these Utes argued; rather, such payments were compensation for the Indians' agreement to surrender their lands and their accustomed way of life. The Ute people were thus legally entitled to these payments, despite the fact that the U.S. government elected to discontinue such support early in the twentieth century.[45] Still smarting from this earlier abrogation of treaty obligations, tribal members at midcentury not surprisingly looked to their tribes—now the recipients of large federal land claims awards and substantial fossil fuel revenue—to assume the obligation that had been renounced by the federal government. Tribal money belonged to the people of the tribe, and they felt they were entitled to their share, unearned or not.

With the influx of money from both family plan funds and per capita payments, considerable improvement in housing conditions occurred on both reservations. Southern Utes built new houses to replace the cramped shacks in which many of them had been living. At Ute Mountain, where the bulk of the population still lived in tents, hogans, and shacks in the early 1950s, many members now moved into houses for the first time. Some 40 new houses were constructed in 1955, and by 1960 a total of 187 homes had been built on the reservation.[46] The council encouraged this development through its 1953 adoption of the Homesite Land Ordinance, which provided fifty-year leases—at $1 per acre per year—to any member who sought to establish a residence.[47] And even though new homeowners would no longer be able to pick up and move with their herds across the reservation as their ancestors had done earlier in the century, they at least retained the freedom to build their homes anywhere they chose on the reservation. Most, however, decided to establish homes in the vicinity of the rapidly booming town of Towaoc.[48] Thus, whereas Southern Ute homes tended to be distributed throughout the reservation on scattered allotments and assignments, a different residential pattern, concentrated in one area centering on Towaoc, emerged on the Ute Mountain Ute Reservation.

Even before receiving claims money, the Ute Mountain Tribal Council had expressed its hope of encouraging tribal members to live in houses. In November 1951, the council noted that Jack House, as a result of the inadequate protection from the elements afforded by his one-room shack, had been sick most of the previous winter and had nearly died. In appreciation for the chief's many years of service to his tribe, the council voted to build a modern house for him, noting that this might have the additional benefit of encouraging others in the tribe to build similar dwellings for themselves.[49] But old habits and beliefs often proved resistant to change. When George Mills, the chairman of the Tribal Council, had the ill luck to have his newly built home struck by lightning in 1954, he and his family refused to reoccupy the house "because of Tribal superstitions." The council then decided to purchase the house from Mills for use as employee housing.[50]

Money from the Ute Mountain Rehabilitation Program also prompted a change in location for the Utes living in the area of Blanding, Utah. These Indians had long resisted the entreaties of the U.S. government to relocate on the Ute Mountain Reservation in Colorado, and superintendents in Ignacio had tried in vain since 1930 to coax these Indians to leave Utah. Despite their insistence on staying put, the situation of these Indians was far from ideal. Those living on allotments in Allen Canyon had long suffered from the isolation and lack of productive land posed by their remote location, while those living near Blanding longed for more and better agricultural land. Beginning in the mid 1950s, rehabilitation funds provided the catalyst for most of the 148 Blanding-area Utes to relocate to White Mesa, 11 miles south of Blanding. Here they used the new funds to erect frame houses.[51] The Ute Mountain Tribal Council moved to bolster the stock-raising activities of the people at White Mesa in 1955 by purchasing a ranch with sufficient grazing capacity for 600 head of cattle.[52] The Utes in this area already held 9,079 acres of allotted land, the only allotted land within the entire Ute Mountain Reservation.[53] Although no longer living in the canyon, the Allen Canyon Utes retained their allotments and continued to graze livestock there. At the close of the century, thirty allotments remained in Allen Canyon, and the White Mesa community had a population of about 350 people.[54]

Both tribes instituted significant changes in educational arrangements as part of their rehabilitation programs. Whereas substantial numbers of Southern Ute children had attended public schools as early as the 1920s, boarding school attendance had continued among Ignacio children, and by the 1954–1955 school year 93 of 164 Southern Ute school children were being educated in the Southern Ute Vocational School, the BIA boarding school at Ignacio.[55] One of the fourteen goals of the tribe's rehabilitation plan stipulated that all Southern Ute children were to "receive the advantages of non-segregated public school education"; accordingly, the tribe entered into negotiations with the Ignacio Public School District in spring 1955 to obtain the transfer of all Ute students from the Ute Vocational School to the public schools.[56] The end result was the consolidation of the Ute Vocational School with the Ignacio Public Schools in 1956, and by the 1958–1959 school year 168 Southern Ute children—up from only 38 in 1954–1955—were enrolled in either the Ignacio or Bayfield public schools. An indication of the tribe's educational progress lay in the fact that 10 Southern Ute seniors graduated from high school in 1959, as compared with only 4 in 1957.[57]

Even more dramatic change occurred in the educational situation in Towaoc, which still lacked a school in the early years of the decade. The Ute Mountain School finally reopened, after an eleven-year hiatus, in 1953. School attendance soon rose dramatically, first at the boarding school in Towaoc, then at public schools in the neighboring town of Cortez. When the boarding school reopened, it included only grades one through six, so older students had to attend either the Ute Vocational School in Ignacio or—as became increasingly common as the tribe encouraged public school attendance later in the 1950s—the public high school in Cortez. One grade at a time, more Ute students were transferred to the public schools each year, sent by bus to Cortez.

By fall 1961, with the removal of the last grade from Towaoc, the conversion to public school education was complete.[58] Thus was effected a tremendous change in Ute Mountain society: whereas almost no one from the long-isolated tribe attended public schools in 1950, and many children at that time were not attending any school; and whereas only 22 out of 176 Ute Mountain students went to public schools as late as the 1954–1955 school year,[59] by 1961 virtually all of the tribe's children were experiencing non-segregated instruction in the public schools of Cortez. The long-standing educational deficit of the Ute Mountain people could not be alleviated overnight by this shift to public schooling, but the ability of the tribe's youth to speak English did improve rapidly.[60]

Health care systems also changed on both reservations. As part of the termination program of the 1950s, the long-standing BIA monopoly in providing services to Native Americans was coming to an end, and tribes would now be dealing directly with other government agencies in addition to the Bureau of Indian Affairs. As part of this shift away from BIA control, the U.S. Public Health Service assumed responsibility for providing health care to Indians in 1955.[61] From this time on, the Indian Health Service, a branch of the Public Health Service, would replace the BIA as the Utes' health care provider.

The Taylor Hospital in Ignacio was closed in January 1955 as part of this transition, prompting a search by the Southern Ute Tribe for an interim arrangement for meeting its people's medical needs. The result was a contract with Blue Cross–Blue Shield that took effect on November 16, 1955. This marked the first time that an Indian tribe contracted for health insurance coverage for its entire membership without any government financial assistance.[62] The Ute Mountain Tribal Council initially contracted in January of 1955 for hospitalization services with the Southwestern Colorado Memorial Hospital in Cortez, but when this proved too costly, the council contracted with Blue Cross–

Blue Shield, shortly after the Southern Utes did so, for health coverage for all its members.[63] Members of both tribes also received some services directly from the Indian Health Service at this time.

Both tribes implemented programs designed to bolster development of their primary economic activities—stock raising at Ute Mountain and farming in the Ignacio area. The Southern Ute council attempted to help its farmers both by adopting a new land code, which provided increased security to those who farmed on assigned tribal land, and by making more land available for farming and stock operations through the assignment to individual members of land in the Oxford Tract that had formerly been administered by the tribe. On the Ute Mountain Reservation, where the biggest problem facing stock raisers had always been the shortage of summer range, the tribe sought to alleviate this situation both by clearing additional range land on the reservation and by purchasing off-reservation ranches, such as the 17,000-acre Pine Crest Ranch located west of Gunnison, in order to provide more summer grazing for the tribe's livestock.[64]

SOCIAL AND ECONOMIC CHANGES

"Another problem of interest is the effect of sudden available spending money on the Ute's philosophy of life." Thus did Dr. George Moore of the Public Health Service highlight in a 1955 report the impact on the Colorado Utes of a suddenly abundant commodity—money.[65] The massive infusion of money during the 1950s on reservations that until this time had been wracked by poverty brought about tremendous change—some of it positive and some negative. The starkness of life on the two reservations in the early years of the decade—before receipt of rehabilitation funds and large per capita payments from energy revenues—was undeniable. Even on the Southern Ute Reservation, long cited by the agency as a shining example of Indian progress, with its homes and farms, living conditions were far from comfortable. Homes were small and crowded, in poor condition, and almost universally lacking in sanitation systems, clean drinking water, electricity, and telephones.[66] The new wealth of the 1950s led to dramatic improvements in the housing situation on both reservations. And soon not only did electricity and telephones become commonplace, but also such amenities as televisions began to appear in reservation homes. Clean drinking water also became the norm, although the water supply at Towaoc remained problematic for many years, requiring the tribe to haul water in by truck each day.

The tribes' newfound wealth certainly brought about a better standard of living, but it did not necessarily result in an increase in the economic self-sufficiency of tribal members. Elbert J. Floyd, who had been agency farmer on both reservations during the 1930s, noted on his return to assume the superintendency in 1950 that the Ute Mountain Indians of the earlier period had owned more livestock and had been "supporting themselves from their own efforts to a greater extent" than they were in 1950.[67] He attributed their diminished self-sufficiency largely to the removal of all government services after 1942, but this trend continued throughout the 1950s, even after the Towaoc agency was reestablished. One troubling measure of the lack of self-sufficiency is the dramatic increase in reliance on unearned income, such as per capita payments, on both reservations from 1950 to 1962. Unearned income, which composed 10 percent of Ute Mountain tribal members' total income in 1950, jumped to a staggering 82 percent share in 1962. Reliance on unearned income increased less drastically among the Southern Utes, from 20 percent of total income in 1950 to 59 percent in 1962.[68]

Claims money enabled Ute Mountain stock raisers to continue increasing the size of their cattle herds, but stock raising did not provide a livelihood for many within the tribe. Cattle herds, which totaled only 91 head in 1933 before increasing to 1,447 head in 1945, continued to grow in size. By 1960 tribal members owned a total of 2,000 head of cattle. The steep decline in the number of sheep raised by tribal members, begun as a result of the federal government's stock reduction program, continued during the 1950s. Thus, sheep stocks fell from over 11,000 head in 1933 to 6,696 head in 1945 and then to only 3,200 head of sheep in 1960.[69] But it was the increasingly minor contribution of stock raising to tribal income that was most alarming. With the tribe's cattle being divided among 70 Ute owners in 1960 and the sheep among 26 owners, few of these stock-raisers had herds of sufficient size to be fully self-supporting. This also left many of the tribe's 817 members with no role at all in the Ute Mountain Indians' main economic activity.[70]

The agricultural economy of the Southern Ute Reservation faced a similar dilemma. Here the big problem was the small size of most Ute farms. In 1954, 70 of 156 families living on the reservation were operating farms, but less than a half dozen of these families had enough land to make farming or stock raising profitable.[71] This situation improved later in the decade, with the number of economically viable Southern Ute farms increasing from only four in 1956 to thirteen in 1958 and twenty-six in January 1960.[72] Even given this progress, with a tribal population of over 600, the vast majority of Southern Utes were unable to support themselves through agricultural operations.

Farmers, stock raisers and other workers on both reservations were hampered in their quest for economic self-sufficiency by economic forces that threatened rural America as a whole. The agricultural economy in America's hinterland was shriveling at midcentury as both farming and ranching were becoming more capital intensive and increasingly dominated by large agribusinesses. As a result, rural unemployment soared. For Indians on reservations, with growing populations and fixed land bases, the situation was particularly difficult. Great Basin reservations such as those of the Utes were left with no viable economy capable of generating steady employment.[73] Unable to earn a solid living, yet unwilling to leave the reservation, tribal members persistently clamored for per capita payments to make ends meet.

Money made possible the improvement of both tribes' standards of living, but it did not bring about an easy or complete adjustment to modern living. A 1955 public health report noted the inconsistency between the Utes' new material wealth and their way of life: "A most interesting point here is that sanitation is generally poor in spite of general material wealth. Television, cars, tractors, washing machines, each may be in evidence but are not in harmony with sanitary practices."[74] The failure of increased wealth to erase such reservation ills as poor sanitation was not the only disturbing trend. The sudden introduction of substantial sums of money among two previously poor tribes wreaked havoc among these people, giving rise to a number of social and health problems. Obesity and diabetes became disturbingly common, as did fatal accidents, alcoholism, and crime. The threat of accidental death was particularly acute in Towaoc, where, unlike the Southern Ute Tribe, the Ute Mountain Tribe was unable to secure auto insurance on the tribal fleet because of the tribe's high accident rate.[75] These troublesome developments resulted in an extremely high death rate among young Ute adults. For those Indians who lived past the age of fifty, however, improvements in health care made it likely that they could look forward to a long life.[76]

Alcoholism stood out as the single most dangerous threat to Ute society on both reservations. Dramatic social and cultural change, the sudden receipt of large amounts of money by individual tribal members, and a 1953 act of Congress legalizing the purchase of liquor by Indians combined to create an environment in which alcoholism thrived, with chilling consequences. The members of the Ute Mountain Tribal Council were alarmed at the prospect of the removal of state and federal prohibitions on Indian alcohol use. Jack House strongly opposed the repeal of these laws and worried that drinking among his people might eventually bring about the demise of the Bear Dance and Sun Dance. The Ute Mountain council members unanimously agreed to vigorously enforce sections of the tribal code prohibiting Indians from bringing alcohol onto the reservation.[77] Given the checkerboard nature of the Southern Utes' reservation, banning alcohol was never a feasible option for this tribe.

Beyond the direct damage to those addicted to drink, alcohol abuse gave rise to a host of additional ills—automobile accidents, crime, broken families, and neglected children. While the Consolidated Ute Agency had reported only a couple of arrests on each reservation in a typical year during the 1930s, increasing to perhaps six arrests a year in each jurisdiction during the mid 1940s, the 1950s produced a veritable explosion of crime. In 1958 fifty criminal cases were recorded on the Southern Ute Reservation alone, and this increased to seventy-two cases in just the first half of 1959. Fully seventy of these seventy-two cases were either directly or indirectly connected with alcohol consumption.[78] Likewise, during 1953 and 1954 twenty-five Southern Ute juveniles were arrested a total of sixty-one times, with forty-six of these incidents involving intoxication. Similar figures emerged from the Ute Mountain Reservation, where seventy-four arrests were made involving twenty-eight juveniles, with liquor being a factor in almost every case.[79] Young children also suffered the effects of alcoholism, as indicated by the large number of neglected children that the Southern Ute Social Welfare Committee was forced to remove from unhealthy home situations—often caused by the drinking problems of parents.

The Tribal Councils in both Towaoc and Ignacio tried desperately to combat alcoholism and its effects on their people. Acknowledging that "it is well known that the Ute Mountain people have not become acculturated or adapted to the use of intoxicating beverages to the point of being able to control their use thereof," the Ute Mountain council in 1955 implored the

Montezuma County commissioners to deny a liquor license application for an establishment located close to their reservation.[80] The following year, the Tribal Council drew up a liquor-sale "blacklist," to be circulated among area liquor sellers. Members with drinking problems were to be added to the list on the request of their relatives.[81] The Southern Ute Tribal Council, for its part, attacked alcoholism among its people by sending tribal members with drinking problems to treatment centers. Despite the many initiatives pursued by both tribes, little headway was made in the war against liquor. Alcohol abuse would continue to ravage the Ute people for years to come.

Drinking also contributed to an increase in problems with neighboring non-Indians. One Cortez resident, who happened to be the son of a former Navajo Springs Agency superintendent, commented that relations between the Ute Mountain Tribe and the people of Cortez had been generally good until the 1950s: "I never really noticed any big problems with the people from Towaoc or the Indians until the drinking came along."[82] In 1955 council chairman Scott Jacket complained about stores in Cortez selling liquor to underaged and drunk Utes, and he also charged the Cortez magistrate with levying heavier fines on Indians for drunkenness charges than on white offenders. The Durango district attorney responded by stating that "our chief troublemakers are drunk Indians," but he denied any unequal treatment of such offenders.[83] Another frequent complaint of tribal members was that Cortez businessmen took advantage of the newly rich Utes by overcharging them on purchases.[84] The Southern Utes, who had always interacted to a much greater extent with their non-Indian neighbors than had the Mountain Utes, experienced fewer such problems, but conflict with local neighbors was not unknown. In 1955 Chairman Sam Burch complained about heavy fines imposed on Indians by officials in the nearby town of Bayfield. He also asserted that the Bayfield police had ordered Indians to keep out of the town.[85]

CULTURAL LOSS AND
CULTURAL REVIVALISM

In the 1940s, Edwin Cloud was one of the last traditional spiritual leaders among the Southern Utes, having long served as a medicine man and as the tribe's Sun Dance chief. His death in November 1946, along with the death of the other remaining healers around that same time, left an immense spiritual void in the tribe. The healing ceremonies of the medicine men began to disappear, and with no new Sun Dance chief taking Cloud's place, this annual dance of great spiritual importance faded from the scene.[86] Although the traditional medicine men were apparently gone forever, many other aspects of Ute culture and spirituality were resurrected as part of a cultural revival on the Southern Ute Reservation beginning in the mid 1950s. The Sun Dance was once again held, under new Sun Dance chief Eddie Box, who was taught how to lead this important ceremony by Sunshine Smith and other members of the Cloud family. Box and other traditionalists in the tribe also adopted the sweat ceremony, once the province of only the medicine men, and reintroduced this ceremony in a modified form with more participants in larger sweat lodges.[87] These same traditionalists, or "nativists" as they are referred to by some anthropologists, also began to show a new interest in using and ensuring the survival of the Ute language.[88]

There was a connection between this cultural renaissance and political divisions within the Southern Ute Tribe. The leaders in this nativist movement, Eddie Box Sr. and Sunshine Cloud Smith in particular, along with others such as Julius Cloud, were the most outspoken leaders of the political opposition to the leadership of John E. Baker on the Tribal Council. Although political factions among the Utes were usually transitory and informal, the factional split in Ignacio pitting nativist leaders against those who declined to embrace the cultural revival was persistent. The Cloud family and the Box family and their supporters were regular participants in traditional activities such as the Sun Dance, the Bear Dance, the sweat ceremony, and the Ute hand game; John Baker and his supporters in the council generally did not participate in such activities.[89]

Spiritual life on both reservations at midcentury continued the eclecticism of earlier decades. In 1960 only perhaps a half dozen Southern Ute families were exclusively Christian, primarily Catholic. The rest of the tribal members were either nominally Christian or, as had been typical of the Utes for some time, practiced an eclectic spirituality combining elements of both native and Christian religion. A dramatic contrast between the two tribes persisted regarding the use of the peyote cactus for spiritual purposes. Southern Ute adherents of the Native American Church still practiced the peyote rite, but they constituted only a small minority of the tribe. After being introduced in Ignacio in the 1910s, at roughly the same time as in Towaoc, peyote use among the Southern Utes had been bolstered early on by the sponsorship of Chief Buckskin Charlie and by the frequent visits of peyote missionaries from Oklahoma during the 1920s. As early as 1930, however, the practice of peyotism had stagnated in Ignacio, and it soon entered a long period of decline.[90] Only fifteen peyote rite participants were reported among the Ignacio Utes in 1954. Peyote use was a source of dissension among the Southern Utes at this time, and even the leaders of the nascent cultural revival opposed its use.[91] The situation was totally reversed in Towaoc at this time, where 90 percent of Ute Mountain tribal members were estimated to be participating in peyote ceremonies in 1954 and where the longtime chairman of the Tribal Council, George Mills, was a peyote priest, or road chief.[92]

A few medicine men lingered on at Ute Mountain throughout the 1950s, but they, too, would soon die, leaving no successors. But in Towaoc traditional ceremonies had not disappeared to the extent that they had in Ignacio. The Sun Dance continued to be held at Ute Mountain, though it had temporarily ceased among the Southern Utes. The Native American Church continued to attract many followers. And the Ute language was spoken in daily life much more than in Ignacio. At the end of 1955, the Consolidated Ute Agency reported that all but 15 of the Southern Ute Tribe's 564 members spoke English, whereas at that same time there were 109 Mountain Utes, out of a total population of 647, who spoke no English. Hence, there was less cause for worry that the Ute language might soon disappear on the Ute Mountain Reservation. The greater retention of traditional Ute culture and language on this reservation could still be attributed at this time to both the greater geographical isolation of the Towaoc Utes and to the much lower incidence among this people of intermarriage with non-Indians. At the close of 1955, fully 98 percent of these Indians were reported to be full-blood Utes, in comparison to a Southern Ute population that was only 60 percent full-blood.[93]

TRIBAL POLITICS

Ute Mountain tribal politics was rather calm in nature during the eventful decade of the 1950s, in contrast to the more tumultuous political atmosphere characterizing other twentieth-century decades. Chief Jack House continued to play a preeminent role on the Tribal Council, wielding more influence than any of the three council members who served as chairmen during this decade: George Mills, chairman of the council from its postconstitution inception until his resignation in 1955; Scott Jacket, who succeeded Mills; and Albert Wing Sr., who was chairman during the final years of the decade.

Chairman Wing presented a stark contrast to John Baker, who was the Southern Ute chairman during this same time. Baker had learned English early in life, had been one of five sons in his family to graduate from high school, had served overseas during World War II, and had attended college. Albert Wing, in contrast, was raised in an environment that did not include much contact with the white world. Born in 1923 near Navajo Springs, he had grown up much like Jack House, living in a tent as he and his family tended livestock in the isolated confines of Mancos Canyon. The young Wing spoke no English when he began attending boarding school in Towaoc, where he studied through the sixth grade. He later attended boarding schools in Sante Fe and in Ignacio, where he continued his education through the eighth or ninth grade. Wing worked on various projects throughout the reservation with the Civilian Conservation Corps, and later the Ute stockman worked for the tribe as a fence rider, patrolling the reservation's western and southern boundaries on horseback to keep trespassing Navajos and their livestock off the tribe's range.[94]

Albert Wing was first elected to the Tribal Council in 1955. In contrast to the sometimes strained relations between the Ute Mountain Tribal Council and Superintendent MacSpadden during the 1940s, Wing later recalled that as a council member he had enjoyed a good relationship with the agency superintendents. He also remembered his service as chairman as having gone fairly smoothly, especially when compared to subsequent developments in tribal politics, which he characterized in 1991 by saying, "The damn thing is all messed up now." Wing was particularly proud of his role in bringing about the construction of a tribal racetrack, rodeo arena, and grandstand in 1957.[95] Even amidst all of the socioeconomic change of the 1950s, the Ute people still loved horse racing and gambling.

One factor behind the relatively good relationship between Chairman Wing and his fellow councilmen, on the one hand, and the agency, on the other, was the appearance in the 1950s of superintendents who were more cooperative and less paternalistic than their predecessors had been. Floyd E. MacSpadden (1940–1950), and to a somewhat lesser extent his successor Elbert J. Floyd (1950–1954), brought an old-style Indian Office approach to dealing with Indians. They were prone to dictating to tribal leaders rather than listening to their concerns, and as a result relations were often quite strained. The arrival of Superintendent Robert L. Bennett in 1954 brought about an almost immediate change in the relationship between the two tribes and the agency. Bennett, an Oneida Indian who would later become commissioner of Indian affairs under Lyndon Johnson, brought to his post a new BIA approach to dealing with the two Ute tribes, one that would be continued by James F. Canan (1956–1961).

The status of the Tribal Councils quickly rose as Superintendent Bennett dealt with tribal leaders in a respectful, rather than paternalistic, fashion. Symbolic of this new relationship was the relocation of the Southern Utes' tribal office from a room in the agency basement to a new room adjacent to the superintendent's office. And no longer did the superintendent insist on signing all Tribal Council minutes, as his more controlling predecessors had done.[96] The arrival of more respectful superintendents in the mid 1950s thus dramatically improved relations between the BIA and the Tribal Councils in both Towaoc and Ignacio.

The Ute Mountain Tribal Council of the 1950s seemed to work fairly well with government officials, as Superintendent Floyd had indicated in his praise for the council's cooperation during the rehabilitation planning process. Council attacks on the Bureau of Indian Affairs, which would later become commonplace, were rarely heard at this time, nor were there many agency complaints regarding the council such as those voiced by Superintendent MacSpadden in the 1940s. One reason for the newly cooperative nature of the Tribal Council in Towaoc, aside from the change in superintendents at the Consolidated Ute Agency, may have been the adoption of a more accommodating posture on the part of the tribe's chief. Jack House, who had been reviled by MacSpadden as the leader of a "reactionary element" and blasted by a geographer studying the reservation in 1945 for his dictatorial control and open hostility to white ways,[97] was presented by 1950s observers in a much more positive light. Journalists and a local historian now depicted the chief not as a reactionary but as a progressive leader of his people.[98] Recognizing that the conduct of tribal affairs was becoming more and more difficult for the tribe's non–English-speaking elders, Chief House acknowledged in 1951 that his people would have to adapt to the ways of the white man in order to survive amid new and rapidly changing conditions.[99]

This does not mean, however, that Jack House and his fellow councilmen were always receptive to BIA proposals. Council members retained a strongly conservative outlook, which often surfaced in response to the entreaties of their superintendent. Council members frequently rejected the advice of Superintendent Floyd, as they did in 1951 when he suggested paving the road from Highway 666 to Towaoc. Jack House led the opposition to this proposal, balking at the cost and asserting that the Indians were perfectly content with the road as it was.[100] Even with such disagreements, however, the council's relationship with its superintendent remained generally amicable.

In addition to the relative absence of tension between tribal officials and the BIA, intratribal disputes were also few and far between during the 1950s. In contrast to the fiery debates of subsequent decades, there was relatively little internal conflict either within the council or between the council and the tribal membership during this period. The financial good fortune of the tribe at this time, compared with the more lean times to come, probably accounts to a large extent for the peaceful political environment in Towaoc during the 1950s.

As indicated by the fireworks attending the adoption of the Southern Ute Rehabilitation Plan, the political situation in Ignacio was a bit more lively at midcentury. Despite the emphasis of the plan on cooperation with the Bureau of Indian Affairs, the Tribal Council of the early to mid 1950s frequently clashed with government officials.[101] Distrust of BIA officials was frequently voiced, and in particular the council did not always feel it could trust Superintendent Elbert J. Floyd. This lack of faith in Floyd led the council members at various times to insist on listening in on calls made by the superintendent on their behalf and on being provided with a copy of a letter that Floyd had said he would send to Washington. At one point, John Baker accused Floyd of manipulating council meeting minutes, changing them to suit his interests.[102]

The Southern Utes had always been more acculturated than their Ute Mountain neighbors to the west, but this did not necessarily translate into more peaceful and cooperative relations with the Bureau of Indian Affairs. The relationship between the Ignacio Utes and the federal government had always been more complicated than this. True, the Southern Utes had generally been less hostile to overtures from the government and more open to considering Indian Office/BIA initiatives, such as the IRA, than the Ute Mountain Utes. This did not mean, however, that the Utes of Ignacio reacted passively and accepted federal policies unquestioningly. To the contrary, whenever Southern Ute leaders perceived that their people had been wrongly treated, they never hesitated to challenge the BIA. This had been the case with land claims in 1896 and again in 1938, with misconduct by the superintendent and failure of the federal government to honor its treaty obligations in 1925–1926, and with the rehabilitation program in the early 1950s.

Most frustrating of all for Southern Ute leaders in the latter instance were those occasions on which the Bureau of Indian Affairs, from which approval was required for major council decisions, either vetoed council actions outright or subjected them to agonizing delays. One example of such interference from Washington was the commissioner's 1954 rejection of the tribe's contract with its attorney, who had just been hired after a long and exhausting search.[103] This BIA veto came at a most unfortunate time since the Tribal Council was then preparing to send a delegation, which was to include an attorney, to Washington to testify on behalf of the rehabilitation plan, which had yet to be approved. Members of the council were likewise annoyed when the

BIA insisted that the council make changes in tribal programs, as it did in 1956 with regard to a tribal credit plan that had been drawn up only after much study and deliberation by the council.[104]

The battle with Washington over the hiring of a tribal attorney spotlighted a new and increasingly important actor working with tribal governments across the country beginning in the late 1940s. More and more, the general counsel, an attorney retained by a tribe on a permanent, full-time basis, was becoming an essential player in the quest for effective tribal self-government. As with the Utes, many tribes first utilized legal counsel during the 1940s as part of land claims litigation. Soon the benefits of such ongoing legal representation, even in the absence of land claims, became apparent, and most tribes began to retain a general counsel. The advantages of retaining a good lawyer in a "statute-stifled society" were obvious, and legal counsel was even more essential for subordinate entities such as Indian tribes that had substantial dealings with state and federal governments. Tribal attorneys soon proved essential to ensuring that tribes were fairly treated by federal agencies.[105] Given this central role in tribal affairs, however, it is not surprising that tribal attorneys would later become embroiled in political controversies in both Towaoc and Ignacio.

Relations between the Southern Ute Tribal Council and the BIA, often stormy early in the 1950s, improved later in the decade and continued to be largely positive into the 1960s. The most significant factor was the new breed of superintendents at the Consolidated Ute Agency, beginning with Robert Bennett's arrival in 1954. The positive and productive relationship between the council and these administrators improved the political climate between the tribe and the federal government considerably. Also, the tribe's rehabilitation plan was now in place, thus removing a source of previous friction.

Much of the conflict at Tribal Council meetings in Ignacio was not between the tribe and the government but rather between various members of the council. The factional split among tribal leaders first evident during the rehabilitation planning process was still a factor in tribal politics as the decade progressed. Particularly apparent was the continuing philosophical divergence between John Baker and his chief rival, Sunshine Smith. Smith, who served as the council's tribal representative to the Consolidated Ute Agency for several years beginning in 1954, shared her older brother Julius Cloud's role as the voice of the Southern Ute people. She was quite sympathetic to their concerns and strongly advocated greater tribal assistance to the people. Baker, by contrast, appeared less interested in satisfying the people's immediate desires than in fostering long-range tribal development. He constantly reminded his fellow tribal members that they could not rely on the tribe to take care of their every need; accordingly, he advocated laissez-faire policies that promoted individual self-sufficiency. He worried over the fact that "first the tribe looked to the government for help and now it looks to the Council, and . . . the tribe cannot become self-sustaining in this way."[106]

Baker and various allies who operated on this philosophical premise were confronted by an opposing group led by Sunshine Smith, Julius Cloud, and Eddie Box Sr. The gulf between these two factions was not just political in nature; it was also cultural. The Cloud family, including Sunshine Cloud Smith, and the Box family both played key roles in the cultural revival that took place on the reservation in the mid 1950s, whereas the Baker family and its political allies generally did not.[107] Yet one must be careful not to read too much into the apparent divisiveness of Southern Ute political infighting, for as an anthropologist observing the Ignacio scene in 1960 remarked, "What looks to the outsider like a serious internal fight will end up with the disputants working together, or keeping up appearances of it, the next day."[108]

John Baker appeared to prevail in this factional political contest when he was elected council chairman following the death of Chairman Sam Burch in 1956. Baker's triumph seemed complete when tribal elections in the fall of that year resulted in something of a changing of the guard: gone were outspoken critics

Julius Cloud and Sunshine Smith, leaving in their place a Tribal Council composed of members who largely supported Baker's policies. As was often the case in Southern Ute tribal politics, however, Sunshine Smith's absence was of short duration. Her relatively quick return to the Tribal Council illustrates the continuity of membership that has characterized this body since its inception in 1936. Members such as Julius Cloud, Sam Burch, John Baker Sr., and Sunshine Smith became semipermanent fixtures on the council; if they failed to win reelection one year, they most likely would be returned to the council in a subsequent election. Contributing to this longevity of council membership was the domination of tribal politics by a few Southern Ute families, most particularly the Clouds, Burches, and Bakers. From 1939 through 1960, every tribal chairman came from one of these families. A similar tendency toward family activism in council politics was noticeable in Towaoc, the most striking example being the presence of four members of the Wing family on the Ute Mountain Tribal Council between 1949 and 1960. Continuity of membership was also a hallmark of this body, with Jack House serving for over twenty years, George Mills serving for nearly fifteen years, and a number of others, including Marshall Whyte, Harry Wall, Scott Jacket, and Albert Wing, serving for extended periods.[109]

A clear contrast between the Tribal Councils of the two tribes lay in the participation of women. Although the initial postconstitution Ute Mountain Tribal Council contained two female members, at no time during the 1950s did women serve on this panel. Women clearly played a more active political role in Ignacio. Euterpe Taylor was elected in 1948 as the first woman to serve on the Southern Ute Tribal Council, and she was soon followed by Sunshine Smith. The extent of popular acceptance of female participation in Southern Ute tribal politics was indicated by the results of the tribal election held in October of 1960: two new female members were elected, resulting in a Tribal Council in which four of the six members were women.[110]

Another characteristic of the Southern Ute Tribal Council was its tendency to monopolize control over tribal affairs. This was largely predetermined by the system of government established by the tribe's constitution, which created no rival governing body. Like most constitutions adopted under the Indian Reorganization Act, the Southern Ute and Ute Mountain Ute Constitutions conferred complete governmental power to the Tribal Council. Such IRA governments lacked any separation of power or system of checks and balances—an arrangement that often led tribal members to complain of abuse of power by their councils.[111] This concentration of power was not altered by the tribes' rehabilitation plans, which created vastly expanded tribal bureaucracies—all under council control. The inability or unwillingness of Southern Ute council members to delegate authority to the tribal committees or to tribal officials outside the council further added to the dominance of this body over tribal affairs—but at the cost of saddling the council with an overwhelming agenda. There was no rival to the power of the Tribal Council in Towaoc either, but here there were two sources of political power: the tribal chieftaincy and the Tribal Council. Since Jack House had always been a member of the council, these two potentially competing institutions had merged their authority into one governing body.

HOPEFUL SIGNS AND OMINOUS TRENDS

In December 1959, the Southern Ute Tribe vacated its old offices in the Consolidated Ute Agency building and moved into a building of its own—the former Taylor Hospital, newly christened the Tribal Affairs Building. Tribal officers and employees reportedly enjoyed "a greater feeling of self-reliance" now that they were carrying out their duties in the tribe's own building rather than in space provided by their longtime overseer and sometime nemesis, the Bureau of Indian Affairs.[112] This was tangible evidence of the tribe's growing independence. It represented a clear departure from the early days of the decade when, following an argument with Superintendent Floyd, the Tribal Council had been banished from the superintendent's office, where it had previously met, and forced to hold its meetings in an unfurnished basement room in which council members sat on packing crates.[113] This move thus symbolized a major step forward in the tribe's quest for self-determination, for these Southern Utes who were eagerly setting up their own office building in late 1959 bore little resemblance to the tribal members of 1933, who, as dependent wards of the federal government lacking any real government of their own, had come to the newly opened Indian Service hospital for medical treatment.

Soon after this, the Ute Mountain Utes of Towaoc were anxiously anticipating the completion of a different sort of facility in Towaoc. A $350,000 building that would house a gymnasium, a swimming pool, and a community center was under construction in summer 1960.[114] This represented quite an advancement for a people who scarcely ten years earlier had been living primarily in tents and earthen hogans.

Indeed, the Southern Utes and Ute Mountain Utes had accomplished a great deal through their rehabilitation programs. Their standards of living had improved dramatically, as had their financial resources, and each tribe had taken significant steps toward assuming responsibility for its own affairs. But ominous trends could be detected in the shadows cast by these shining accomplishments: alcoholism and its associated evils showed no signs of abating, the tribes were expending funds at an alarming rate, and the Southern Ute Tribe was in danger of going bankrupt. For all the tribes' expenditures, however, disappointingly few tribal members had achieved economic self-sufficiency, many instead becoming disturbingly dependent on tribal per capita payments. Thus, despite substantial accomplishments, the Ute Indians of Colorado still faced some daunting challenges.

6

TRIBAL ECONOMY
AFTER 1960

As some fifty members of the Southern Ute Tribe assembled for a General Council meeting on July 21, 1960, their attention was focused on the troublesome economic situation facing the tribe. The people found themselves listening to a lecture delivered by Chairman John Baker, a man who never hesitated to speak his mind no matter how unpleasant the message:

> You know that the membership have a group of people who is the Tribal Council that is supposed to be looking after all the members, the range, and the money. We have our Charter, our Constitution and By-Laws and our Council meetings which we try to follow. Remember, when I say we are out to help you, it does not mean we will do everything for you. We can not chop wood for you, irrigate for you, haul coal for you, or cook for you. The Council receives many requests for money for help with bills or for other things, but if they decided to do all of this they would be working far into the night. The day would not be long enough.

Baker then pointed to a clump of grass displayed at the front of the room. This grass represented the tribe's range, a resource that

Baker felt the tribe was not using productively: "The grass setting here does not do us any good, it is just a waste. An effort has been made to set up a good range program but in the past the tribe has only received peanuts from it."[1]

John Baker, who often spoke at great length during such meetings, was not yet finished; he addressed his people sternly, decrying what he perceived as their lack of individual enterprise: "As we drive along the roads on the reservation we can pick out what is Indian land. Even though there is a nice home and machinery it can still be recognized as Indian land because the alfalfa has not been watered, the fences are down, and many horses are grazing there. Cattle are there without supervision. I am talking about quite a few of you now, and maybe I am making you mad but if this is necessary to get you to do something I am glad I am making you mad."[2] Baker was not the only one present to voice concern over the decline of tribal agricultural operations and an apparent lack of initiative on the part of many tribal members. Leonard Burch, recently returned from service with the air force, bemoaned the state of Ute farming and stock raising. Where he had seen Indian cattle in abundance in the mid 1950s, he now saw idle farms devoid of cattle; and more and more tribal pasture land was being leased to non-Indians. Many people, the young veteran felt, took an interest in nothing other than collecting their per capita payments.[3] In an effort to stop this trend and reap more economic benefit from the tribe's farms and range, John Baker and program director David Box proposed the establishment of a tribal herd, to be run as a tribal enterprise. The response to this suggestion was fairly positive among those in attendance.

This scene, taking place in Ignacio in 1960, is indicative of the economic situation confronting both the Southern Utes and the Ute Mountain Utes throughout the entire post-1960 period. Both tribes faced a lack of economic activity and jobs on their reservations, partly as a result of their own tribal policies and the actions of their members and partly as a result of greater economic forces beyond their control. Midcentury changes in the nation's agricultural economy produced severe dislocation and increased unemployment throughout rural America. In a time marked by increasingly large-scale, capital-intensive farming and stock raising, it no longer made economic sense for the Utes to attempt to support themselves through agriculture.[4] The post-1960 experience on both reservations was thus marked by the pursuit of economic diversification. With large numbers of tribal members unable to support themselves and thus dependent on their tribal government for subsistence, each tribe embarked on a perpetual search for new business enterprises to provide revenue for the tribe and employment for its membership.

ECONOMIC ACTIVITY ON THE RESERVATIONS

The decline of agriculture, long the pillar of the reservation economy, repeatedly aroused concern among Southern Ute tribal members in the later decades of the twentieth century. Having already undergone one fundamental economic transformation—from hunting and gathering to farming and stock raising—the Ignacio Utes were again faced with reorienting their economy as the latter mode of living increasingly disappeared from the reservation or continued under non-Indian operation through the leasing of tribal land and individually held allotments to white farmers and ranchers. The contrast with the past was clear and sometimes painful. A 1986 article in the tribal newspaper tracing the history of the annual Southern Ute Fair contrasted the impressive agricultural exhibits in fairs of the 1920s with the relatively small number and diminished quality of farm products entered by tribal members in recent fairs.[5] And a 1993 letter to the editor of the *Southern Ute Drum* expressed one tribal member's lament regarding the existing socioeconomic situation, in which people were no longer farming and appeared to be neglecting both the land and their children.[6]

A key factor in the steadily diminishing role of agriculture in the Southern Ute tribal economy was the limited size of most allotments and assignments. As Councilman Guy Pinnecoose Jr. commented at a 1977 General Council meeting, "Most people only have 80 acres—you can't make a living on 80 acres."[7] A comparison of the numbers of Southern Ute families involved in agriculture in 1952 and in 1965 clearly shows the results of this situation. While the number of Ute families living on farms increased from 74 to 101, only 18 of the latter families were full-time farmers, compared with 47 such families in 1952. Seventy-one other families were engaged in agricultural pursuits part of the time in 1965, and the remaining farm residents in that year did no farming at all.[8] During the 1960s, then, only a small minority of Southern Utes was fully supported through farming, and this minority was growing ever smaller.

A similar situation was unfolding in Towaoc, where the traditional mainstay of the reservation economy, stock raising, continued to be actively pursued, but only by a steadily declining fraction of the Ute Mountain tribal membership. Here, as in Ignacio and the Los Pinos River valley, the biggest problem was the supply of land. The arid reservation, still lacking the water that had long been promised by the U.S. government, contained very little summer range for the tribal members' herds of cattle and sheep. The tribe acted to alleviate this situation by using some of the oil and land claims wealth it had received during the 1950s to purchase seven higher-elevation ranches totaling more than 25,000 acres. Most of these ranches were located in the Hesperus-Mancos area north and east of the reservation; the largest by far was the more distant 18,749-acre Pinecrest Ranch, located between Gunnison and Montrose.[9] These relatively well-watered ranches provided much-needed summer range for the tribe's stock raisers, who would truck their cattle to Pinecrest and the other ranches each summer after grazing their animals on the winter range located on the reservation. This arrangement yielded little revenue for the tribe since most of the proceeds from cattle sales went to the individual cattle owners, who were not charged grazing fees for their use of the reservation range or the ranches. Even with the added stock-carrying capacity provided by the high-country ranches, relatively few Mountain Utes owned cattle—and sheep were disappearing quite rapidly—as the tribe entered the final quarter of the century. For example, only 76 tribal members out of a population of 1,150 owned and raised livestock in 1970, and only 12 of the 76 possessed large enough herds to be considered full-time stock-raisers.[10] And nearly two decades later, at a time when the tribe numbered some 1,600 people, only 38 different brands were represented among the cattle sold at the 1989 tribal cattle auction.[11]

The shrinking role of agriculture in the reservation economies of the two Colorado Ute tribes was symptomatic of a nationwide decline in Indian farming and stock raising. In 1940, nearly one-half (46.7 percent) of all Indian males had been classified as either farmers or farm managers; by 1960 only 9.5 percent of Indian men were farming. As a result of this trend, only slightly over one-third of the gross agricultural production on Indian lands in 1968 was the work of Indians. In other words, the bulk of Indian agricultural land was being leased to non-Indian farmers and ranchers.[12]

Thus, it is clear that in the late twentieth century most Southern Utes were only marginally involved with agricultural activities and most Ute Mountain Utes did not raise livestock. This left wage work as the predominant economic activity among the people of both reservations. When seeking jobs, most tribal members stuck close to home, only rarely seeking employment off the reservation in Durango or Cortez or in more distant cities. The most common employer for the Utes of Colorado were the two tribes themselves. Beginning with the receipt of the land claims and oil and gas windfalls during the 1950s, both tribes had built up substantial bureaucracies to implement newly established tribal programs; from this time on (with some notable fluctua-

tions) many Utes would look to their tribal organization for employment. In 1977, for example, the Ute Mountain Tribe had 185
employees on its payroll; unfortunately, however, the tribe's financial woes required that 80 of these employees be laid off that
year.[13] Once the tribe's budgetary difficulties had passed, tribal
employment rebounded dramatically, and by 1993 the tribal workforce had mushroomed to 861 employees and a gross payroll for
the year of $16.306 million.[14] As Tribal Chairperson Judy Knight-
Frank explained following the 1992 opening of the Ute Mountain Casino, which employed 79 tribal members, "Our people are
reluctant to leave their homes so the tribe had to bring the employment to them."[15] Although not resulting in such impressive
employment figures, the same trend toward increasing numbers
of tribal jobs was evident in Ignacio. Also, on both reservations
many tribal members who did not work in the tribal organization
obtained employment with the Bureau of Indian Affairs.

Even though many jobs were created by each tribe, not all of
these jobs were filled by tribal members, and this would prove
to be a persistent source of irritation among the people of both
reservations. For example, the new casino in Towaoc employed
79 members of the tribe when it opened in 1992, but 171 of the
facility's 250 jobs went to nontribal members.[16] And when Ute
employees were hired, they typically were placed in lower-paying
jobs as both tribes relied on white professionals to fill many
higher-paying positions. Although officials of both tribes pledged
to hire their own members wherever possible, critics in both
Ignacio and Towaoc frequently charged that tribal members were
consistently passed over in favor of outsiders. "Tribal preference
is a joke," complained Bertha Grove at a 1993 General Meeting
of the Southern Ute Tribe. "You always find tribal members in
the lowest paying jobs."[17]

Many Utes worked for their tribe or the federal government,
but these two sources did not provide sufficient employment to
put all of the reservations' nonagricultural members to work. Un-

able to find employment on the reservations and either unable or unwilling to find it off the reservations, many of these tribal members were left without jobs. As a result, unemployment rates were exceedingly high—over 50 percent on both reservations for most of the post-1960 period. A 1965 tribal report highlighted the inability of most Southern Utes to earn a living. Out of a total of approximately 250 Indian families on the reservation, 155 families had neither tribal land assignments nor jobs.[18] When one recalls that only a handful of those with land were able to support themselves through farming, the economic picture becomes even more bleak.

A FINANCIAL ROLLER-COASTER

Given this dearth of both agricultural activity and wage work on the two reservations, the Ute people became increasingly dependent on their tribal governments for economic support. Despite the efforts of tribal leaders such as John Baker or Judy Knight-Frank to spur members into self-sufficiency, the Tribal Councils in both Ignacio and Towaoc were overwhelmed with requests for assistance from members. Per capita payments to individual members had grown dramatically in size during the 1950s financial bonanza, and they came to be regarded by the people not as a luxury but as a necessity since for many tribal members these payments were the only source of income. Hence, the Ute people loudly protested any proposed decrease in such payments. Even though the Bureau of Indian Affairs had always stressed that per capita payments were to be made only when the tribes realized surplus revenues, the people of the two reservations had come to look on them as a fact of life, regardless of budgetary fluctuations. The Tribal Councils accordingly soon discovered that per capita distributions could be tampered with only at great political peril. Thus, council members were extremely reluctant to reduce the size or frequency of these payments—even when tribal revenues did not justify such distributions. The net result was a recurrent budgetary nightmare.

Tribal income fluctuated greatly in both Towaoc and Ignacio throughout the latter half of the century. This boom-and-bust cycle resulted from the almost total reliance of the two tribes on revenue accruing from a single commodity: petroleum. Unfortunately for the Utes, the vagaries of oil and gas discovery and production, along with tremendous swings in market price, made for extreme variability in the revenue obtained through leases, bonuses, and royalties. Since the Southern Ute Tribe was heavily dependent on natural gas revenues, which constituted 87 percent of tribal income in 1987 and an astonishing 97 percent in the mid 1990s, the tribal budget was extremely vulnerable to drastic swings in the price of natural gas. The fall in gas prices accompanying the energy bust of the 1980s was particularly devastating to the tribe's financial picture, as it caused the tribe's income from natural gas in 1987 to drop to only about one-half the amount received in 1982.[19] The tribe derived some income from other sources, such as timber harvesting, leasing of grazing rights, and catering to tourists and hunters, but these revenues paled in significance compared with the tribe's energy income. The same situation confronted the Ute Mountain Tribe, which was almost totally dependent on oil and gas revenues for its tribal budget. The tribe had been receiving oil income since the first well was drilled on its reservation in 1921.[20] Since livestock proceeds went primarily to individual tribal members, the tribe had no other significant source of revenue. This remained the case for most of the post-1960 period, despite tribal attempts to bring about economic diversification.

Another source of funds for both tribes, one even more irregular than oil and gas leasing, was legal action waged on behalf of the Ute Indians seeking monetary compensation for past government seizures of Ute land. The Confederated Bands of Ute Tribes, through their attorneys, had filed additional land claims beyond the four that had resulted in final judgments in 1950. In the 1960s and early 1970s, two suits were decided by the U.S. Court of Claims in favor of the Ute tribes. As with the 1950 judgments, a plan had to be formulated by each tribe to show how the proceeds of each case would be used, although in this case the ensuing plans were nowhere near as substantial as the 1953–1954 rehabilitation plans. One suit, docket number 327, yielded the Southern Utes $1,556,855, which they received in 1967; the Ute Mountain Utes received their $1,441,002 share from this case the following year.[21] In 1970 a favorable judgment was issued regarding docket number 47567, resulting in the receipt of $979,360 by the Ute Mountain Tribe by the end of that year and a slightly lesser amount received later by the Southern Utes on approval of their plan.[22] One additional claim, this one pursued on behalf of the Southern Utes alone, sought compensation for reservation land that had been opened to homesteading. After a favorable decision from the Court of Claims, this judgment was overturned by the U.S. Supreme Court in 1971.[23]

When the sporadically occurring land claims judgments of 1953–1954 and 1967–1971 were added on top of the already erratic cycle of oil and gas income, the result was a level of tribal income that, over the course of the latter half of the century, alternately rose and fell like a roller-coaster. When the additional factor of persistently high per capita distributions was figured in, the tribal budgetary picture became even more convoluted. Given the lack of alternative means of support, the size of these payments became, out of necessity, quite large, and the total bill was staggering.

Beginning to feel the pinch of high per capita outlays, the Southern Ute Tribal Council adopted a declining schedule of payments beginning with $1,000 in 1959 and decreasing by $100 each year through 1964.[24] Even at such reduced levels as the $800 per capita issued in fiscal year 1961, the total sum was still substantial, amounting in this case to $520,000 out of a total budget of $1,226,255.[25] As a result, Representative Wayne Aspinall

(D-Colo.) warned the tribe in 1960 that its funds might soon
be depleted. Aspinall pointed out that the financial situation in
Towaoc, where energy revenues continued to pad the tribal treasury, was much brighter.[26] In 1964 the BIA Central Office approved the scheduled Southern Ute per capita distribution of
$400 but notified the tribe that future per capita payments would
be approved only on the basis of tribal earnings.[27] Accordingly,
over the next several years the council was only able to make
fairly small per capita—or "dividend"—distributions whenever
budgetary surpluses were realized.

With an explosion of natural gas revenues during the energy
boom of the 1970s, the council was once again able to make substantial per capita payments, but when energy prices plummeted
in the following decade, the people continued to demand 1970s-
level per capita amounts. The council relented in the face of
these demands until the late 1980s, by which time the tribe's
General Fund had diminished from its 1983 level of $13 million
to less than $3 million in 1988. Payments of $3,000 per capita had
been budgeted for the latter year, and when the Tribal Council
voted to reduce this amount, it sparked an uproar. At the current
rate, council members estimated, the tribe would be broke within
twelve to eighteen months.[28]

A parallel budgetary odyssey, although later in developing,
was taking place in Towaoc. After beginning the decade with
a healthy balance in the tribal fund, the Ute Mountain Tribal
Council was forced as early as 1964 to cut back on operating expenses in the interest of obtaining sufficient funds for a per capita distribution. Even with such cutbacks, the council was still
forced to engage in what would become an oft-repeated ritual—
withdrawal of funds from the tribe's reserves in the U.S. Treasury—in order to procure enough of a surplus to make a $900
payment to each enrolled member.[29] Steady tribal population
growth increased the cost of making such payments, and continued withdrawals from the U.S. Treasury gave rise to a rather bleak

economic and budgetary picture by the close of the decade, when the Tribal Council released its plan delineating how the tribe would use its proceeds from claims case 47567. The plan reported that between 1952 and 1969 the tribe had received a total of nearly $52 million from oil and gas royalties, claims awards, and other minor sources. Despite this immense infusion of money, the economic outlook in Towaoc remained dismal. As of 1969 the tribal unemployment rate had recently risen to 68 percent, only some twenty tribal members were working for employers other than the tribe, and for the majority of families per capita payments constituted the only form of income.[30] The council's efforts to provide for its largely nonworking membership had been an expensive proposition. Tribal expenditures had exceeded income every year since 1960, and the tribe's balance of funds was decreasing precipitously. The claims case plan of 1970 summarized the tribe's predicament:

> We exist in a dilemma. We do not have promising employment opportunities. Our oil and gas reserves are rapidly declining. Our range resource can only support a very limited number of our residents. Our population grows, in numbers, in health, in education, in desire, and in need. We owe our population every opportunity to live in comfort and in mental and physical strength.
>
> We want to conserve our assets. We also want to see our assets grow.
>
> We must provide for our members until they can provide totally for themselves.

But the Tribal Council's attempts to provide for its members had seriously eroded the tribe's assets. The plan ominously predicted that if current budgetary trends continued, "we can expect our cash reserves to disappear by 1977."[31]

This feast-followed-by-famine budgetary nightmare in Towaoc, as in Ignacio, was typical of the situation facing tribes across the country. Having distributed to the membership most of the $52 million received between 1952 and 1969, the Ute Mountain

Tribe was facing insolvency. Other tribes, having shared the Utes' predilection for per capita distribution of tribal wealth, were left facing similar financial woes. Nationwide, out of a total of $106 million in land claims money awarded to tribes by the Indian Claims Commission between 1950 and 1966, $42 million had been distributed in the form of per capita payments. Likewise, over one-half of all tribal income from resource extraction—chiefly oil and gas—between 1949 and 1966 had been paid out in per capita payments to individual tribal members.[32] Thus, by 1970 most tribal balance sheets had little to show for the energy, and land claims, windfalls of the previous two decades.

At Ute Mountain the budgetary pattern persisted, and yearly deficits continued to mount. In 1971 BIA officials, increasingly concerned by the tribe's dire financial straits, urged budgetary discipline, specifically the collection of grazing fees from tribal stock raisers and, most important, the elimination or drastic reduction of per capita payments.[33] Neither recommendation was followed by the council, which instead voted to increase the per capita payment amount for the budget in question from $1,000 to $1,250.[34] As a result, in spring 1977 the gloomy prediction issued in the 1970 plan proved all too accurate: the tribe's financial roof came crashing down. The last bimonthly per capita checks were issued in April of that year, and in the summer the tribe was forced to lay off one-third of its workforce. "We're broke," acknowledged tribal treasurer Henry Jacket. To add insult—and political scandal—to economic injury, the Federal Bureau of Investigation (FBI) moved in on two occasions that spring to seize tribal documents as part of a federal investigation into alleged misuse of funds by tribal officials.[35]

A 1982 oil and gas deal worth nearly $7.7 million inaugurated the return of good financial times at Ute Mountain and the resumption of large per capita distributions.[36] Tribal members once again became accustomed to hefty payments and opposed any reduction in their size when falling energy prices ravaged the tribal budget later in the decade. In 1990 the interest earned on the Tribal Investment Fund was sufficient only for a per capita distribution of $250; but people demanded a larger payment, and the council obliged by presenting the membership with four payment options from which to choose: $700, $1,000, $1,700, or $2,200 per capita. If chosen, the latter amount would wipe out the entire investment fund, which had been established in 1984 to provide tribal members with yearly interest income. In the ensuing tribal election, the people voted to accept payments of $1,700 each, thus liquidating much of the investment fund's principal.[37]

The financial turbulence of the latter half of the twentieth century posed a difficult challenge for the Ute Mountain Ute and Southern Ute Tribes. The two Tribal Councils were forced to take a variety of drastic steps in an ongoing attempt to keep their respective financial heads above water, while at the same time maintaining the all-important per capita payments. Operating expenses were slashed, tribal programs were terminated, the federal government was asked to make up for cuts in tribal funding for various programs, and investments were withdrawn—often at substantial penalty—to meet immediate needs. Tribal leaders were alarmed at the depletion of tribal assets, yet they remained committed to meeting the substantial needs of their people. The situation facing council members in both Towaoc and Ignacio in the years following 1960 was aptly described by the Ute Mountain Tribal Council in 1970: "We exist in a dilemma."

ECONOMIC DEVELOPMENT PROGRAMS

John Baker, always the advocate of individual self-sufficiency, expressed concern in 1956 regarding the increasing tendency of tribal members, previously dependent on the federal government, to look to the Tribal Council for their support. In the post-1960 period, this trend accelerated to the point where there was no doubt as to the almost total economic reliance of the Southern

Ute and Ute Mountain Ute peoples on their respective Tribal Councils.

Given this situation, each council embarked on a steady stream of projects designed to meet the economic needs of its people. Two goals were targeted: jobs for tribal members and additional sources of revenue for the tribe. New income sources were sought with hopes of reducing the almost total dependence of the two tribes on the energy industry, with its often painful boom-and-bust cycle, and preparing the Colorado Utes for the day when their oil and gas deposits would run out.

One development strategy involved soliciting outside businesses to locate on the reservation to provide jobs for tribal members. The Southern Ute Tribe actively pursued such arrangements in the late 1960s and early 1970s. At this time, not only the tribe but also the Ignacio community as a whole was suffering from a stagnant economy. In 1969 funding from a Labor Department grant paved the way for Durango-based Southwest Data Institute (SDI) to open a keypunch operation on the grounds of the tribal headquarters. This facility employed 150 Utes, Hispanics, and Anglos in a paid training program.[38] Around this same time, the tribe began considering plans for going into the egg business as another means of bringing jobs to the reservation. This proposal called for a joint venture with Quality Farms and the investment of $800,000 in tribal funds. Neither SDI nor the Egg Production Program, however, provided the employment that the tribe so desperately sought. SDI soon faded from the scene, and the tribe never did enter the egg business, as the latter plan was unanimously rejected by skeptical tribal members at a meeting of the General Council.[39]

More frequently pursued by both tribes were plans for new business ventures to be initiated by the tribes themselves. Even though such tribal enterprises yielded mixed results in terms of generating income for the tribes, they did provide jobs for a number of tribal members and come to play an increasingly important

role in the tribal economies. The Ute Mountain Tribe's first tribally owned enterprise was the Ute Mountain Pottery Corporation, formed in 1970, which sought to bring the tribe a share
of the regional tourist trade through sales of southwestern Indian–style pottery (ironically, the nomadic Utes of the past had
never made much pottery themselves).[40] Beginning as a small
operation in a former clinic building in Towaoc, the pottery enterprise soon moved into a large new facility in the tribal industrial park located on Highway 160 east of Towaoc. After a slow
start, sales of the handmade pottery boomed in the mid 1980s
and took off even more dramatically after a 1988 deal under
which King Soopers, a supermarket chain operating along Colorado's Front Range, began selling Ute Mountain pottery in some
of its stores. This led to a doubling of the operation's workforce
from fifteen to thirty tribal members.[41]

Another potential source of revenue for the tribe were the
countless archaeological ruins left by the Utes' ancient predecessors in southwestern Colorado—the Anasazi. The Ute Mountain Reservation had originally included much of Mesa Verde, part
of which was set aside by the U.S. government as Mesa Verde National Park in 1906. Soon after its creation, federal officials sought
to incorporate into the new park the impressive architectural ruins
located in the adjoining Ute reservation. A land swap was negotiated with the Ute Mountain Tribe, and the cession of 14,354
acres of tribal land to be added to Mesa Verde National Park was
finalized on May 10, 1911. In compensation, the Utes received
20,167 acres of land on the northern half of Ute Mountain.[42]

Even with the loss of the spectacular Anasazi cliff dwellings at
Mesa Verde, the Ute Mountain Reservation still contained a
treasure trove of Anasazi structures dotting the cliffs of Mancos
Canyon and its many side canyons. Given the traditional aversion to spirits of the dead, the Utes, while aware of these ruins,
generally avoided them up until the late 1960s, when some tribal
members began to consider their economic potential for the

tribe. Chief Jack House, who initially opposed development of the reservation's archaeological resources, finally assented to the plan, and in the early years of the following decade the Ute Mountain Tribal Park slowly began to take shape.[43]

The story of the Tribal Park's formation offers a glimpse into tribal attitudes toward economic development at Ute Mountain. Many tribal members welcomed the jobs and revenue, but others strongly opposed opening their homeland to intrusion by the non-Ute world. Ernest House, chairman of the tribe throughout most of the 1980s and a member of a family that had long lived in the midst of the Anasazi ruins, pushed for establishment of a park but acknowledged the objections of many of his people. House, who later became director of the park, recalled the isolationist nature of tribal sentiment against development in the early 1970s: "The whole reservation is our homeland. This is where we live. So if you let other people come in it's just like you invite people into your house: you don't want people looking around in your bedroom. . . . Now a lot of our old Indian people didn't want people wandering around here. What business is it for people to be wandering around here? This is our land. This is our reservation."[44] Longtime Tribal Park superintendent Arthur Cuthair concurred with this assessment of tribal members' resistance to the park: "They didn't want the reservation opened to the outside people. You might say that it's a closed reservation."[45] Opposition occasionally took a violent form. Around the time of the park's creation, angry tribal members burned Jack House's old hogan located in the park and fired gunshots at Arthur Cuthair's house.[46]

Park proponents prevailed, however, and the 125,000-acre Ute Mountain Tribal Park—roughly twice the area of Mesa Verde National Park—was established in 1971. With the assistance of archaeological experts, the tribe started stabilizing the Anasazi ruins, and Ute guides then began conducting tours of the cliff dwellings.

These tours, however, produced no income bonanza. Tour revenues for March–July 1987, for example, amounted to little more than $10,000; and in 1992 the total number of Tribal Park visitors, some 3,000 people, paled in comparison to the 742,080 tourists passing through nearby Mesa Verde.[47] The potential for financial gain was greatest at Soda Point, a section of the Tribal Park bordering Mesa Verde National Park and, by virtue of a federal surveying error, located adjacent to a heavily traveled loop road in the national park. Initial construction of the park's Chapin Mesa road had placed the road 5 miles outside the national park boundary, and even after being rerouted in the 1960s, the road still crossed over onto Ute land, according to a subsequent survey.[48] The Utes took advantage of this surveying error in 1986 by establishing a facility along the road that offered souvenir and refreshment sales and helicopter tours. The Soda Point operation proved to be more lucrative than the tours of more remote sections of the Tribal Park. During May and June 1987, for example, helicopter tours and souvenir sales at Soda Point brought in over $34,000.[49] Thus began a battle over Soda Point between the tribe and the Park Service, which did not welcome this uninvited and unregulated concession in the midst of a popular area in the national park. After announcing an intention to relocate the road once again to bypass tribal land entirely, the Park Service ultimately entered into a pact with the tribe in 1988 by which the two neighbors agreed to coexist under the present arrangement, with some restrictions placed on the tribe's concession and helicopter tour operations at Soda Point.[50]

After the initial ventures in pottery and tourism, the Ute Mountain Tribe established several additional tribal enterprises to further the reservation's economic development. By far the most successful of these was the Weeminuche Construction Authority, established by the Tribal Council in 1985.[51] Business for the new enterprise quickly boomed, amounting to over $3 million in contract work in fiscal year 1987 alone, and by 1993 Weeminuche had grown to such an extent that it boasted a workforce of 190 permanent employees.[52] This company clearly brought the tribe substantial revenue and provided employment for many tribal members; but critics decried the fact that this enterprise was managed by a white-owned firm in Cortez that claimed much of the operation's profit, and they also protested that Ute employees tended to remain in the lowest-paying jobs.[53] Other tribal enterprises begun during the 1980s included a high-stakes bingo hall with a seating capacity of five hundred, which opened in 1984, and the tribal Farm and Ranch Enterprise, chartered in 1987 to increase the tribe's agricultural revenue and employment.[54]

The Southern Ute Tribe, which investigated at great length the prospects for a tribal cattle enterprise in the early 1960s, never took any action on this proposal; and agriculture continued to diminish in economic importance for the Utes of Ignacio. Instead, the Tribal Council increasingly regarded tourism as offering the greatest potential for economic development of its reservation, and it soon embarked on a number of tribal enterprises seeking to bring tourists to the reservation. Lake Capote, purchased by the tribe and opened to the public for fishing in 1963, was the first such enterprise. A campground and other facilities were constructed on this site, and the lake, located along Highway 160 northeast of Ignacio, was regularly stocked with fish by the tribe.[55] A much larger economic development project was undertaken in 1970 with the groundbreaking for the tourist motel complex, called the Pino Nuche Pu-Ra-Sa, which opened the following year. In addition to the thirty-eight-unit Pino Nuche (meaning Pine People) Motel, this complex eventually included several other tourist-oriented enterprises: an outdoor pool (later converted to an indoor pool), a restaurant and lounge, an arts and crafts shop, and a museum. The complex, located immediately south of the tribal headquarters, also contained a community center at which a variety of tribal gatherings were held and which doubled as a convention facility for visiting groups.

The Southern Ute Tribe was quite successful in obtaining federal grants to finance large building projects such as the Pino Nuche, later renamed the Sky Ute Lodge. The tribe was awarded a grant from the Economic Development Administration in 1974 to fund the construction of another large facility, the $668,000 Horse Training and Conditioning Center, to be built on the site of the tribal fairgrounds and racetrack situated along the Los Pinos River just east of Ignacio.[56] This facility, initially consisting of an indoor arena and 100 horse stalls, was later expanded and rechristened Sky Ute Downs. Tribal leaders hoped that the Downs and the Sky Ute Lodge would complement each other, each producing more tourist customers for the other. The tribe also initiated several smaller business ventures to increase both tribal revenue and employment. The Southern Utes' first off-reservation enterprise, a Shell service station located in Ignacio, was purchased by the tribe and opened in 1975.[57] A tribal retail facility, the Sky Ute Country Store, opened in 1986 directly across the highway from the Sky Ute Lodge complex.[58] The tribe briefly operated the Sky Ute Marina on Navajo Reservoir, located southeast of Ignacio along the Colorado–New Mexico border, and like the Ute Mountain Tribe, the Southern Ute Tribe began operating weekly bingo games at the Sky Ute Lodge complex in the mid 1980s.

The tribe was more successful in obtaining federal funding for new enterprises than in making the resulting ventures profitable. Substantial amounts of money from a variety of federal agencies other than the BIA became available to Indian tribes beginning in the 1960s. For the first time, tribes became eligible for funding that was not targeted specifically at Native Americans. The Office of Economic Opportunity (OEO), part of Lyndon Johnson's Great Society, provided millions of dollars—free from BIA control—to the nation's tribes. One OEO program gave Indians funding to establish Community Action Programs to fight poverty on their reservations.[59] Another new source of grant money, the Economic Development Administration, offered funding for projects aimed at the economic development of Indian reservations. This agency, part of the Department of Commerce, soon overshadowed the OEO as a source of tribal funding, ultimately providing some $122 million in grants.[60] This windfall of newly available federal funding, however, was often rather ineffective in stimulating economic activity on Indian reservations. The rush to obtain grant money sometimes gave rise to poorly conceived projects and mismanagement of funds.[61] One example of a questionable tribal development project, made possible by federal grant money, was the Southern Ute Tribe's Pino Nuche Motel.

The Pino Nuche and other tribal enterprises in Ignacio proved somewhat more problematic than their counterparts on the Ute Mountain Reservation. Unlike the highly profitable Weeminuche Construction Authority and the successful Ute Mountain Ute Pottery enterprise, the Southern Utes' business ventures consistently lost money. The motel and restaurant at the Pino Nuche rang up losses year after year, and after four years of operation they still required monthly cash infusions in the neighborhood of $12,000–14,000 just to remain afloat.[62] Nor did this situation improve as the years went by. The performance of the Sky Ute Downs was similarly disappointing; here, too, monthly losses were the norm.

Failure to realize a profit was not the only problem associated with the tribal enterprises. Management difficulties were endemic. After only four years of operation, the motel was already on its fifth manager—all four of his predecessors had quit in the face of criticism from tribal members or the Pino Nuche board of directors.[63] On one occasion in 1982, Sky Ute Downs was temporarily shut down after a management dispute left the staff there in fear of suffering "physical abuse."[64] Management problems also afflicted Lake Capote, which had a poor year in 1979 owing partly to its early closure that season following the premature departure of its managers.[65] Despite these losses and administrative

shortcomings, the various enterprises yielded one important benefit—jobs for tribal members. However, even this positive contribution to the reservation economy became a source of controversy. Tribal members constantly bombarded the Tribal Council
with complaints that they had been passed over while outsiders
were hired for jobs at the tribal businesses.

Given the abundant difficulties associated with these ventures,
the Tribal Council frequently considered and sometimes acted
on proposals to terminate tribal enterprises. The Sky Ute Marina
lasted for only one season and the tribe's Shell station, a mere
three years. The tribe elected to forego operation of the Sky Ute
Country Store after only one year, preferring in 1987 to lease the
store to the Thriftway Company.[66] That same year, the Tribal
Council actively sought—without success—to lease both the
Sky Ute Downs and the Sky Ute Lodge to outside operators.[67]
In the face of persistent losses from these ventures, some tribal
members began entertaining the thought of simply shutting
them down. At a 1989 meeting, Tribal Council member Clement
Frost worried that expenditures were getting out of hand. "We are
spending too much money trying to make a go of the enterprises
and not getting anywhere," he asserted. Perhaps, he suggested, it
was time to consider closing down the enterprises.[68] While bingo
games yielded some revenues to the tribe, the remainder of the
Southern Utes' tribal enterprises proved persistent sources of
frustration.

The Southern Utes' disappointing experience with economic
development projects was not unusual. Problems abounded as
tribes across the country attempted to establish businesses on
their reservations throughout the 1960s and 1970s, often with
the financial assistance of federal development programs such as
those offered by the Area Redevelopment Act, the Office of
Economic Opportunity, the Economic Development Administration, and the BIA, which established the Indian Business Development Program in 1970. Most of these new businesses failed

to meet expectations. The overall closure rate for tribal enterprises during this period was 20–25 percent per year. Virtually all Indian tourist complexes, like the Pino Nuche/Sky Ute Lodge and the Sky Ute Downs, operated at a loss; and tribal industrial parks stood empty or underutilized. Even the employment picture was discouraging: tribal enterprises throughout the country employed more non-Indians than Indians.[69]

THE BATTLE FOR WATER

Many economic development projects were precluded by the lack of adequate water supplies on each reservation. Water limitations barred the expansion of farming and ranching operations as well as the mining of vast and largely untapped coal deposits. The Ute Mountain Tribe had always suffered the economic consequences of its reservation's aridity; the tribe was even forced to haul drinking water by truck from Cortez to Towaoc daily until 1990. And even though the water situation appeared to be much less problematic on the Southern Ute Reservation, crossed as it was by a number of substantial streams—the La Plata, Animas, Florida, Los Pinos, Piedra, and San Juan Rivers—the tribe nevertheless found itself without adequate water for the development of its reservation. The problem here, as with the Mancos River flowing through the Ute Mountain Reservation, was that the senior rights of the Indians to the water of these rivers, as guaranteed by the Winters doctrine, existed solely on paper, while the actual water had long been used by parties upstream.[70] The Pine River Project of the early 1940s, through the construction of Vallecito Reservoir, had provided the Southern Utes with much-needed irrigation water, but this project did not fully meet the tribe's water needs; and those of the Ute Mountain Tribe had never been addressed by the federal government.

Thus, the stage was set for a lengthy battle for water, waged by the Tribal Councils of both tribes throughout the 1970s, 1980s, and 1990s. Rather than insisting on their senior water rights to the many streams crossing their reservations, a stance that would seriously threaten the interests of non-Indian water users upstream from the Ute reservations, the tribes opted for a compromise solution. In negotiations with state and federal officials, the two tribes agreed to defer their claims to water flowing through streams such as the Los Pinos River and the Mancos River in exchange for another arrangement guaranteeing water for the Utes. The federal government pledged to provide the two tribes with water diverted by the Dolores and Animas–La Plata (A-LP) water projects.[71] The Colorado Ute Indian Water Rights Settlement Agreement, signed by all parties in December 1986 and enacted by Congress November 3, 1988, spelled out the terms under which the water rights of the two tribes would be satisfied. The tribes would receive both irrigation water and municipal and industrial water from the two federal projects. Water from the Dolores Project would enable the Mountain Utes, who at the time the settlement was negotiated had only enough agricultural water to irrigate a mere 200 acres, to irrigate at least 7,500 additional acres; and even more acreage could later be irrigated on the arrival of water from the Animas–La Plata Project. The Southern Utes, who would not benefit from the Dolores Project, were to obtain roughly 26,500 acre feet of municipal and industrial water and 3,400 acre feet of irrigation water each year from the Animas–La Plata Project. The Ute tribes would also split a $60.5 million development fund to be used for economic development of their reservations. The Mountain Utes would reap the additional benefit of a $6 million pipeline carrying municipal water from Cortez to Towaoc.[72]

Construction for the Dolores Project's McPhee Reservoir, located on the Dolores River north of Cortez, had begun in 1976, so this reservoir was already in existence at the time the water settlement was enacted; hence the Ute Mountain Tribe soon began to enjoy the fruits of this agreement. The pipeline from

Cortez, constructed by the Weeminuche Construction Authority, was completed in 1990, furnishing Towaoc with a safe and reliable supply of municipal water for the first time. Thus, after nearly a century of delay, the federal government finally made good on its promise to provide the tribe with water.[73] No longer did tribal members need to set out buckets each day to be filled by the water truck. Also at this time, the tribe eagerly anticipated the arrival of irrigation water from McPhee Reservoir. As early as 1987, the tribe's Farm and Ranch Enterprise planted and harvested a test crop of oats utilizing new side-roll sprinklers.[74] A $31,909,400 Bureau of Reclamation contract for completion of the 34-mile Towaoc Canal, designed to carry this irrigation water to the reservation, was awarded to the Weeminuche Construction Authority early in 1992.[75] This canal soon channeled water to the arid and barren country to the south and southwest of Sleeping Ute Mountain. By 1994 this flat, open stretch of the reservation, previously covered only with scattered clumps of grass, had become a verdant oasis of wheat, barley, and other crops. Meanwhile in the Montezuma Valley, the arrival of municipal water as part of the water settlement made possible the 1992 opening of two new tribal business enterprises—a new casino and an adjacent convenience store and gas station, both located along Highway 160 east of Towaoc.[76]

While the Ute Mountain Tribe quickly reaped the benefits of the Colorado Ute Indian Water Rights Settlement Agreement, the Southern Utes became impatient with the lack of progress toward obtaining their share of water. Even though the tribe soon began to receive its economic development funds, there was not a drop of water in sight. The controversial Animas–La Plata Project, slated to deliver water to the tribe as part of the agreement, had yet to materialize. The Animas–La Plata Project had originally been authorized in 1968, some twenty years prior to congressional approval of the Water Rights Settlement Agreement, but the project had been stymied by a succession of obstacles.

One such hurdle came in 1990 when the U.S. Fish and Wildlife Service found the project in violation of the Endangered Species Act because of the threat it posed to two federally protected fish species living downstream. Then in 1992 the Sierra Club and several other environmental groups filed suit against the Bureau of Reclamation in an attempt to block the project.[77] A new challenge to A-LP arose in 1995 when the economic feasibility of the project was called into question by the Bureau of Reclamation. A draft economic analysis completed by the Bureau predicted that every dollar invested in A-LP by taxpayers would produce benefits worth only thirty-six cents.[78]

Tribal chairman Leonard Burch fumed over such delays and adamantly insisted on construction of the Animas–La Plata Project. "The Southern Ute Tribe will not allow the United States Government to again break a treaty obligation to the Indian people," he vowed. Burch brushed aside suggestions that the tribe accept a monetary settlement in lieu of A-LP water. The Utes had once made this mistake with respect to their land, ceding it to the government in exchange for money, he explained. "We are unwilling to repeat the mistakes of the past with regard to our water."[79] The Southern Utes hoped to gain some additional irrigation water from Animas–La Plata, but they were most anxious to obtain industrial water, which would enable them to develop the immense coal deposits underlying the reservation.[80] As the twentieth century neared its conclusion, however, the tribe was still without adequate water and thus was unable to tap this vast fossil fuel treasure.

The battle over water continued at this time at Ute Mountain, despite the tangible improvement in the tribe's water situation under the Colorado Ute Indian Water Rights Settlement Agreement. In December 1994, the Ute Mountain Ute Tribe announced that it would commence litigation over the failure of the federal government to satisfy the tribe's water rights. Tribal officials claimed that only 40 percent of the lands to be irrigated with Dolores Project water had in fact been reached by water as of the May 1, 1994, completion date for the project.[81]

TAPPING AN UNDERGROUND TREASURE

In 1992 the Southern Ute Tribe utilized some of its economic development funds received under the Water Rights Settlement Agreement to form its own energy company, Red Willow Production Company. The tribe had long been in the energy business, but in the past it had typically had little control over the terms of this business. This was about to change. The establishment of Red Willow inaugurated a promising new chapter in the tribe's drive for economic autonomy, and in this respect the Southern Ute Tribe was emerging as a leader in the nationwide movement toward tribal control over energy development.

Oil and gas reserves had long been tapped on both reservations, beginning with the first oil well drilled at Ute Mountain in 1921, but the arrangement under which fossil fuels had been developed on the Ute reservations tended to minimize both the profits and control enjoyed by the two tribes. As the pace of petroleum extraction increased throughout the West in the 1940s and 1950s, oil and natural gas found on Indian reservations was developed under the terms of the 1938 Omnibus Tribal Leasing Act. This legislation gave tribes the power of consent over oil and gas development on their reservations, but it did not allow them to control the conditions under which their resources were leased to energy companies. Oil and gas leasing between 1938 and 1982 was controlled within the Department of the Interior by the BIA and the U.S. Geological Survey (USGS), and a number of problems emerged for energy tribes such as the Utes of Colorado under this arrangement. Tribes were bound by long-term agreements that precluded renegotiation of lease terms, and they were forced to accept government-imposed standard leases, even when oil companies likely would have agreed to contracts more favorable to the Indians. Lacking the expertise and information needed to maximize returns, mineral-rich tribes were forced to rely on federal bureaucrats to obtain and enforce the favorable lease terms. But USGS and BIA officials typically failed to protect Indian interests through the course of the leasing process. Two independent studies during the 1970s found that Indian mineral resources were being mismanaged and leased at prices far below their market value.[82]

In general, the mineral leasing system established under the 1938 Omnibus Tribal Leasing Act forced Indian tribes into a subordinate role in which they were merely the passive recipients of royalty payments as per lease agreements concluded and overseen by the Department of the Interior.[83] Despite being forced into a passive role in this process, both Colorado Ute tribes actively endeavored to protect their interests. A 1975 Federal Trade Commission report described the two tribes as being "quite sophisticated" in their energy dealings, noting that, whereas the USGS rarely rejected any oil or gas bid, the Southern Utes and Ute Mountain Utes had both done so when faced with unfavorable bids.[84]

During the 1970s, the Utes and other energy tribes began to take action to reform this unfavorable system. The two Colorado Ute tribes joined with other energy-rich tribes on September 18, 1975, to form the Council of Energy Resource Tribes (CERT). This organization was formed to improve the position of its member tribes in their energy dealings through sharing information, obtaining scientific and technical expertise, and gaining political clout. By 1988 forty-three tribes had become members of CERT.[85] Another way in which tribes sought to increase their return from energy development was through the negotiation of leases with more favorable terms than the standard Interior Department lease. The legality of such alternative leases, however, remained in question until Congress passed the Indian Mineral Development Act in 1982. This act, which authorized tribes to conduct their own negotiations with energy companies, finally allowed Indians to play an active role in the development of their own energy resources.

Both Ute tribes quickly moved to take advantage of their new freedom under the 1982 mineral legislation. The Ute Mountain Ute Tribe negotiated a quite favorable lease with the Wintershall Corporation in the mid 1980s. The tribe obtained a number of beneficial terms, including a $5 million bonus, escalating rentals and royalties, a $200,000 investigation (paid for by Wintershall) to clear up the lease status of tribal lands, an agreement that the tribe's construction company would be utilized by Wintershall for this project, and an annual work commitment of $1.5 million. The tribe also wisely included a safeguard feature in the lease by retaining the oil and gas rights to one-quarter of every other section within the area being leased.[86] These terms helped protect the tribe from the risks that came with negotiating on its own without federal protection. The Southern Ute Tribe likewise took advantage of the new entrepreneurial freedom made possible by the Indian Mineral Development Act. The Ignacio tribe became one of the first in the nation to acquire complete ownership of oil or gas wells, being one of only four tribes to hold total ownership in wells as of 1988.[87]

The Southern Ute campaign to assume control over energy development on the tribe's reservation culminated in the 1992 creation of the Red Willow Production Company. The tribe was embarking on a bold new economic development strategy: assuming ownership and direct control over much of the tribe's energy resources. In what some sources described as the first such deal of its kind for an American Indian tribe, the Southern Utes purchased interests in fifty-one active gas wells within the exterior boundaries of their reservation in January 1993; twenty-one of these wells were to be operated by Red Willow, and the tribe would hold royalty interests in the remaining thirty.[88] This deal, along with a second acquisition made several months later, reversed the historical pattern for development of Indian energy resources. Instead of being a passive spectator in business dealings, sitting back to await the results of Interior Department negotiations with an outside energy company, the Southern Ute Tribe had now dispensed with both the Department of the Interior and the energy company. With the 1993 purchases by Red Willow, the tribe finally achieved complete control over the operation of some of its gas wells.[89] The tribe expected to recover its initial investment within three years and to profit from the recently acquired wells for a period of twenty-four years.[90] This represented a substantial step toward economic autonomy for the Southern Ute Tribe.

A NEW GOLD RUSH: INDIAN GAMING

Colorado voters probably did not realize when they voted to amend the state constitution in 1990 to allow limited-stakes gambling in three mountain communities that they were also paving the way for the establishment of casino gambling on the state's two Indian reservations. The possibilities opened by this 1990 referendum certainly did not escape the detection of the Ute Mountain Utes and the Southern Utes. Both tribes were eager to participate in the nationwide trend toward Indian gaming facilities. This burgeoning new Indian industry had been made possible by the Indian Gaming Act, passed by Congress in 1988. Under this act, Indian tribes located in any state that already allowed gambling would be permitted to conduct their own gambling enterprises. Tribes all across the country were turning to gaming for their economic salvation—some with notable success. By 1994 eighty-eight tribes had signed gambling pacts with nineteen states.[91] The 1990 limited-stakes gaming amendment to the Colorado Constitution gave the Colorado Ute tribes the opening they needed to join tribes all across the country in participating in this new economic gold rush.

The Ute Mountain Tribe was the first of the two Colorado tribes to open a casino, converting the pottery plant in the tribal industrial park into a 30,000-square-foot casino complete with 300 slot machines and 14 blackjack and poker tables. One unusual aspect of the Ute Mountain Casino was the absence of alcoholic beverages since alcohol was still prohibited on the reservation.[92] Operated by Texas-based Full House Limited, the Ute Mountain Casino welcomed an opening-night crowd of more than 1,000 people on Labor Day weekend 1992. With 250 employees, including 79 tribal members, and an estimated annual payroll of $3 million, the effect on both the tribal and local economy was immense.[93] Crowds continued to flock to the casino throughout its first year of operation, no doubt generating considerable revenue for the tribe, but the tribe did not release any financial data to the public. A member of the Ute Mountain Gaming Commission contended that earnings had been above average for a casino of this size, but the tribe—a sovereign entity not subject to state regulation—was under no obligation to report its earnings, and it showed no inclination to do so.[94]

Lacking a ready-made facility such as the former pottery plant in Towaoc, the Southern Utes moved more slowly, but with equal determination, toward the opening of their own tribal casino. There was no immediate consensus regarding the site for such a facility. The new tribal gaming committee initially formulated plans for a large casino-hotel complex on Highway 550 south of Durango near Bondad, but their focus soon shifted back to Ignacio—with the hope of solving an old nagging problem. Sky Ute Enterprises had been subsidized by the tribe for over twenty years. The Sky Ute Lodge (formerly the Pino Nuche Motel) and the Sky Ute Downs horse racing facility had both been a perpetual drain on the tribal budget. In fact, several months later a rather reluctant Tribal Council approved yet another infusion of tribal funds into the ailing enterprises. The gaming committee contended that by locating a smaller casino at Sky Ute Lodge, these operations could be made profitable for the first time ever.[95] Keeping alive the possibility of building a larger casino in Bondad at some future time, the tribe began construction of the Sky Ute Casino in May 1993. The casino, which was to be managed, along with the Sky Ute Lodge and restaurant, by Great Western Casinos, opened to the public on September 1, 1993. Just under one-half of the facility's 170 employees on opening day were Southern Ute tribal members.[96]

The Sky Ute Lodge and Casino proved highly successful in its first year of operation, yielding revenues of twice the amount that had been forecast for the new venture. The $4.1 million that the tribe had loaned itself for start-up costs were repaid in full by August 1994, far ahead of schedule. Despite this success, some familiar problems surfaced. The casino's general manager and controller were replaced because of disagreements with the Tribal Council, which acted as the tribe's gaming committee.[97] Nevertheless, the tribe was sufficiently encouraged to launch a $4 million expansion of the Sky Ute Casino to accommodate the crowds, which had often strained the capacity of the new facility. The casino expansion would triple the number of slot and video poker machines, add new blackjack and poker tables, and provide room for the return of bingo games.[98] The Southern Ute Tribe's newly enlarged gaming facility opened for business in summer 1995. At this time, the Indian gaming industry still looked to be a profitable one for the Utes of Colorado.

Both tribes had sought for several decades to profit from tourism in the Four Corners area, and they now hoped that gambling would bring more tourists to their reservations. The Ute Mountain Utes, who a quarter century earlier had agonized over whether to open their homeland to outside visitors, now sought to offer new amenities in order to attract more tourists to the Towaoc area. The Sleeping Ute RV Park opened adjacent to the tribe's casino in 1994, and an Indian village that would showcase traditional dancing and crafts was soon under construction nearby.[99]

Having only recently entered the gaming business, the Ute Mountain Tribe in 1993 entertained the idea of becoming involved with another entirely different sort of economic activity—storage of radioactive nuclear waste. The Mountain Utes were one of nine tribes across the country to apply for $200,000 grants for examining the feasibility of storing spent nuclear reactor fuel on their reservations.[100] This endeavor of the Ute Mountain Ute Tribe clearly reveals the strength of the modern imperative for economic development of Indian reservations. Despite the intense and enduring affection of the Ute people for their homeland, tribal leaders actively pursued a venture that involved potentially ominous environmental implications. Nothing came of this proposal, yet the fact that it was seriously considered by the Ute Mountain Ute Tribe is revealing. More than anything else, perhaps, this initiative epitomizes the intensive efforts of both Colorado Ute tribes to diversify their economies and develop their reservations during the latter part of the twentieth century.

Members of the Southern Ute Tribal Council in 1960. Seated is Chairman John E. Baker Sr.; standing from left to right are Sunshine Cloud Smith, Anna Marie Scott, Anthony Burch, Bonny Kent, and Clifford Baker. John Baker was the driving force behind the ten-year Southern Ute Rehabilitation Plan, which was instituted in 1954. (Courtesy, Colorado Historical Society, F24501.)

Albert Wing Sr., a longtime member of the Ute Mountain Tribal Council and chairman of this body for much of the 1950s and 1960s. The work of Albert Wing and his fellow council members during this time was made more difficult by their lack of education and limited English-language proficiency. (Courtesy, *Denver Post.*)

Jack House, the last chief of the Ute Mountain Utes. The state of Colorado honored the Ute chief by placing this stained-glass portrait in the State Capitol. As chief of his tribe for thirty-five years (up until his death in 1971) and also a perennial member of the Tribal Council, Jack House dominated Ute Mountain tribal affairs throughout the often-turbulent midcentury period. (Richard Young photograph.)

An exhibit created by the Tribal Committee on Alcoholism for the 1960 Southern Ute Tribal Fair. Alcoholism took a heavy toll among the Ute people throughout the latter half of the century, in spite of persistent efforts in both Towaoc and Ignacio to combat this problem. (Courtesy, Colorado Historical Society.)

A sweat lodge, located adjacent to the Southern Ute Tribe's alcoholism treatment center, the Peaceful Spirit Lodge, 1993. Sweat ceremonies are a focal point of traditional Ute culture and spirituality, and such rituals were sometimes utilized in the war against drug and alcohol abuse. (Richard Young photograph.)

A Sun Dance lodge near Ignacio, 1960. Each year a new willow lodge is erected on the Sun Dance grounds in preparation for this annual summer dance of great spiritual importance. Adopted from Plains Indians around the turn of the century, the Sun Dance was conducted on both reservations for most of the twentieth century. (Courtesy, Colorado Historical Society, 30367.)

The Ute Mountain Bear Dance, June 1993. This traditional Ute dance dating from the aboriginal period is still performed each spring in both Towaoc and Ignacio. Conducted inside a large juniper-walled corral, the Bear Dance begins with a line of men facing a line of women. Both lines shuffle forward and then backward in synchronized fashion. (Richard Young photograph.)

The Ute Mountain Bear Dance, June 1993. The second part of this dance begins on the signal of a "catman," who breaks individual couples apart from the two lines. The couples then dance forward and backward across the corral. (Richard Young photograph.)

Card games at the Ute Mountain Bear Dance, June 1993. Gambling has always been a favorite pastime among the Ute people, and this continued to be the case late in the century. The annual Bear Dance is usually accompanied by gambling activities, such as card games or the traditional Ute hand game, conducted under large shade houses. Here spectators at the Bear Dance in Towaoc play a card game called "fives." Ute Peak is visible in the distance. (Richard Young photograph.)

Judy Knight-Frank (known as Judy Pinnecoose in the 1970s), the first female chairperson of the Ute Mountain Ute Tribe. Once an outspoken critic of the Tribal Council, Knight-Frank took over the reins of tribal government first in 1979 and then again in 1989. As chairperson, she actively promoted economic development of the reservation. (Courtesy, *Denver Post*, Kit Miniclier photograph.)

Leonard Burch, the dominant figure in Southern Ute tribal politics from the mid 1960s through the mid 1990s. An ardent advocate of economic development and tribal water rights, Burch served as tribal chairman for thirty straight years with only one constitutionally mandated three-year interruption. (Courtesy, *Denver Post*, Kit Miniclier photograph.)

The Ute Mountain Ute Tribal Office Complex in Towaoc, 1993. This impressive adobe-style structure, built at a cost of $1.8 million, was dedicated in October 1988. (Richard Young photograph.)

The Ute Mountain Casino, located on Highway 160 just east of Towaoc, 1993. This facility was an economic boon to the tribe following a September 1992 opening. The Southern Ute Tribe entered the gaming business one year later with the inauguration of the Sky Ute Casino in Ignacio. (Richard Young photograph.)

Terry Knight, preparing to conduct a sweat ceremony at his home near Towaoc in 1994. A significant figure in the spiritual life of the Ute Mountain Ute people during the final decades of the century, Terry Knight was one of many Ute Mountain "roadmen" who led tribal members in the peyote rites of the Native American Church. He also became the tribe's Sun Dance chief in 1980. (Richard Young photograph.)

Ernest House Sr. speaking to Tribal Park visitors during a tour of the Bone Awl House ruin in 1994. A grandson of the Ute Mountain Ute Tribe's last chief, House served as tribal chairman for seven years during the 1980s. He later became director of the Ute Mountain Tribal Park, an immense preserve inside the reservation that is dotted with Anasazi ruins. (Richard Young photograph.)

A parade by Southern Ute veterans on Memorial Day, 1993. Large numbers of tribal members from both reservations served in the armed forces throughout the twentieth century, beginning primarily with World War II. Among tribal leaders, in particular, military service was quite common. (Courtesy, *Southern Ute Drum*, Robert Baker photograph.)

7

TRIBAL POLITICS
AFTER 1960

On October 6, 1961, 122 members of the Southern Ute Tribe convened in the tribe's recreation hall to hold the annual Tribal Council election. This building had originally served as the tribe's Council Hall before being converted into a recreation facility in 1955. Old rivals Sunshine Smith and John E. Baker Sr. were both up for reelection at this meeting, their three-year terms having expired. The results of the voting were a resounding triumph for John Baker. While Smith was defeated in her bid for reelection, Baker was overwhelmingly reelected in a separate race against two challengers, one of whom was Sunshine Smith's brother, Ralph Cloud.[1] At this time, the tribe was seven years into its ten-year rehabilitation program, which had been spearheaded from the start by John Baker. The outspoken Southern Ute leader was so strongly identified with this program in the minds of tribal members that some of Sunshine Smith's own relatives informed an anthropologist observing the 1961 election that they had voted for Baker because they feared that without him there would be no program at all.[2] Baker, who had served as chairman of the council from 1956 to 1960 before relinquishing that position to Anthony Burch, was once again elected to the chairmanship by his fellow council members soon after the 1961 Tribal Council election. John Baker, however, soon withdrew from this primary leadership role, and another member of the Burch family stepped forward to fill the resulting political void.

As the 1960s began, many of the long-familiar contrasts between the Southern Ute and Ute Mountain Ute Tribal Councils were still in evidence. Continuing the trend of the 1950s, all seven members of the Ute Mountain Tribal Council were men, whereas in Ignacio the October 1960 election left the Southern Utes with a council composed of four women and two men. Language usage also remained a point of contrast between the two bodies. Most business in the Southern Ute Tribal Council was conducted in English, as it had been since at least the mid 1950s; and John Baker was forced to admit at a 1960 General Council meeting that his knowledge of the Ute language was "not too good."[3] English was spoken much less frequently at meetings of the Ute Mountain Council. Jack House, the aging chief of the Ute Mountain Tribe who had never gone to school and spoke virtually no English, was beginning his third decade on the tribe's council (in addition to his years of service on preconstitution councils), and he still wielded tremendous power in council deliberations.[4] Albert Wing Sr., the stockman and former CCC worker, was still chairman of the Tribal Council in Towaoc.[5] Whereas Chairman Wing did not have a high school education, his counterpart in Ignacio, John Baker, had both a high school diploma and some college experience and in fact would soon be resuming his college studies.

Despite these striking contrasts, the two councils also shared some common characteristics. Both panels profited from the experience of individuals with long tenures as council members. Both councils also benefited from the participation of armed service veterans, with two of seven Towaoc councilmen in 1960 having served in the military and fully half of the six Southern

Ute council members being veterans. Certainly the political situation on the two reservations differed in many respects throughout the post-1960 period, but, despite the persistence of significant social and cultural disparities, these political differences became less apparent as the years went by. Tribal politics in Towaoc and Ignacio during the latter half of the century increasingly came to be characterized by the same issues and concerns, the same challenges, and the same turbulent factionalism.

SOUTHERN UTE POLITICAL LEADERSHIP

Even before assuming the chairmanship in 1956, John E. Baker Sr. clearly began dominating the proceedings of Southern Ute Tribal Council meetings, and this continued to be the case during the early 1960s; but the era of dominance by Baker soon faded. When his colleagues on the council voted in 1962 for his continuation as chairman, the forty-four-year-old World War II veteran asked if it would be possible to take the position on a temporary basis, explaining that he felt the tribe was due for a change.[6] Baker subsequently resigned from both the council and the chairmanship on two separate occasions—in 1963 and again in 1966—to resume his college education at Arizona State University, where he studied political science. Never able to withdraw for long from his tribe's political scene, Baker's absences were of short duration; and in each case he returned to the Tribal Council to serve, with only a few brief interruptions, through 1982.

The departure of John Baker in 1966 paved the way for the beginning of a new era in Southern Ute politics, one that was dominated by Leonard C. Burch. Son of the late chairman Sam Burch, Leonard Burch was an air force veteran who had served his country from 1953 to 1957, mostly in the Middle East. After completing his tour of duty, Burch returned to the reservation and worked briefly for the BIA before becoming a realty officer for the tribe in the early 1960s. In fall 1966, Burch was elected to

the Tribal Council and then promptly chosen by his fellow council members to be the chairman of this body. At the age of thirty-
two, Burch was the youngest person ever to achieve this position.[7]
Thus began his extended reign as chairman, one that would persist, with one constitutionally mandated three-year interruption,
well into the 1990s. Only Jack House can rival the longevity of
Leonard Burch in the postconstitution history of leadership
among the two Colorado tribes.

The triumph of Leonard Burch, son of a tribal chairman and
brother to another, illustrates the persistence of family dynasties
in Southern Ute politics during the latter half of the twentieth
century. This characteristic of tribal leadership had first emerged
among the prereservation Southern Utes as the increasing use of
horses led to band consolidation and a tendency toward hereditary chieftaincy.[8] In addition to the three Burch family members
who served as chairmen beginning in the 1940s, another member of the family, Everett Burch, joined the Tribal Council for a
time in the 1970s.[9] The Cloud family, too, continued to send representatives to the council, with two family members, Sunshine
Smith and her brother Ralph Cloud, being elected in 1963. Although Neil Cloud was elected to the council in 1977, the Cloud
family was by this time becoming less active in council politics.
The Baker family, however, maintained a strong council presence
throughout the entire period. The election of brothers John and
Chris Baker in 1965 meant that fully one-half of the six council
members were Bakers, cousin Clifford Baker having joined the
council in 1964. John E. Baker Sr., who narrowly lost to Leonard
Burch in the 1981 election for tribal chairman, continued to
serve on the Tribal Council with only brief intermissions until
November 1982, when he stepped aside to yield his seat to son
John E. Baker Jr., who had just been elected to the panel. Chris
Baker became a fairly permanent feature on the council, and he
served one three-year term as chairman when a new constitutional term-limit provision forced Leonard Burch to step down in

1984. Other family names, such as Taylor, Box, Jefferson, and Frost, were also repeatedly seen on the Tribal Council roster in the years following 1960.

Even though John E. Baker Sr. sought to unseat Chairman Burch in the 1981 tribal election, the triumph of Leonard Burch in Southern Ute politics actually represented the continuation of John Baker's tribal agenda. Both leaders favored a strong and active tribal government, and both ardently opposed termination of the tribe's legal status. Accordingly, both strongly asserted tribal sovereignty in the face of challenges from federal, state, or local governments. At the same time, however, both Baker and Burch advocated close cooperation with the Bureau of Indian Affairs. Like Baker, Leonard Burch at times bemoaned the lack of initiative on the part of some tribal members and their inability to support themselves. To improve the tribe's financial and employment picture, Burch championed various economic development projects, ranging from the Sky Ute enterprises and the Animas–La Plata water project to Red Willow Production Company and the introduction of casino gambling. Thus, many of the goals toward which Burch strove during his lengthy tenure as tribal chairman were quite similar to those targeted by Baker in the 1950s and early 1960s. This does not mean that the two Southern Ute leaders always saw eye to eye. To the contrary, John Baker often assailed Leonard Burch for accumulating too much power as chairman and for engaging in "abuse of power."[10] Nevertheless, such disagreements pertained more to the manner in which leadership was exercised rather than to the goals toward which it was directed.

Leonard Burch may have resembled his older predecessor as a military veteran and as a leader determined to achieve tribal economic development, but in other ways he represented a departure from John Baker. Unlike Baker, who shunned traditional cultural activities, the young air force veteran embraced his cultural heritage, participating, for example, in the tribe's Sun Dance. In this respect, Leonard Burch's rise to power brought together both sides in the nativist-nonnativist factional split so evident in tribal politics during the 1950s. His ascension also demonstrates the limits of family rivalry in Southern Ute politics. Leonard Burch, a nephew of Sunshine Cloud Smith, was first tapped as chairman by a Tribal Council dominated by three members of the Baker family. The breadth of Burch's support, crossing both cultural and family divides, did not, however, bring an end to political turmoil in Ignacio. These two characteristics now gave less impetus to factional conflict, but factionalism continued along other lines.

UTE MOUNTAIN UTE POLITICAL LEADERSHIP

Unlike the Southern Ute Tribe, whose last chief died in 1961 after a long but politically insignificant reign, the Ute Mountain Tribe continued to have a politically powerful chieftaincy throughout the 1960s. Jack House, who had served on Tribal Councils beginning as early as 1921 and continuously since the 1930s, remained a member of the Ute Mountain Tribal Council through 1964. Even after leaving the council, he continued to be an influential leader until his death in 1971. Jack House was to be the last chief of the Ute Mountain Ute Tribe. As the institution of the chieftaincy faded from the scene in Towaoc, the political system at Ute Mountain came to resemble the one already existing in Ignacio: the Tribal Council, led by its chairman, was the sole political institution of importance within the tribe. Two resilient council veterans, Albert Wing Sr. and Scott Jacket Sr., both first elected to the council in 1955, alternated as chairman from the time of George Mills's resignation in 1955 until 1974, when Marshall Whyte assumed the leadership of the council for one year. Scott Jacket, a veteran of U.S. Army service as well as service on behalf of his tribe, was again selected by his colleagues to be chairman the next year, and he served in this capacity until late in 1979.[11]

The longevity of council members and the recurrent presence of particular families that characterized the Southern Ute Tribal Council were also evident at Towaoc. Not only did Scott Jacket Sr. serve as tribal chairman for large parts of three consecutive decades, his brother Henry Jacket also enjoyed a long tenure as a council member and as tribal treasurer. Not even the controversy surrounding the 1977 FBI investigation into tribal finances could topple the towering presence of the two Jackets from the heights of tribal leadership. Henry Jacket remained on the council until 1982, and Scott Jacket did not end his twenty-eight-year career as councilman until 1987. Other family names were a recurrent sight on the council roster in the years following 1960; Whyte, Dutchie, House, Cantsee, Hammond, and Knight all appeared frequently.

Ute Mountain tribal leadership was remarkably stable during the first four decades under the tribe's constitution. Only four chairmen presided over the Tribal Council from 1940 through 1978, with three individuals accounting for thirty-eight of these thirty-nine years. This stability gave way to a period of rapid change beginning in the late 1970s. To some extent, this may have resulted from the passing of the older generation, which had led the tribe through a time of substantial change. Albert Wing had served on the council since the mid 1950s and had helped lead this body through an important transitional period that saw it gain steadily more responsibility over tribal affairs. Even more significant during this period was the stabilizing presence of Jack House. Bringing the traditional prestige and authority of the tribe's chieftaincy to the deliberations of the new Tribal Council, the aging chief had helped facilitate consensus among the members of this elected body. After Jack House left the council in 1964 and then after the institution of the chieftaincy died with him in 1971, the political scene in Towaoc was left with a substantial void, which was accentuated by the departure of familiar council veterans such as Albert Wing. This major change in the political landscape in Towaoc occurred at the same time as the tribe was beginning to encounter serious financial difficulties. Declining energy revenues and perennial budgetary deficits were threatening the continuation of the all-important per capita payments, and a day of reckoning was approaching. It is hardly surprising that a financial crisis, coinciding with the passing of the tribe's chief and its veteran council leaders, would bring about an increase in political conflict. The latter years of the century would witness a higher level of tension both within the tribe and between tribal leaders and Washington. As a result of this heightened political conflict, the Ute Mountain Tribal Council and the office of tribal chairperson would be characterized by higher turnover among officeholders during the 1970s and 1980s.

New faces thus appeared on the Tribal Council in the late 1970s. In 1978 two members of the Knight family, brothers Terry and Carl, won election to the council. Their sister Judy Pinnecoose—who would later go by the name of Judy Knight and then, after remarrying, by the name of Judy Knight-Frank—joined the council the following year. The thirty-six-year-old single parent of two was selected by the council members that year to serve as chairperson.[12] Terry Knight, an air force veteran and a spiritual leader among the Ute people, succeeded his sister as chairman in 1981. The following year Ernest House Sr., grandson of Chief Jack House and another veteran of military service, began a seven-year reign as tribal chairman.

Even though two women had served on the Ute Mountain Tribal Council during the early 1940s, female council members had been a rarity since that time, with none during the 1950s and only a couple in the 1960s and 1970s up to the time of Judy Knight's election in 1979. During this same period, women were frequently elected to the Southern Ute Council, with the presence of two female members being quite common. Thus, Judy Knight's selection as chairperson in 1979, her continued service on the council during the 1980s, and her election as chairperson

again in 1989 represent something of a departure from tribal tradition. Judy Knight-Frank had left the reservation in the mid
1960s with her first husband to live in California, where she
worked for Aetna insurance.[13] After returning to Ute Mountain,
she became an outspoken critic of the Tribal Council, to which
she twice sought election before finally succeeding on her third
attempt in 1979.[14] Whereas it had been her fellow council members who tapped her to be chairperson in 1979, Knight-Frank's
return to the top leadership position of her tribe in 1989 was
by tribal election, the tribe's election procedures having been
changed in the interim. In October 1992, Judy Knight-Frank prevailed in a contest pitting her against three challengers, including her brother Carl, to win reelection to a second three-year
term as chairperson.[15]

EXTERNAL RELATIONS

"The tribe must continue to work with the BIA," declared Leonard Burch in an acceptance speech following his reelection to
the council in 1974. "I think that as a tribe we can gain strength
here if we continue to work together with the BIA. Certainly we
have our differences but they can be worked out."[16] This summarized the approach followed by the Southern Ute Tribal Council in its dealings with the Bureau of Indian Affairs in the years
following 1960. Throughout this entire period, council members
and chairmen continually expressed the need for cooperation
with the BIA, and they bitterly resisted proposals for "termination"—elimination of the tribe's sovereign status and of special
federal programs from which the tribe benefited. The idea of
tribal termination had first been brought forward in the 1950s,
and it continued to surface throughout the early 1960s. Most
often these proposals came from outside the tribe, from various
government officials; but occasionally the anti-BIA sentiment
that had been strongly articulated by opponents of the rehabili-

tation plan in the early 1950s resurfaced later among tribal members in the 1960s. The Tribal Council noted disapprovingly in 1964 that a group of tribal members was discussing the possibility of termination. The council members, who unanimously agreed to go on the record opposing termination shortly after this, expressed the opinion that many tribal members did not realize how fortunate they were to be receiving the benefits of the current arrangement—benefits not provided to non-Indians.[17]

Another reflection of the tribe's close and amicable relationship with the BIA was the hostile response of both council members and other Southern Utes to the actions of the American Indian Movement (AIM) during the early 1970s. After AIM representatives were invited to Ignacio in 1972 by a Pawnee Indian student who attended Ignacio High School, they convened a "grand jury" to hear complaints of discrimination against local Indians by the school board and other groups. The AIM group met with a rather unfriendly reception from many of the Southern Utes in attendance, several of whom reminded the AIM people that they had not been invited to the reservation by Utes.[18] Later that same year, the tribe's leaders vehemently denounced AIM's takeover of the BIA office in Washington, issuing a press release describing the actions of AIM as "irresponsible" and "deplorable" and the organization's demands as "unreasonable."[19] The Tribal Council's opposition to AIM is hardly surprising given the belief of leaders such as Leonard Burch that the tribe's fortunes were tied to the BIA. Whereas AIM members regarded the Bureau of Indian Affairs as an oppressive enemy, most Southern Utes now saw the BIA as an ally—albeit a sometimes troublesome one—and a source of assistance.

One reason for the Southern Utes' more positive outlook toward the BIA at this time was that the tribe was less beholden to the bureau than in previous years. In contrast to the old days when the Indian Office enjoyed a monopoly over the administration of Indian affairs, the BIA of the 1960s and later decades was no longer the only avenue through which tribes could deal with the federal government. This erosion of BIA control had begun in 1955 with the transfer of responsibility for Indian health care to the Public Health Service and had accelerated in the 1960s. During the Johnson administration, Indian tribes became eligible to receive services and funding from a variety of federal agencies other than the BIA; and this trend continued under later administrations. Community Action Programs were established through the Office of Economic Opportunity to bring the nation's War on Poverty to Indian reservations, and by 1968, 129 reservations were being served by 63 Community Action Agencies; reservation development projects were funded by grants from the Economic Development Administration; nutritional programs to help Indian mothers and children were provided by the Department of Agriculture; tribal housing authorities were funded by the Public Housing Administration; Head Start programs were begun on the reservations; and tribes were able to administer several federal worker training programs through the Comprehensive Employment and Training Act of 1973.[20] Tribal dependence on the BIA was further reduced by the Indian Self-determination and Educational Assistance Act of 1975, also known as Public Law 638. This legislation enabled tribes to receive federal funds to operate programs that had previously been carried out by federal employees. Tribes could now provide services directly to their own people instead of relying on the BIA to do so. With tribes no longer solely reliant on the BIA for federally supplied services and funds, the bureau was no longer omnipotent; and relations between the Southern Ute Tribe and the BIA improved greatly.

Despite these developments, the mood in Towaoc was often unfriendly toward the Bureau of Indian Affairs in the 1960s and 1970s. Members of the Ute Mountain Tribal Council frequently chafed under perceived interference by the BIA and complained bitterly that the bureau was not serving the interests of the people or the council. "The Tribal Council does not feel that it is being treated as a governing body but as a kind of meddler in its own affairs," the council angrily asserted in a 1961 resolution passed in the midst of a struggle with the BIA over access to records pertaining to the tribe. That same year, the council also strongly protested the government's slowness in crediting interest on the tribe's funds in the U.S. Treasury, delays that were costing the tribe money.[21] In a 1964 resolution, the council bitterly criticized Consolidated Ute superintendent Jose Zuni and asked for his removal on several grounds: he had failed to cooperate with the council, he had caused dissension between the council and tribal members, he had caused tribal officials to lose the respect of the people, he had caused considerable delay in carrying out tribal business, and so on. Such harsh rhetoric toward federal officials echoed the distant past when Ute Mountain leaders such as John Miller had vehemently denounced the Indian Office and its policies. Yet unlike pre-IRA times, tribal leaders of the 1960s and later decades did acknowledge the necessity of the BIA's presence on their reservation. For example, despite the council's apparently abundant dislike for Jose Zuni, the 1964 resolution went on to charge that the superintendent did not visit the reservation often enough.[22] This problem of having an absentee superintendent, stationed 85 miles away in Ignacio, continued until 1969, when the Consolidated Ute Agency was dissolved and replaced by two separate agencies—the Southern Ute Agency in Ignacio and the new Ute Mountain Ute Agency in Towaoc.

Even though the open hostility expressed in these resolutions became more infrequent as time went by, the relationship between the tribe and the bureau remained rather strained in the 1970s. In 1977 Judy Pinnecoose, who had yet to be elected to the council, charged, "You can't get anywhere with the bureau." And Joe Otero, then superintendent of the Ute Mountain Ute Agency, acknowledged that "the Utes have not looked to us as a major source of assistance."[23] Given these divergent responses of the two Colorado tribes to the BIA, it is not surprising that bureau officials would feel more confident about the performance of the Southern Ute Tribal Council than about its counterpart in Towaoc. In 1967 Consolidated Ute superintendent Ray deKay explained his many absences from the Ignacio agency to the members of the Southern Ute Council by stating that his presence was more necessary at Ute Mountain: "You people have been running this show for a long time. . . . The situation over there [in Towaoc] is quite different, and I think that I need to be over there a little more, perhaps, than I do here."[24]

Dealing with the federal government could easily be a source of frustration for tribal leaders, but interactions with state governments could prove even more trying. Former Ute Mountain chairman Ernest House Sr. recalled the difficulties of getting caught in a web of overlapping federal and state authority. The status of tribal sovereignty supposedly removed the tribe from state authority, yet the tribes were frequently confronted with attempts by state governments to assert control over various tribal affairs. In such situations, the tribe had to "put its sovereignty up front," as House described it, and fight to assert its unique status.[25] Such was the case when the state of New Mexico attempted to collect taxes on oil pumped from the portion of the Ute Mountain Reservation lying within that state. The Ute Mountain council refused to pay the tax but ultimately lost this battle when it went before the U.S. Supreme Court.[26] The Ute Mountain Tribe also came up on the losing side of a conflict with both the U.S. government and the Navajo Tribe over the reservation boundary in New Mexico. As a result of a federal surveying error, both tribes claimed possession of the same tract of land, and substantial oil revenues were at stake. When this dispute was decided in favor of the Navajos, it cost the Ute Mountain Tribe $7 million in lost oil royalties. After the Tribal Council sought compensation for this loss from the federal government, Congress eventually passed legislation providing the tribe with an award of both land and money.[27] One area that brought both Ute tribes into conflict with the state of Colorado, beginning in 1990, was casino gambling and the question of the state's authority to regulate casinos located on reservations in Colorado. The state maintained that tribal casinos were subject to the same betting limitations applied to the states' other limited-stakes gaming establishments. Officials of both tribes rejected this position, citing tribal sovereignty and asserting that state-imposed restrictions could not be applied to tribal gaming operations. When the two tribes subsequently negotiated gaming compacts with the state of Colorado, the betting limitations were included, but court challenges to these provisions remained an option open to the tribes.[28]

The Ute Mountain and Southern Ute Tribes also had to coexist with neighboring communities and their governments. At times relations with local governments were cooperative and positive. The Southern Utes and the town of Ignacio, by virtue of their close geographical proximity, had little choice but to work together on a number of issues. The Tribal Council, for example, authorized the cross-deputization of tribal police officers and officers of the La Plata County Sheriff's Office in 1980 to increase law enforcement efficiency both on and off the reservation.[29] Cooperation between the tribe and the town, however, sometimes proved a difficult matter. A major dispute over water rates emerged in 1975 regarding an arrangement by which the town of Ignacio purchased its municipal water from the tribe, which had a new $1 million water plant. Under the leadership of a mayor who was highly critical of the Southern Utes, the town board proceeded with controversial plans to construct its own water treatment facility, and these plans were not scrapped until a new mayor was elected.[30] Conflicts between the tribe and the Ignacio school board were also common. Disagreements between the tribe and local governments were sometimes eased, however, by the participation of tribal members in the various governing bodies. For example, Chris Baker, in addition to being a tribal councilman, was also a member of both the town board and the local school board during the mid 1970s.

Relations between the Ute Mountain Tribe and the local governments and community groups in neighboring Cortez were often more strained than between their counterparts in Ignacio. Despite efforts by both sides to promote good relations—for example, the Cortez Chamber of Commerce honored the tribe as its 1986 "Citizen of the Year"—there was, as Chairman Ernest House remarked in 1986, an "invisible curtain" between the tribe and the local non-Indian community. Here, where there had never been the consistently close interaction between communities that had long characterized life in Ignacio, it was still a matter of "you take care of your problems and we'll take care of ours."[31] A persistent area of friction was the way in which the local public school district served the tribe's children. Tribal dissatisfaction with school policies was all the more frustrating for the Utes given the tribe's inability to elect one of its own members to the Montezuma-Cortez school board. After Indian candidates were defeated in both the 1985 and 1989 elections, eight tribal members filed a lawsuit against the school district. They charged that the district's at-large voting system denied them the opportunity to elect a representative of their choice to serve on the school board. In 1990 a U.S. District Court judge approved a settlement of the suit under which an election subdistrict, to include the entire reservation, was established. This arrangement gave the Utes a voting majority in the new subdistrict, thus greatly increasing the chances of a tribal member being elected to the school board.[32]

DIVISIVE ISSUES

Although sparks could sometimes fly in the course of political interaction with the federal government and other outside entities, it was the internal politics of the Southern Ute and Ute Mountain Ute tribes that generated the most turbulence in the latter half of the twentieth century. The same intense level of debate that had characterized the battle over adoption of the Southern Ute Rehabilitation Plan was often evident in the political life of both tribes throughout the years following 1960. Council members in both Towaoc and Ignacio quickly found out just how demanding their constituents could be, and there was no issue that aroused more intense popular pressure than per capita payments. This was a matter that placed the Tribal Councils, which were responsible for their tribes' fiscal health, sharply at odds with tribal members, who had grown to depend on these payments for their subsistence. Council members soon discovered this was a political sacred cow that, if threatened, would evoke a tremendous popular outcry.

A parade of leaders, including John Baker and Leonard Burch in Ignacio and Judy Knight-Frank in Towaoc, expressed a desire to wean the people from their dependence on these tribal payments. Motivated by financial necessity, by worry over the debilitating effects of their people's reliance on unearned income, or by both of these concerns, these leaders were rarely able to effect any substantial change in the status quo. "I would love to run the tribe as a business," Judy Knight-Frank asserted in 1989, "but there is no way to do it. The council has always taken care of them [tribal members]. How do you get past that?"[33] In addition to encountering expectations of regular per capita payments, Knight-Frank sometimes found herself confronted with an old custom— the practice of tribal members visiting the homes of their council representatives in search of cash handouts.[34]

Council members were under tremendous pressure to increase—or at a minimum to maintain—the amounts of payments made to tribal members. Superintendent Espeedie Ruiz wrote on behalf of the Ute Mountain Tribal Council in 1971 urging BIA approval of a requested per capita payment—despite the fact that the council had not yet submitted a budget for the period in question. The superintendent explained that the Tribal Council was "currently under tremendous pressure to make a per capita payment in early August 1971," and he implored the BIA area director to "consider the possible problem facing the council if a per capita payment is not made."[35] Clearly, the superintendent did not relish arousing the wrath of the Ute Mountain people. Again and again the Ute Mountain council received demands pertaining to per capita distributions. For example, a budget resolution in 1975—at a time when the tribe had been running up annual budget deficits for 15 straight years—acknowledged that "the tribal membership has instructed the Council Members to provide per capita payments of $1,000 per member for F.Y. 1976." The council accepted and acted upon this "instruction."[36]

The Ute Mountain council still felt compelled to yield to such popular demands in 1990 when it handed the question of a per capita payment out of the Tribal Investment Fund back to the members by calling for a special election. Tribal members were asked to choose from one of four payment options. In this way the council permitted the membership to cast votes resulting in the liquidation of much of the tribe's investment fund.[37] This tendency of the elected council to defer to tribal opinion harks back to the traditional Ute preference for government by consensus, and it is reminiscent of the leadership style of Chief Jack House. Often when the Tribal Council was meeting with federal officials on a specific matter, Jack House would refuse to make a decision, stating that he first needed to consult with the people of his tribe.

A similar situation regarding per capita payments prevailed in Ignacio. Unable to find jobs on the reservation, Southern Ute tribal members relied on distributions of tribal funds to support themselves. Here, in addition to frequent verbal expressions for continued or increased per capita payments, the Tribal Council was continually bombarded with petitions articulating the same demands. In 1986 after the council responded to a steadily deepening budgetary crisis by reducing a scheduled $2,000 per capita payment to a new level of only $250, the result was predictable. Two petitions demanding, among other things, the resignation of Tribal Council members and the per capita payment of $2,500 in April of that year were promptly submitted to the council. The situation was complicated by a third petition, affirming support for the tribal government, which was submitted with more valid signatures than either of the two protest petitions.[38] The council replied with a statement that it would be "fiscally irresponsible" to acquiesce to the demand for such a large per capita payment, and it took no further action.[39] A similar petition arrived before the council a year later, this time demanding a per capita payment of $1,500 by April 10, 1987. The council, which had budgeted a payment of $600, split the difference with the petitioners and authorized a payment of $1,000 to each member.[40]

The Southern Ute Tribal Council, which largely held firm in 1986 and gave in only halfway to popular demands in 1987, was not always so fiscally prudent. Between 1982 and 1988, it authorized payment of roughly $17 million in per capita distributions, resulting in a steady depletion of the tribe's funds, which shrank from $13 million to less than $3 million during the same period.[41] Dissatisfaction with the level of per capita payments surfaced again in 1989 when it helped inspire a petition that led to a recall election for five of the seven members of the Tribal Council.[42] Thus, in both Ignacio and in Towaoc, tampering with per capita payments was playing with fire.

Another important issue on the political agendas of both tribes—one that could also be divisive at times—was constitutional reform. Beginning in 1970, both tribes sought to amend their tribal constitutions, originally adopted three decades or more earlier under the Indian Reorganization Act. Some amendments to the tribal constitutions, such as changes in the procedure for electing tribal chairpersons, were not controversial as most tribal members wanted to increase their say in the conduct of tribal affairs. Accordingly, both tribes scrapped the old system involving selection of the chairman by the members of the Tribal Council, replacing it with direct election of the chairperson by the tribal membership. At the same time, the length of the chairperson's term was increased from one to three years. The Southern Utes instituted these changes when they revised their constitution in 1975, and the Ute Mountain Tribe amended its constitution to this effect in 1983. The Southern Utes made additional changes in their electoral process in 1975 in a further attempt to increase tribal democracy. A three-term limit for the tribal chairperson was imposed, and procedures for the recall of council members were adopted. No such provisions were added to the Ute Mountain Ute Constitution. Another 1975 change in the Southern Ute Constitution—one that at the time generated surprisingly little discussion either in council or general meetings or in the tribal newspaper—was a somewhat less democratic provision granting the chairperson veto power over decisions made by the Tribal Council.[43]

A more controversial area of constitutional change acted on by both tribes was the blood quantum requirement for enrollment of individuals as members of the tribe. The Southern Ute Constitution, as adopted in 1936, stipulated that individuals had to have at least one-quarter Southern Ute ancestry to qualify for tribal membership. In 1970 Southern Ute voters narrowly approved increasing the constitutional membership requirement from one-quarter Southern Ute blood to one-half tribal blood.[44] This was an emotionally charged issue affecting not only the size of one's share when per capita payments were distributed but also, in many cases, whether one's children could be enrolled as members of the tribe. Many mixed-blood parents saw their children excluded from tribal rolls under the one-half tribal blood quantum approved in 1970. Tribal members subsequently had second thoughts on this question, for when they voted 92 to 55 to approve a 1975 overhaul of the tribe's constitution, one of the revisions included in the package was a return to the less restrictive one-quarter Southern Ute blood requirement. Apparently the blood quantum change had been the only issue on the minds of many voters in 1975, and one council member asserted that many of the people had not understood all of the other revisions.[45] The Ute Mountain Tribe similarly eased its membership criteria by amending its constitution in 1984 to decrease the required blood quantum from one-half to one-quarter Ute Mountain Ute blood.[46] Revision of the Southern Ute Constitution again became a major topic of discussion in the late 1980s, but nothing came of these efforts other than a minor amendment approved in 1991 clarifying the procedure for calculation of blood quantums.

Another item frequently appearing on council agendas was the matter of tribal enterprises. This was often a hotly debated topic, especially in Ignacio, where the enterprises were less successful and more of a problem than in Towaoc. Southern Ute tribal members often fumed over business ventures that seemed to absorb the tribe's money and the council's attention while yielding no significant benefit. One persistent critic of the council, Bertha Grove, complained in 1972, shortly after the opening of the Pino Nuche, that all the council ever talked about was the motel, and as a result the older people felt ignored and uncertain as to where the tribe was headed.[47] In Towaoc a similar concern over Tribal Council preoccupation with development was expressed by future Ute Mountain councilman Michael Elkriver in 1991: "Instead of addressing gambling issues, the Tribal Council needs to take care of the problems that require immediate attention."[48] Persistent deficits aroused opposition to the Southern Ute enterprises, and one of the architects of the 1989 Tribal Council recall campaign, Ray C. Frost, reiterated a frequently heard complaint about the drain on tribal finances posed by the enterprises. He asserted the tribe could no longer afford "to bail out the financial[ly] struggling enterprises."[49] The hiring policies of tribal enterprises were another frequent subject of political protest. Tribal members on both reservations resented the hiring of outsiders to fill the best jobs.

At times tribal members worried about the side effects of tribal enterprise operations, particularly with respect to the presence of alcohol. The issue of liquor sales by Southern Ute tribal enterprises—the Pino Nuche–Sky Ute Lodge lounge, Sky Ute Downs, and the Country Store after it was leased to the Thriftway Company—produced schisms among both the general membership and the membership of the Tribal Council. Most council members, eager to increase revenue from the ailing enterprises, favored liquor sales, but others, such as Lillian Seibel, were more concerned with the tribe's alcoholism problem and thus voted against such sales.[50] In Towaoc Councilman Arthur Cuthair voted against opening a casino on the Ute Mountain Reservation for largely the same reason: "I fear that we bring too much liquor onto the reservation, mainly through the casino. It's going to ruin us."[51] Most tribal leaders in both Towaoc and Ignacio eagerly anticipated the arrival of casino gambling as a new source of revenue and jobs; however, Arthur Cuthair and other members of the two Ute tribes did not necessarily see casinos as welcome additions to their world. Opposition was particularly strong among Southern Utes when it was learned the tribe planned to open its first casino at the Sky Ute Lodge. Many Utes were not anxious to have a casino located virtually in their backyard: "It's too close to our schools, too close to our tribal offices," John Baker protested.[52] Elders such as Sunshine Smith did not relish the establishment of a casino on what they considered to be "sacred ground"—the low-lying area on both sides of the Los Pinos River encompassing the agency-tribal affairs complex, the cemetery, and the Bear Dance grounds.[53]

In Towaoc the very success of a tribal business such as the new casino could become a source of controversy. As business boomed at the Ute Mountain Casino following its opening in 1992, questions began to arise as to the amount of income produced by the casino and where this money was going. Since the tribal casino

was not subject to state oversight, the tribe was not obliged to reveal the casino's financial records. This situation created suspicion among many Ute Mountain Utes. Tribal members attending
a 1994 general meeting expressed a lack of confidence in the
Tribal Council's conduct of business and were particularly worried by the lack of accountability concerning casino revenues.[54]

Behind the particular details—profits or losses, number of jobs,
presence or absence of alcohol—regarding specific tribal enterprises, there always lurked the fundamental question of whether
economic development of the reservation was in itself good for
the tribe. The Ute Mountain council election of 1987 represented
a contest between two contrasting philosophies regarding this
question: incumbent Judy Knight stood for economic development, while challenger Arthur Cuthair was wary of the costs of
development and placed a greater value on tradition. Knight, classified by one observer as "the most liberal of the Ute leaders," had
been a constant advocate of change and had pushed for advances
in job training and education. Cuthair did not necessarily oppose
such programs, but his priority was preserving the distinctive Ute
way of life. Judy Knight, like Leonard Burch in Ignacio, ardently
championed the building of the Animas–La Plata Project as a
means of providing the tribe with a substantially increased water
supply. "Animas–La Plata is the Utes' only hope for the future,"
she affirmed. "It must succeed." A skeptical Arthur Cuthair opposed the project: "Animas–La Plata will never help the tribe."[55]
Judy Knight prevailed in the 1987 election contest, but two years
later Arthur Cuthair led all candidates in the balloting for three
council seats. Apparently both tradition and development held
some appeal for the Ute Mountain people.

POPULAR UNREST AND POLITICAL TURMOIL

In April 1977 FBI agents suddenly descended on the offices of
the Ute Mountain Ute Tribe in the isolated and normally quiet

town of Towaoc. As part of a federal investigation into possible mishandling of funds by tribal leaders, the agents executed search warrants in April and again in June, confiscating tribal financial records. Two former tribal employees, a bookkeeper and a secretary, painted an alarming picture of corruption among the tribe's leadership. They claimed that council members had abused their positions for their own gain and that of their relatives and that councilmen had withdrawn substantial sums from tribal accounts for their personal use. The bookkeeper accused all seven members of the council of engaging in this practice, obtaining sums ranging from $91,857 in the case of Chairman Scott Jacket to $950 allegedly withdrawn by Jack Cantsee. Other disturbing reports emerged from the reservation. Charges of nepotism were made against tribal officials, and it was alleged that witchcraft was regularly used as a means of obtaining political power within the tribe.[56]

Nothing came of the grand jury investigation, and none of the seven council members was charged with any crimes; nevertheless, this episode spotlighted a tribal political system that many people at Ute Mountain found rather disturbing. "We've gotten leaders who have worked for themselves and kept the rest of us down," complained Judy Pinnecoose bitterly.[57] The incident proved divisive, as indicated by the decidedly mixed response of the Indians at White Mesa in Utah to charges that their council representative Jack Cantsee had embezzled $950 of tribal funds. Even though this amount paled in comparison with the dollar figures alleged to have been withdrawn by other council members, this did not lessen the outrage felt by some of Cantsee's constituents, one of whom wrote disapprovingly in the tribal newspaper about the councilman's subsequent reelection: "Most people were hoping Anna Marie Nat would get elected to office. Since knowledge of Jack's involvement in the embezzlement case in Towaoc. Some people say Jack borrowed the money and payed [sic] it back but two wrongs don't make one right. Ever since the embezzlement news hit White Mesa, the people have split in two and I don't think will ever rest until they see another person in the seat of councilman of White Mesa." Another tribal member responded in Jack Cantsee's defense: "Many people here strongly believe, with the information available, that Mr. Cantsee is not guilty of the so called "Embezzlement" of the Tribal funds. . . . Conclusion: Add here that every parent and each member of the Ute Mountain Tribe may be the guilty ones in the misuse of the trust funds.[58]

The electoral consequences of this controversial incident were as mixed as the sentiments of tribal members. The allegations probably contributed to the election of a group of new council members in the late 1970s and to the subsequent election of such newcomers—Judy Knight, Terry Knight, and Ernest House—as chairpersons. At the same time, however, the principal leaders of the 1977 council, Scott and Henry Jacket, continued to be elected to the Tribal Council into the 1980s.

Even without allegations of corruption or other such scandals to provoke the ire of tribal members, the people of both tribes often voiced disenchantment with their Tribal Councils. One early 1960s observer of the political scene in Ignacio reported that one-half of the Southern Ute membership appeared to be "estranged" from tribal affairs. These individuals, who did not vote in tribal elections, seemed to regard the tribal government of the 1960s in the same way they had thought of the BIA in the past—as a complicated bureaucracy that dispensed tangible benefits, on the one hand, and punishment for rules infractions, on the other.[59] Those who did participate in tribal politics were often highly critical of their tribal government. Tribal members complained time and again throughout the latter half of the century that their council members did not listen to them and that the council did not keep the people informed about tribal affairs.

Such complaints were especially prevalent among the Southern Ute membership and were articulated most loudly and persistently by Bertha Grove, sister of Chairman Leonard Burch and an active participant in the Native American Church. She repeatedly accused the Tribal Council of various deficiencies: being more concerned with tribal enterprises than with tribal members, ignoring the needs of the people, and losing its Indian ways and behaving like white people.[60] She also claimed to be voicing the concerns of other tribal members who were afraid to come forward and speak out. For her part, Bertha Grove was certain that she would suffer "persecution" as a result of her status as a "troublemaker."[61]

Grove was not the only Southern Ute to fear retribution in the event of speaking out against the Tribal Council; this concern was evident in 1993 when the council's plan to open a casino at Sky Ute Lodge was made public. Tribal members who worked for the tribe—a substantial number of people—were unwilling to go on the record in opposition to the plan for fear they would lose their jobs as a result of speaking out.[62] Given a similar dependence on tribal employment at Ute Mountain, the same reluctance to openly oppose the Tribal Council was also in evidence there. Tony Tallbird, who would later be elected to the Ute Mountain council, deplored this situation in 1987, declaring, "I don't think tribal members should live in fear of the Council."[63]

The political tensions on both reservations were further heightened by the prevalence of factionalism among the Ute people. "The Southern Utes are one people. I hate to say it, but the Southern Utes are very prejudiced against one another. They're kinda like them hillbillies, you know, to be fighting years and years and years, and then some of them don't know why they were fighting all the time."[64] Thus did Bertha Grove describe the tendency toward factional dispute that had survived not only among the Southern Utes but also among the Ute Mountain Utes. Criticizing a rather sensationalist account of Ute factionalism that had recently been published, historian Robert W. Delaney wrote in 1981 that "factionalism and family feuds have always plagued the Utes."[65] Others saw the situation differently.

Historian Floyd O'Neil sensed a double standard in all the talk of
Indian factionalism: "Fighting in Washington, D.C., between political factions, is called politics, but fighting over some of the
same issues on Indian reservations is called factionalism."[66]

Whether any more "factional" than political battles in Washington or not, political infighting clearly continued to be prevalent both in Towaoc and in Ignacio throughout the latter half of
the twentieth century. A statement of tribal goals for the Ute
Mountain Ute Tribe for fiscal year 1989 concluded with an ardent plea for tribal unity: "Tribal members, we have to work together cooperatively to build a better future. If we are divided, we
will fail, and we will continue to have the same old problems
which we have had for years."[67] Political schisms often negatively
affected the performance of the Tribal Councils, as Southern
Ute economic director Bill Manning bitterly complained when
he resigned his position in 1982. Manning decried the "long-
standing political conflict within the Council," and he cited the
existence of "a powerful tension and negative energy that affects
the attitude and ability of the entire staff" as being one of the reasons for his resignation.[68]

Internal squabbles often divided the membership along family
lines, but on many occasions political battles also pitted members
of the same family against one another. This was clearly evident
in Ignacio, where Chairman Leonard Burch's most vocal critic
was his sister Bertha Grove and where John E. Baker Sr. ran
against his brother Chris for the chairmanship in 1984 and later
spoke out against the Tribal Council, of which both his brother
and son were members.[69] Ute Mountain was also the scene of in-
trafamily political battles. For example, Carl Knight challenged
his sister Judy Knight-Frank in the 1992 election for chairperson.

Indications of another social and political cleavage within the
tribal memberships, this one between full-blood and mixed-
blood members, surfaced at a 1980 General Council meeting of
the Southern Utes. One tribal member provoked loud applause

by asking why the "half-breeds" did not complain about their problems and by wondering if this was because they were being well taken care of by the council. A tribal member of mixed Ute and Spanish blood shot back, "I have learned to depend upon myself to do the work instead of crying to the council for help like you full bloods."[70] Tensions between full- and mixed-blood members of the Southern Ute Tribe were nothing new, as this issue had previously been considered by tribal leaders on such occasions as a 1960 workshop addressing the problems of alcoholism. Participants at this meeting suggested mixed-blood Utes had a more serious problem with alcohol abuse than full-blood members because those in the former category were often rejected by Indians and non-Indians alike.[71] Such a full blood–mixed blood schism was much more significant in Southern Ute politics than in Ute Mountain politics since the Ignacio Utes had a substantially larger fraction of mixed-blood members.

CHALLENGES TO TRIBAL COUNCIL POWER

On December 5, 1989, the Southern Ute Tribal Council, which had received numerous petitions from tribal members over the years, received yet another petition, one that represented the most serious challenge yet to its power. Renee Baca presented a "Petition for Better Tribal Government" calling for the recall of all members of the Tribal Council; the petition had been signed by 206 tribal members out of a total of 620 eligible voters in the tribe. The ambivalence of the tribe's membership toward the tribal government was indicated not only by the presentation of a counterpetition through which some signers of the original petition now sought to remove their names from that document, but also by the fact that on November 3, at the very moment the recall petition was being readied for submission, tribal members voted to reelect both council incumbents whose terms had expired.[72] Despite these contradictory signs, the council notified

the membership on January 3, 1990, that it had accepted the petition as valid and that a recall election for five of the seven council members—excluding Orian Box and Lillian Seibel, who had
just been reelected—would be held on February 2.[73] The Southern Ute Tribal Council's political life was now on the line.

The recall petition listed a long litany of abuses justifying the
removal of the council members, and many of these items had
been the subject of past complaints. These alleged abuses ranged
from general failures such as mismanagement of governmental
operations and tribal funds to such specific improprieties as in-
consistent enrollment and blood quantum changes. Additionally,
recent reductions in the level of per capita payments had helped
spark the recall effort, and many other backers of the petition
were disappointed by the council's failure to follow through on
attempts to amend the tribal constitution begun in 1986. One
person who supported the recall campaign for the latter reason
was John E. Baker Sr., who accused the council of "abuse of
power." Baker was particularly incensed by the council's failure to
address a key provision of the revised constitution of 1975 that
granted the tribal chairman "extraordinary powers"; Baker regarded this provision as a "loophole."[74] The particular loophole
to which Baker referred was the chairperson's veto power, and he
was not the only member of the tribe to be worried by this provision. Sunshine Smith, too, was concerned by the veto provision
in the constitution, and she supported the recall effort. On this
issue these two longtime political rivals were in agreement.[75]

While clearly opposed to the recall campaign, some council
members shared these same concerns about the tribe's governing
document. In a strongly worded statement made at a November 1,
1989, council meeting, Guy Pinnecoose Jr. vigorously asserted
the need for constitutional reform and lamented the fact that the
council had failed to accomplish anything in this area. Then Lillian Seibel launched into an impassioned attack on the current
constitution:

[When they voted on] the Constitution, when it was amended in 1975, people were not looking at all the other changes that were being made. They were only looking at lowering the blood quantum from 1/2 to 1/4 so that they could get their children enrolled. They didn't look at all the other things that were being included in there. Like I said a lot of power needs to go back to the six Councilmembers. I'm not afraid to say that because I feel that I don't have any control as an elected official and I can't represent my constituents in a good way because I can't do anything when they come to me. I see something is wrong in the organization and I can't say anything because what good is it going to do? I am only going to be looked at as the bad guy. But if there's six people that can vote on something that can make decisions who can direct then that's good.[76]

Seibel went on to charge that the constitution was not working and, furthermore, that the current government was one that "oppresses" its people. Seibel clearly viewed the veto power wielded by the chairperson as precluding effective and democratic operation of the council.

The result of the February 2, 1990, recall election was a razor-thin victory, 183-182, for the recall forces. It appeared to be the end of an era in Southern Ute tribal politics with the toppling of the previously all-powerful Tribal Council, but the political waters were soon muddied by an incredible sequence of events. An election official came forward and admitted that, fearful of becoming the victim of a supernatural spell, she had allowed Bertha Grove to cast a ballot on behalf of her husband, who had not been present at the polls.[77] Grove, who acknowledged that many people still believed in witchcraft, adamantly insisted she had neither threatened to cast a spell nor intended to commit any voting impropriety.[78] The situation became even more complicated as events unfolded following this revelation. In a move that outraged backers of the recall campaign, the Tribal Council proceeded to discard the questionable vote and declare that the resulting tie vote constituted defeat of the recall measure.[79] The Committee for Better Tribal Government (CBTG), organizers of the recall petition, then took the matter to the Southern Ute Tribal Court, but the tribal judge declared the recall election void and remanded the issue back to the Southern Ute Election Board. The issue was not fully resolved until September 1991 when the Southwest Inter-Tribal Court of Appeals upheld the actions of the Southern Ute Tribal Council and the tribal election board in handling the recall election.[80] The recall campaign had failed, and the Tribal Council—by the skin of its teeth—had prevailed.

Having survived the 1977 financial collapse and the resulting federal investigation and allegations of corruption, the Ute Mountain Tribal Council did not face any subsequent challenge to its power as serious as the Southern Ute recall drive. At roughly this same time, however, the integrity of the Ute Mountain council and its members was being threatened by electoral controversy. As the tumultuous history of the Southern Ute recall election showed, Ute tribal elections could be highly contentious affairs inviting accusations of impropriety. This had often been the case in Towaoc, where a BIA official, taking extra precautions against voting fraud in the 1987 tribal elections, observed, "The Utes are very distrustful people."[81] Tribal election campaigns in Towaoc grew increasingly ugly in the late 1980s and early 1990s as "rumor or slander sheets" began to be circulated by opponents of Judy Knight-Frank. These surreptitious documents, containing various personal attacks and unsubstantiated charges, first appeared before the 1989 tribal election in which Knight-Frank was elected chairperson. In 1991 disgruntled tribal members upped the ante by submitting complaints of misconduct by tribal officials, including the chairperson, to the FBI, which subsequently mounted an investigation that yielded no indictments. Later that same year, a petition against Chairperson Knight-Frank began to be circulated selectively and secretly among the tribal membership,

with some members complaining of intimidation by those circu-
lating the petition.[82]

Not surprisingly, given these developments, the 1992 election
for tribal chairperson proved a highly controversial affair. Incumbent Judy Knight-Frank was challenged by former chairman Ernest House, by Councilman Arthur Cuthair, and by her brother
Carl Knight, who was against the proposed tribal casino that
Knight-Frank strongly favored.[83] Judy Knight-Frank won reelection in the October contest with 242 votes, compared to 139 for
Cuthair, 110 for House, and 67 for Carl Knight. Arthur Cuthair
filed a grievance with the Tribal Election Board, charging that
Knight-Frank had bought votes with tribal funds. Similar accusations were voiced by Carl Knight, who allegedly criticized his sister for "dishing checks out"; unlike Cuthair, however, Knight did
not file a grievance with the election board.[84] Arthur Cuthair, an
army veteran and former Tribal Park superintendent, contended
that bribes had been paid by the incumbent chairperson under
the guise of advances on per capita payments, but the election
board rejected the grievance on the grounds that Cuthair had
failed to produce any evidence to back up his allegations.[85]
Cuthair insisted that the election had been bought: "And what
happens here is [at] election time they'll bring that money out
where it's been hidden. Then they'll start to buy votes with it. I
can't sit here—because I'm broke—I can't buy votes. Their [the
incumbents'] votes would be $500 a vote, and I don't have a
chance against somebody with that kind of money. . . . That's
what happened here. Votes were bought off."[86]

Arthur Cuthair was not the first person to make allegations
of vote buying in Towaoc. One year before Tony Tallbird was
elected to the Tribal Council, he wrote an open letter to tribal
members in reference to the upcoming 1987 tribal election:
"Election time is approaching us rapidly and with the traditional
payoffs from the tribal office being made my suggestion is this, 'If
you are offered money to vote for this individual take the money

its [sic] yours, but you don't have to vote that way.'"[87] Thus, as the
two tribes began the 1990s, tribal members were making serious
allegations against council members and challenging the authority of both Tribal Councils.

THE TRIUMPH OF COUNCIL POWER

On November 2, 1990, just nine months after the disputed tie
vote in the February 2 recall election, Chairman Leonard Burch
was easily reelected to the chairmanship with a resounding 243
to 133 victory over recall leader and prominent council critic Ray
C. Frost and over two other challengers, who polled far fewer
votes. This represented a political comeback of substantial proportions for the longtime chairman who had been one vote away
from repudiation and ouster earlier in the year. One other council incumbent, Vida Peabody, was also reelected, while another,
Richard Jefferson, met defeat.[88] And in Towaoc, despite charges
of election improprieties, the fact remained that Judy Knight-
Frank had survived a series of slander sheets, petitions, and an
FBI investigation to win reelection in 1992 by a wide margin.
Having weathered a number of turbulent storms, the Tribal Councils in both Towaoc and Ignacio remained the unrivaled centers
of power for each tribe. The Tribal Council, led by the chairperson, retained a virtual monopoly on tribal political power.

While council critics such as Ray Frost in Ignacio had been
frustrated in their efforts to topple the seemingly omnipotent
Tribal Council, they found an alternative course of action in the
old saying "If you can't beat 'em, join 'em." Ray Frost was defeated
in the election for chairman in 1990, but he persevered, and in
the 1992 council election he was the second-highest vote recip-
ient in a seven-person race. Under the old election format, in
which the top two candidates were the winners, Frost would have
won one of the two contested seats outright; but confronted by a
lawsuit filed by Frost's own Committee for Better Tribal Govern-

ment, the Tribal Council had revised the election code to provide for runoff elections when one of the top two candidates received less than 25 percent of the vote.[89] His victory ironically
delayed by the impact of the CBTG lawsuit, the Vietnam veteran
finally was elected to the council in the ensuing runoff election
in February 1993. Vowing to "bring the government back to the
people," Ray Frost became a member of the body he had for so
long assailed.[90]

A similar state of political affairs prevailed in Towaoc, where
council critics were frustrated with perceived abuses of power on
the part of tribal officials but were often able to win election
to the Tribal Council themselves. Judy Knight-Frank, the object
of derision by challengers in 1992, had herself first been elected
to the council in 1979 after years of attacking what she felt to be
flawed policies and corruption on the part of council members.
Similarly, outspoken critics of the Ute Mountain Tribal Council
continued to win election to this body in the 1980s and 1990s, as
did Tony Tallbird in 1988 and Arthur Cuthair in 1989. Defeated
by Judy Knight-Frank in the contest for chairperson in 1992,
Cuthair was back on the Tribal Council once again in 1994 after
he far outpaced the other nine candidates competing for two
council seats.[91] Thus, even though members of both tribes might
decry the monopolistic power of their Tribal Councils and possible abuses of power emanating from these bodies, the fact remained that the Tribal Council, while apparently impervious to
change from the outside, was at times susceptible to change from
the inside.

In Ignacio, in addition to the apparently unassailable power of
the Tribal Council, a second feature of the Southern Ute political landscape was becoming more and more clear—the growing
dominance of the tribal chairman. Already the longest-reigning
chairman in tribal history, Leonard Burch sought one last term as
the top official in the tribal government in 1993. Unable to secure an outright majority in the five-man race for chairman on

November 5, 1993, Burch faced a runoff election the following month against former councilman and outspoken critic Guy Pinnecoose Jr. A former physical education teacher and fifteen-year council veteran, Pinnecoose claimed to be running against two people—Chairman Burch and longtime tribal attorney Sam Maynes, whom the challenger claimed had "pulled our present Chairman's strings for many years." Pinnecoose complained that tribal members were being left "in the dark" by behind-the-scenes deals and secret contracts, and he derided the Animas–La Plata Project, strongly championed by Burch, as an "impractical and expensive scheme."[92]

When 422 of 706 registered voters cast runoff ballots on December 17, 1993, Leonard Burch prevailed once again in the contest for tribal chairman. He had held this position since 1966 with only one three-year break mandated by a term-limit clause added to the tribal constitution in 1975. Burch's moment of triumph at the subsequent inauguration ceremony lost some of its luster when Councilwoman Lillian Seibel launched a diatribe at the chairman following Burch's successful move to have Seibel replaced as tribal treasurer. Councilman and longtime Burch critic Ray Frost added to the unpleasantness of the scene by vowing, "I will be a thorn in the side of the council for the remainder of my term." Several tribal members were embarrassed by this airing of dirty laundry at a public inauguration ceremony.[93] This incident clearly revealed that neither the recent economic successes afforded by the Sky Ute Casino and the Red Willow energy company nor the political continuity provided by Burch's extended leadership had done anything to calm the turbulent nature of Southern Ute tribal politics.

Such public quarrels among councilpersons, however, did not diminish the unrivaled dominance of Leonard Burch in the governance of his tribe. Burch planned to retire in 1996, bringing to a conclusion twenty-seven years of service as tribal chairman. Aside from this unparalleled longevity, Burch had clearly risen to

an unequaled position of power, thanks partly to the 1975 constitutional amendment that had given him veto power over Tribal
Council decisions. Clearly, a significant development in Southern Ute political history had taken place in the latter half of
the twentieth century—the rise of the strong chairmanship.
This situation had not yet evolved—if indeed it ever would—at
Ute Mountain. The appearance of this new institution echoed
another political development in Ignacio one hundred years earlier—the rise of the powerful chieftaincy. Leonard Burch's persistence as tribal chairman triggered memories of an earlier long-
reigning tribal leader—Buckskin Charlie, who had been chief of
the Southern Utes for forty-six years. Yet the new institution of
the strong chairmanship exerted a different sort of power.
Whereas Buckskin Charlie's power had relied mainly on the
force of his personality and his ability to forge tribal consensus,
the office of tribal chairman at the close of the century wielded
immense institutional power, particularly the veto, even in the
absence of consensus. It remains to be seen whether the strong
and durable chairmanship will endure beyond the retirement of
Leonard Burch.

8

TRIBAL SOCIETY
AND CULTURE
AFTER 1960

In the predawn darkness of June 17, 1993, a fire broke out in the Towaoc post office complex. The blaze spread quickly, causing an estimated $300,000–400,000 in damage to the building. In addition to the post office, this old building dating from the second decade of the century contained two other units, a residence and a store, both vacant at the time of the fire. While the post office suffered mostly smoke and water damage, the two unoccupied sections of the building were completely destroyed, despite the efforts of two local fire departments. In practical terms, this was not a particularly devastating loss for the people of Towaoc, nor could the fire be regarded as a major development in the Ute Mountain Tribe's history. But it was in many respects a rather troubling sign of the times. The old store had been a palpable part of the tribe's history, the focal point of memories for many older tribal members. Operated for many years by the trader Frank Pyle, a trusted friend and adviser of the Mountain Utes, the store had long been a gathering place for the people of Towaoc. It was at this trading post, for example, that Superintendent D. H. Wattson in 1934 had found Chief John Miller and members of the Tribal Council "loafing" instead of attending a meeting with him to discuss the upcoming IRA election, and the old store had been the scene of impassioned debates between the chief and the superintendent over the merits of this new government policy.[1]

Thus, the tribe had lost a tangible piece of reservation history dating from before 1920. The loss was even more painful because of the suspicious nature of the blaze, which one of the Cortez firemen suspected to be the result of arson.[2] An editorial in the tribal newspaper lamented the disturbing nature of this occurrence: "The Store held remnants of the Tribe's past and to see it burned so senselessly and the memories destroyed was both a sad and lonely day for the Tribe: sad, because it was a part of Towaoc that can never be replaced. Lonely, because a connection to our earlier days and our Elders at Towaoc has been lost forever."[3]

Arson was not a stranger to the Towaoc community, which had endured many deliberately set fires in recent years. For example, even the new $1.8 million tribal office complex had been the target of arsonists during its construction in 1988.[4] The destruction of the old trading post was worrisome for two reasons: it was a stark manifestation of the tribe's loss of its past, and it was symptomatic of unsettling social problems that had emerged as a consequence of revolutionary changes in the way of life practiced by Utes on both of the Colorado reservations.

TWO TRIBES FACING
A DIFFICULT TRANSITION

"When we got this money, everything changed." In this way did one sixty-eight-year-old tribal member aptly summarize in 1990 what had happened to life at Ute Mountain in the latter half of the twentieth century.[5] Much the same observation could be made with respect to the Southern Ute experience during this period. In 1993 Arthur Cuthair, the former Ute Mountain coun-

cilman and frequent critic of his tribe's leadership, cited the impact of money on his people:

> They have too much money, you might say, on the [Ute Moun-
> tain] reservation. People worship money. I don't know if that's the
> right way to put that, but it has ruined the Ute people with too
> much money. Also, it dates back to the 1950s when they received
> individual money—they call it per capita payments. The Ute
> [Mountain Ute] people used to be scattered all over the reserva-
> tion. They rejected development of any kind. Any outside contact
> off the reservation—they rejected that. The Southern Utes to the
> east are about twenty years ahead of us. They got involved in edu-
> cating their people and sending their kids to college about twenty
> years ahead of this reservation here. So they're ahead of us.
> They're into development. They're into farming. They're into al-
> lotted land. That's one of the things we rejected.[6]

The sudden infusion of millions of dollars in land claims money
and oil and gas income produced a social and cultural revolution
on the two reservations, and people such as Arthur Cuthair were
not pleased with the results. Both Ute tribes experienced the
same sort of drastic changes, and both suffered many of the same
resulting problems; yet with the persistence of the long-evident
acculturation gap between them, the new realities faced by tribal
members on the two reservations were not identical.

Substantial cultural differences between the Southern Utes
and Ute Mountain Utes, apparent since the late nineteenth century, continued to exist throughout the latter half of the twentieth century. The Ute Mountain people, still more geographically
isolated and living in a more closed society, retained much more
of their traditional culture and were more suspicious of development than were their cousins in Ignacio. The latter group, by
virtue of having settled on allotments in close proximity to non-
Indian neighbors and sustaining a relatively high rate of marriage
outside the tribe, had undergone a greater cultural transformation. Efforts to promote tribal economic development had given

further impetus to cultural change. In a society marked by rapid change and abundant contact with outsiders, the Southern Ute Tribe became much more culturally heterogeneous than the neighboring tribe to the west. Tribal society in Ignacio embraced a wide range of lifestyles, characterized by varying degrees of retention, or abandonment, of traditional Ute culture.[7]

CULTURAL DISLOCATION
AND SOCIAL PROBLEMS

The two Ute tribes of Colorado witnessed housing booms on their reservations during the 1950s. They each established housing authorities to oversee construction of public housing projects in ensuing decades as they sought to obtain sufficient housing to meet the needs of their growing populations. Both tribes thus added large numbers of housing units to their reservations, but the new housing developments represented a much greater social and cultural change for the Ute Mountain people than for the Utes of Ignacio. Whereas members of the latter group had long been settled in permanent housing—albeit cramped and of substandard construction—very few Mountain Utes at midcentury were accustomed to this mode of living. As late as the 1940s, most tribal members were scattered over the reservation, still living primarily in tents or hogans. Thus, the shift to a settled existence in permanent homes closely situated in and around a single town, Towaoc, meant a totally new way of life for the Ute Mountain people. For Southern Utes, by contrast, the post-1950 housing boom represented an improvement in the quality and size of their homes, not a fundamental change in their mode of residence. Unlike the Mountain Utes, whose houses centered on a single town, the Southern Utes continued the allotment-era practice of dwelling in homes dispersed throughout their reservation.

The new pattern of residential life in Towaoc struck at the very core of traditional Ute culture. Whether built with family plan money from the 1953 land claims award or with Department of Housing and Urban Development (HUD) grant money obtained in later decades, modern rectangular houses situated on streets required a major psychological and cultural adjustment for people used to tents or hogans. Culturally based taboos and aversions, such as fear of spirits and fear of lightning, complicated this residential transformation and had to be assuaged. For this reason, the new houses had to be blessed by a spiritual leader such as Terry Knight. Failure to do so would leave residents vulnerable to haunting by spirits. Calling on tribal spiritual leaders to make a new home livable is an example of the adaptive change so often initiated by the Ute people throughout the twentieth century. Confronted by new practices or institutions—in this case, modern American single-family housing—the Utes adopted this new development and fit it into their existing cultural structure.[8] Yet even the traditional blessing of new homes could not alter the fact that the lifestyle of the Ute Mountain people was undergoing radical, and irreversible, restructuring. "After awhile, we'll all live like white men," Terry Knight lamented. "We'll live in a square house and pay mortgages and live by the golden dollar."[9]

Cultural dislocation and adaptation were not the only sources of stress in the lives of the Ute people. The economic realities of modern living struck heavily on the people of both tribes. Reluctant to leave their people and their beloved homeland, yet provided with very few opportunities for supporting themselves economically on the reservation, the Southern Utes and Ute Mountain Utes suffered extremely high rates of unemployment. The Southern Ute Tribe reported unemployment rates of 55 percent in 1974 and over 56 percent in 1982.[10] Unemployment was even more rampant at Ute Mountain, where the tribe reported annual jobless rates ranging from 46.4 percent to 86.8 percent for the latter part of the 1960s and where other sources cited unemployment rates ranging from 57 percent to 80 percent for the late 1980s.[11] Furthermore, when tribal members managed to find jobs, they often found it difficult to adjust to the demands of regular employment in the modern world of business. For instance, a 1985 tribal staff meeting in Towaoc addressed the problems of tardiness, neglect of responsibilities, unauthorized leave, and other examples of poor work habits exhibited by tribal employees.[12] The same complaints were also frequently voiced by tribal officials in Ignacio. Such problems could often be traced to the long-standing cultural divergence between Indians and business corporations. The values and attitudes inherent in modern industrial capitalism were culturally foreign to Indians such as the Utes who were more familiar with an egalitarian system based on kinship ties and who had different concepts of time and land use.[13]

Persistently high levels of unemployment gave rise to widespread poverty. In 1980 only one-quarter of Ute Mountain tribal members age sixteen or older earned more than $5,000, and a majority of the people lived below the federally defined poverty level.[14] Economic ills such as unemployment and poverty in turn combined with the distressingly rapid pace of social and cultural change to create a host of acute social problems. A survey of 1987 statistics from the Ute Mountain Reservation reveals the scope of the problem: 80 percent of tribal members suffered from drug or alcohol addiction; 98 percent of Ute deaths over the previous three years had been alcohol related; the rate of teen pregnancy was double the national average; three out of four Ute Mountain children dropped out of school before finishing high school; the number of criminal cases in 1987, with 97 percent involving alcohol, was so overwhelming that the Tribal Court dismissed nearly two-thirds of the cases; and the average age at death was only thirty-seven.[15] Alcoholism and its associated high rate of accidental death contributed to this frighteningly short life expectancy, as did the frequency of suicide. Much the same situation existed in Ignacio, although the statistics there were slightly less bleak. Clearly, the rapid introduction of modern Euro-American socioeconomic institutions was exacting a terrible toll on the people of the two Ute tribes.

The Ute Indians of Colorado were not alone in facing these trying circumstances. Their plight was typical of most Native American peoples in the late twentieth century. Depressing social and economic statistics were the norm for reservation-dwelling Indians, although in some cases tribal figures for the Southern Utes and Ute Mountain Utes were even more grim than for other tribes. This was particularly true for the unemployment rates of the two tribes during the later years of the century. Ranging from just below 50 percent to as high as almost 90 percent, unemployment among the Colorado Utes greatly exceeded the overall 1980 unemployment rate of 13.3 percent for all American Indians in the thirty-three reservation states.[16] Ute Mountain health and economic statistics for the 1980s were especially alarming relative to comparable figures for Native Americans as a whole. Whereas Mountain Utes lived on average only 37 years, the overall life expectancy for Indians in the United States in 1980 was 71.1 years.[17] And whereas the median household income for American Indian families was $11,471 in 1979, approximately three-quarters of adult tribal members in Towaoc earned less than $5,000 per year at this time.[18]

The extent of drug and alcohol abuse and crime at Ute Mountain, while certainly worrisome, was not unusual among Native American populations. Alcoholism took a terrible toll on Indians of all tribes. The 1988 death rate for Indians as a result of alcoholism was more than five times higher than the rate for Americans of all races.[19] Similarly, the dramatic increase in crime on both Ute reservations was experienced by most American Indian tribes. The BIA revealed that the total number of assault reports on all Indian reservations rose by more than 25 percent from 1991 to 1992, and the number of murders increased by over 60 percent.[20] Nor were Ute health problems of the early 1990s unusual for a Native American population. Diabetes, for example, was a serious health threat, affecting roughly one-quarter of Colorado Utes over age forty-five. This pales in comparison, however, with the much higher incidence of this disease among the Pima Tribe of Arizona—more than one-half of those over age thirty-five were afflicted.[21] Thus, the grim conditions on the two southwestern Colorado reservations were in many respects symptomatic of general trends among American Indians.

The tribal governments in both Ignacio and Towaoc actively sought to protect their people from the destructive side effects of modern society. One anthropologist described the Southern Ute Tribe as a "cradle-to-grave service organization," providing both income and services to its members and also acting as an intermediary between individual members and the external world.[22] This was also true of the tribal government in Towaoc, which came to play a similarly dominant role in the lives of its members. Both tribes assumed steadily greater control over the administration of government services on their reservations by contracting with the Bureau of Indian Affairs to operate programs previously implemented by the BIA. By the 1980s, both tribes had taken over administration of such services as police protection, road maintenance, tribal courts, social services, housing, and education. Sometimes, however, the tribes elected to return such programs to BIA control, often as a result of tribal budgetary deficits. Contracts were also returned to the bureau when tribally run programs failed to perform adequately. Such was the case at Ute Mountain in 1991 when the Tribal Council voted to return the law enforcement program and the tribal court system to the BIA, acknowledging that "the current court system is not providing adequate social and public safety to the Ute Mountain Ute tribal members."[23]

A number of programs were launched to meet the special needs of particular segments of the tribal membership. The Southern Ute Tribe constructed special housing units and a community center for elderly members, and the Sunrise Youth Shelter was opened at Ute Mountain to help the tribe's troubled youth.[24] Tribal resources were frequently employed to combat the most serious and pervasive threat to the membership: alcoholism. Tribal efforts to address this menace began in the 1950s, and as the problem persisted, so did programs to alleviate its harmful effects. The Southern Ute Tribe, whose Committee on Alcoholism had hosted Alcoholics Anonymous meetings as early as 1960, opened the Peaceful Spirit Lodge, an alcoholism treatment center, in 1971. A large HUD grant in 1986 financed the construction of a new facility tò house this program.[25] The Southern Utes, by virtue of the substantial non-Indian presence in Ignacio and throughout their reservation, faced a more difficult task in fighting alcoholism than did officials on the more isolated Ute Mountain Reservation; banning liquor from such a checkerboard reservation was simply not feasible. The tribe's Committee of Elders once recommended to the Tribal Council that the tribal alcoholism center and halfway house be moved from its existing location in Ignacio, where nearby liquor stores and bars posed too much of a temptation.[26] The new Peaceful Spirit Lodge, located in the tribal complex north of town, put this source of temptation at a greater distance.

The Ute Mountain Tribe, blessed with a large and continuous block of land and with no towns on its immediate doorstep, was in a somewhat better position to control the flow of alcohol. The tribe was thus able to ban liquor from its reservation. An attempt by the Tribal Council in 1987 to reverse this ban produced a tremendous outcry among the membership, and the ban remained.[27] The threat of liquor sellers popping up just outside the reservation boundary surfaced periodically, spurring the council to protest to the county commissioners as it did concerning one such liquor license application in 1992.[28] Some tribal members, such as Arthur Cuthair, feared that the Ute Mountain Casino, which opened as an alcohol-free establishment, would eventually become a vehicle through which liquor would be introduced onto the reservation.[29]

Traditional Ute culture and spirituality were sometimes seized on as possible solutions to the tribes' alcohol and drug problems.

Eddie Box Sr.—Southern Ute Sun Dance chief, a spiritual leader, and also a councilman during the 1970s—was a strong advocate of this approach. Box himself had been a heavy drinker before he began participating in the Sun Dance. Box then had a dream instructing him both to take part in the dance and to abstain from alcohol, so he subsequently stopped drinking and became the tribe's Sun Dance chief.[30] In an attempt to combat drug and alcohol abuse among tribal youth, Eddie Box reintroduced young tribal members to the Indian way of life by including traditional rituals such as the sweat ceremony in a two-day spiritual workshop in 1979. This same rationale led tribal leaders to schedule a 1986 gathering for recovered alcoholics to coincide with the annual Sun Dance.[31] A similar approach was often taken in Towaoc, where sweat ceremonies were conducted at the youth shelter in an attempt to give troubled teens a positive direction for their lives.[32]

EDUCATION

One possible answer to many of the Utes' social problems was education; thus both tribes continually promoted increased education for tribal members. The Ute people remained far below national averages in their accomplishments in this area. All of the Indian graduates from Ignacio High School in 1982 were in the lower half of their class, and during that same year only 19 of 123 Southern Utes between the ages of eighteen and twenty-two attended college.[33] Educational statistics from Ute Mountain were even more bleak: in 1980 the average amount of schooling among tribal members was six years, in 1989 it was estimated that only 30 percent of adults in Towaoc had finished high school, and as of 1989 only two tribal members had ever graduated from college.[34] In comparison, the Southern Ute Tribe claimed a total of sixteen college graduates as of 1982.[35]

Public school education in both Ignacio and Cortez was a perpetual source of frustration for the Ute people. Even though Utes made up only 7 percent of the student body in the Cortez public schools as compared with a plurality in Ignacio—42 percent of Ignacio public school students in 1982 were either Southern Utes or members of other tribes—the same complaints were voiced by tribal members concerning both school systems.[36] For most of the post-1960 period, neither district employed any Ute teachers, and although Southern Utes were occasionally elected to the Ignacio school board, no one from Ute Mountain had ever won a seat on the Montezuma-Cortez school board. "They're prejudiced," charged Cynthia Kent, the Southern Ute Tribe's educational coordinator from 1975 to 1981, speaking of Ignacio school officials in 1983. "They have been and always will be."[37] John Baker expressed a similar level of exasperation with the Ignacio school board, deriding the board members as "a bunch of bigots" when they failed to address his concerns at a public meeting.[38] The same discontent was proclaimed in Towaoc with respect to the Cortez schools. School officials denied the existence of a problem in Cortez, but Tribal Chairperson Judy Pinnecoose complained in 1980 of these same officials, "They just won't work with us."[39]

School officials in Cortez and Ute Mountain tribal members were unable to see eye to eye. While tribal members were protesting in 1980 that the school district was making no attempt to understand them or to meet their needs, a school counselor in Cortez was contending that poor performance by Ute children in school was the result of unstable home situations and a lack of interest on the students' part. A school board member asserted at about the same time, "There's a tendency on the Indians' part to cry wolf and discrimination."[40]

Another persistent source of conflict between the two tribes and their respective school districts was the question of how Johnson-O'Malley funds—federal funds provided annually to school districts with large Indian populations—would be utilized. Indian parents fumed when this funding was not used in ways specifically benefiting their children.[41] Cultural conflicts, such as disputes over long hair worn by Indian boys, further pitted local Indians against school officials.

Even though children of both tribes had been attending public schools since at least 1961, their educational experience continued to be marked by a substantial degree of segregation. For many years following consolidation of the BIA school and the public schools in Ignacio, it had been the school district's policy to retain most Indians and Hispanics in the first grade; and ability grouping had consistently tended to segregate students of these two groups from their Anglo schoolmates. Furthermore, once students reached the fourth grade or thereabouts, they tended to stay within their own ethnic groups, rarely mixing with students from other backgrounds.[42]

The Southern Utes successfully pushed for the establishment of special programs focusing on Ute language, culture, and history in the Ignacio schools, but the results were disappointing. The effectiveness of the bilingual/bicultural program of the late 1970s was limited by a number of factors: there were no certified teachers of the Ute language, with the program relying instead on Ute aides; the program was limited to fifteen minutes per day; and a greater emphasis was placed on the Spanish language than on Ute. As a result, the program had been abandoned by 1981.[43] A Ute history, language, and culture class was begun later in the 1980s at Ignacio High School, but this class did not attract large numbers of students.[44] Both tribes already operated their own Head Start programs, and given the disappointing results of the special programs in the Ignacio schools and the general climate of distrust and hostility between both Ute tribes and their school districts, it is not surprising that some tribal members began to consider the possibility of establishing tribally operated schools. A 1990 survey of Ute Mountain tribal members revealed that 54.2 percent of respondents favored the establishment of the tribe's own elementary school on the reservation.[45]

ATTEMPTS AT CULTURAL PRESERVATION

Chief Antonio Buck Sr. died on February 6, 1961, and with him died the chieftaincy of the Southern Ute Tribe. The son of Buckskin Charlie, having served as the tribe's chief from 1936 up until his death, was laid to rest by his people in a manner combining traditional Ute burial practices with those of the modern Anglo-American world, which had long since intruded on the reservation. His body was not secretly and hastily buried in a crevice as had been done with Ouray's body in 1880—only for the bones to be reburied in the tribal cemetery in a well-attended 1925 ceremony. Instead, a funeral was held in the local Presbyterian church, followed by burial in Ouray Memorial Cemetery, located across the Los Pinos River from the agency and adjacent to the tribe's Bear Dance ground. In addition to Christian rites, traditional elements from the Ute past were also evident in the burial ceremony. The chief's body was dressed in a beaded buckskin shirt, and an ochre stripe was painted on one side of his face, extending from hairline to chin. With him were his redstone pipe and a fringed tobacco pouch. Two of the chief's most prized possessions, his eagle-feather warbonnet and his rawhide drum, were not buried with the chief but were instead presented by his daughter, Frances Buck, to the director of the State Historical Society, whose presence she had requested at the funeral. These items, some of which were later returned to the Southern Ute Tribe for display in its own museum at the Pino Nuche, were exhibited at the Historical Society's Ute Museum in Montrose, Colorado.[46]

Unlike Jack House of the Ute Mountain Tribe, Antonio Buck Sr. had long ago ceased to play a major role as tribal chief in the conduct of his tribe's affairs. His death thus held no political significance for the Utes of Ignacio, but the passing of the tribe's last chief was a sad milestone in the cultural evolution of the modern Southern Ute Tribe. It highlighted the cultural loss being experienced by the Ute people as they sought to find a place for themselves in twentieth-century American society. It also reinforced the fact that as elected Tribal Councils and an array of committees replaced chiefs and subchiefs, much of the tribe's heritage was passing from the scene. In the years following 1960, many aspects of the Ute past disappeared, but at the same time much effort was devoted to preserving what remained.

One of the biggest concerns was that the Ute language—regarded by many as the core of tribal culture—would disappear. A meeting of the three Ute tribes—the Southern Utes, the Ute Mountain Utes, and the Northern Utes of Utah—was convened in 1977 to explore intertribal cooperation toward preserving their common language and cultural heritage. Southern Ute elder Ralph Cloud worried on this occasion about the prospect of losing his native language, which he reminded those in attendance had been a gift to the Ute people from the Creator. In the "olden days," he explained, children routinely learned the language and traditions of the Utes from their parents. But children today no longer do this, he related: "Now they don't have time; they go watch T.V."[47]

The Ute language faced less immediate danger of disappearance among the more culturally conservative Mountain Utes, whose Tribal Council members still required the services of an interpreter into the 1980s;[48] but even among this people there were individuals who feared their native tongue was "dying." Norman Lopez, grandson of one of the tribe's last medicine men and editor of the tribal newspaper, worried about this prospect. Lopez asserted that young people in Towaoc were no longer learning the language. Since many of them no longer lived with their extended families, as had been the custom in the past, they lacked the opportunity to learn the old ways from their grandparents as children had previously done.[49] Tribal historian Alden Naranjo of the Southern Utes voiced this same concern in 1993. In past years, he explained, children had been watched by their grandparents and had learned their native tongue from these older relatives, but in late-twentieth-century society grandparents were rarely able to spend this valuable time with their grandchildren.[50]

The most ambitious efforts to preserve the Ute tongue were undertaken in Ignacio, where the language was already fading from the scene with alarming rapidity. In 1975 the Southern Ute Tribal Council resolved to follow the tribal planning commission's recommendations calling for the utilization of an outside expert to transform the Ute language into written form. Commission members contended, "If the language is not written, the language will surely die, as not too many members of the tribe, under 30 years of age, speak their native tongue."[51] The resulting Ute Language Project led to the creation of an alphabet and then a Ute dictionary, copies of which were distributed to all tribal households in 1979. Following this accomplishment, the next goal of the tribe's Ute Language Committee was to computerize the language.[52] The tribe was less successful with its attempts to increase Ute language fluency among its children through the public school bilingual program. Given the apparent failure of this program, along with the fact that most children were no longer learning their native language at home, tribal members in 1979 raised the prospect of establishing a Ute language school to be run by the tribe.[53]

Language was not the only area in which the Utes of Colorado sought to reaffirm connections with their past. Another such area involved hunting and the bison—key components of the traditional prereservation Ute economy. Both tribes established small bison herds on their reservations—although the Ute Mountain herd proved to be rather short-lived—and the Ute Mountain Tribe paved the way for expanded hunting by its members through the negotiation of a 1978 agreement with the state of Colorado. This pact permitted year-round hunting by tribal members over a vast 3.4 million-acre area to the north and east of their reservation—an area constituting much of the tribe's traditional hunting grounds.[54]

The Southern Utes and Ute Mountain Utes further acknowledged their past in 1976 by concluding some long-unfinished business—the formulation of a peace treaty begun by their ancestors more than one hundred years previously. At this time, a Ute delegation had met with leaders of their long-standing enemies, the Comanches, in an attempt to bring the hostilities between the two tribes to an end. This diplomatic initiative, however, had reportedly been derailed by the firing of a shot, which triggered a resumption of fighting.[55] At the time of these abortive peace talks, the Utes and Comanches had been fighting each other intermittently for more than a century and a half. At times during the eighteenth century, they had been allies, but for the greater part of the century, particularly from 1727 to 1786, the increasingly aggressive Ute people and their Comanche neighbors to the east and south incessantly engaged each other in war. Often during this period, Ute warriors assisted their Spanish allies, serving as guides for Spanish punitive expeditions against the Comanches. This state of war became so entrenched, in fact, that the Ute term for an adversary, *ko ma ntci,* meaning "anyone who wants to fight me all the time," was adopted by the Spaniards as a name for the tribe that was then their common enemy. This Ute word was eventually corrupted into what has since become the accepted name for this southern Plains tribe—Comanche.[56] To bring this state of war to an end once and for all, leaders of all three Ute tribes came to Oklahoma in September 1976 bearing peace pipes. In a solemn ceremony conducted in front of a large tipi, tribal leaders officially terminated the long period of hostilities between the Ute and Comanche peoples.[57]

Heightened interest in Ute heritage surfaced in other aspects of modern tribal life. In 1993, for example, "in order to better reflect the Ute Mountain Ute heritage," the tribal newspaper in Towaoc underwent a name change and a facelift. The name of the paper was changed from *Echo,* which held no particular significance for the tribe, to *Weenuche Smoke Signals—Weenuche* meaning "old Ute" or "the Indians of long ago." Additionally, the portrait of Chief Ouray, which had long graced the newspaper's masthead along with that of Chief Jack House, was replaced with the image of a chief who had been more directly involved in the history of the Ute Mountain Ute Tribe: Chief Ignacio.[58]

SPIRITUAL LIFE

In years past, the Ute people had turned for help to individuals such as Walter Lopez, a Ute Mountain medicine man who used traditional methods to cure Utes, Navahos, and other Indians. Lopez, who lived a simple life at Mariano Springs on the southwest flank of Sleeping Ute Mountain, had used these old ways to heal people afflicted with either physical or spiritual maladies— the Utes, after all, did not differentiate between the two. For example, Terry Knight remembered as a young child seeing Lopez conduct a medicine ceremony to remove gallstones from his mother's abdomen. But with the death of Walter Lopez in the late 1960s and the passing of others like him, the Ute Mountain people were left without any medicine men.[59] The Southern Utes had already faced this same loss two decades earlier, and now neither tribe could call on the services of such traditional healers. Should a Ute man or woman require Indian medicine, he or she now had no choice but to seek help from outside the tribe, most likely from Navajo medicine men, who charged sometimes hefty fees—anywhere from $75 to several hundred dollars—to cure various dysfunctions.[60]

The spiritual life of the Colorado Utes, however, did not come to an end with the passing of the last medicine men. They and their knowledge of the healing arts were indeed gone, but a new actor, often referred to as a "spiritual leader," arose to at least partially fill the void. In the early 1990s, there were four or five such individuals on the Ute Mountain Reservation, and one of these was Terry Knight.[61] The former councilman and tribal chairman was uncomfortable, however, with this label people were now applying to him: "Spiritual leader—that's a non-Indian term. Where they get that term, 'spiritual leader,' is that that's the kind of life I lead and the things I do week in and week out, during the summer and during the winter. And somebody said, 'Hey, this guy does that, and he is leading so many people, so he must be a spiritual leader.' And I say I am not anybody. I'm just doing what I have to do . . . and [following] how I believe in the Creator."[62]

In this modern spiritual leadership role, Terry Knight often conducted sweat ceremonies—previously the realm of only medicine men—and he complained that such ceremonies were more and more frequently being staged by leaders who lacked the proper training and hence the "right" to lead sweats. The sweat ceremony, perhaps the oldest of all Ute spiritual ceremonies, had undergone the same transformation at Ute Mountain that had accompanied its revival at Ignacio in the 1950s. Traditionally part of the medicine ceremony, the sweat had evolved during the post–medicine man period into a separate ceremony of its own, but it was still conducted "strictly for doctoring, for medicine purposes, or if you need a purification ceremony."[63] The sweat ceremony, something of a spiritual sauna, is conducted in a dome-shaped structure consisting of a hooplike frame of curved boughs covered by hides, blankets, or canvas. Participants sit around a central pit, filled with at least twenty-four fire-heated rocks, in the dark interior of the sweat lodge. An intense cloud of hot steam, sweet with the scent of cedar and sage, engulfs the participants as water is splashed over the hot rocks. As those in attendance sweat profusely and are thus physically purified, prayers are recited and traditional Ute songs chanted to help bring about "spiritual enlightenment, purification, [and] rejuvenation."[64]

In addition to being widely recognized as a spiritual leader of his people, Terry Knight was also one of a number of "roadmen" (persons who lead Native American Church ceremonies) on the Ute Mountain Reservation. Such ceremonies typically begin around 9:00 P.M., most often on Saturday, and continue through the night. Participants, both men and women, sit around the floor of a tipi on either side of the roadman, who faces east toward the tipi door. In the center of the tipi floor a fire burns, and between the fire and the roadman lies an earthen altar in the shape of a crescent moon. The roadman is surrounded by various items—a staff, a decorated rattle, an eagle-feather fan, and an eagle-bone whistle—which he uses as he conducts the ceremony. A drummer sits to the roadman's right. The ceremony, which is not set in writing and thus varies from one roadman to another, begins with the consumption of peyote. Each participant usually eats four buttons of the hallucinogenic cactus and also partakes of peyote tea, which is passed around the circle. After the peyote has been consumed and the celebrants have smoked tobacco, songs are sung, first by the roadman and then by others in the tipi. Singing may comprise from one-half to two-thirds of the entire ceremony. Later, prayers may be offered. The ceremony continues until dawn, when participants emerge from the tipi to welcome the rising sun.[65]

The peyote religion has been described as "a pan-Indian, semi-Christian, nativistic movement." It is pan-Indian in that it stresses the common bond among all Indians regardless of tribe. It has a strong Christian component, as is evident in symbolism employed during the ceremony and in prayers that refer to God, Jesus Christ, and the Virgin Mary. Despite these Christian elements, however, the peyote ritual is also nativistic; it is clearly an Indian way of reaching God, and the peyote religion thus serves as a vehicle for the assertion of participants' cultural identity.[66] The curative power of peyote, a small cactus growing in a few areas of northern Mexico and southern Texas, is the principal motivation behind participation in Native American Church ceremonies. Since following the "peyote road" can bring good health, peyote meetings are often sponsored by individuals who seek to cure illness in their family.[67] Much as Christians partake of the body and blood of Christ when they take Communion, peyotists eat the peyote cactus—a sacrament provided for Indians by God—to establish communion with God. As Christians believe God sent Christ to save humanity, followers of the Native American Church believe that "God reveals Himself in Peyote."[68]

With roughly thirty roadmen on the Ute Mountain Reservation in the early 1990s and possibly as many as one-half of the people there taking part in such ceremonies at one time or another in their lives, the Native American Church continued to play an important role in the spiritual life of the Ute Mountain people throughout the latter half of the century.[69] As in earlier times, participation in this church was much more limited among the Southern Ute people, with perhaps ten families in the Ignacio area holding ceremonies of this sort in the early 1990s.[70] Here, then, was another indication of the cultural divergence between the two Colorado Ute tribes: peyotism, which for many Utes served as a rallying point for cultural preservation, was widely accepted as a part of life at Ute Mountain but existed only on the fringes of Southern Ute society.[71] In Ignacio peyotism remained a much more divisive issue than in Towaoc, with social rifts sometimes arising among Southern Ute tribal members over the issue of participation in the Native American Church.[72] The peyote ritual was rejected in Ignacio even by some of the tribe's spiritual and cultural leaders. Sun Dance chief Eddie Box Sr., for example, suggested that peyote and the Sun Dance did not mix.[73] No such incompatibility was perceived at Ute Mountain.

Another important institution in the spiritual life of people on both reservations—and another key focal point for the assertion of one's Indian identity—was the annual Sun Dance.[74] Conducted by a Sun Dance chief—Eddie Box Sr. of the Southern Utes (from the mid 1950s through 1994) and Terry Knight of the Ute Mountain Utes (after 1980)—this dance was held each summer at different times on all three Ute reservations. For many Utes, the Sun Dance is the most important event of the year.[75]

Although only a small fraction of the tribe's men may actually dance, participation in this spiritual event is not limited to dancers. From the time that advance preparations begin during the winter to the conclusion of the postdance feast the following summer, hundreds of tribal members will have been involved in the Sun Dance as committee members, corral builders, dancers, singers, orators, or spectators.[76] Thus, the Sun Dance is a collective effort by a large segment of the tribal population, one that is directed toward both individual and collective ends. The main focus of the dance is the acquisition of power, both spiritual power and physical good health, for the individual dancers as well as for the tribe as a whole. In addition, for the men who actually dance, taking part in the Sun Dance can provide a rare opportunity for gaining prestige.[77]

The modern Sun Dance begins after nightfall, typically on a Friday night in July. A round willow corral, called a Sun Dance lodge, is constructed around a prominent central pole earlier in the day. The center pole, which often holds a bison head or a stuffed eagle, is regarded as a source of supernatural power; and the Christian component of the Sun Dance is indicated by the names that are used to refer to this pole: "God's brain," "Jesus," or "the crucifix."[78] Dancers, who have experienced dreams calling them to join in the dance, face a grueling test of endurance. They will dance for the better part of four days, repeatedly shuffling forward to the center post and then back to their place along the edge of the corral. During this period, they will take no food or drink and will have only brief periods of rest. The forward-and-backward dance is repeated continuously as the dancers blow eagle-bone whistles and are accompanied by singing and drumming. A large crowd of spectators assembles in and around the lodge to share in the experience and to lend encouragement to the dancers. Excitement mounts, and the dance pace quickens on the final day as the nearly exhausted dancers push themselves in a final quest for a vision—the ultimate religious experience offered by the Sun Dance. Dancers who receive visions fall to the ground unconscious and are carried back to their individual stalls along the side of the lodge. As the dance concludes, a final prayer and blessings are uttered, and dancers and spectators alike drink of sacred water. Then gifts are distributed to Indians visiting from other reservations, and a feast is held the next day.[79]

As with other aspects of Ute culture, the Sun Dance attracted more participation at Ute Mountain than in Ignacio during the latter half of the twentieth century. A comparison of the 1966 Sun Dances on both reservations reveals the relative popularity of this spiritual institution among the two tribes. Only 9 Southern Utes danced in their tribe's 1966 dance compared with 13 Ute Mountain Ute dancers. There was a similar contrast in spectator support. Some 400 Southern Utes were among the 1,030 spectators at the Ignacio Sun Dance, as compared with the 920 Ute Mountain tribal members, out of a total crowd of 1,280 people, who turned out to witness the Towaoc dance.[80] Aside from this difference in the level of participation, other contrasts were apparent between the two dances held in 1966. The Southern Ute Sun Dance, which was described as being "small and serene," was attended by non-Indians as well as Indians, and it evoked a Christian overtone both through speeches uttered during the dance and through Christian symbols used or worn by the dancers. The Ute Mountain dance, by contrast, was a secretive affair held in a meadow high up on Sleeping Ute Mountain. An observer noted of this tribe's Sun Dance, "The Ute Mountain people are especially hostile to whites, and so few whites ever attend." He described the mood of the dance as "very intense," observing that participants here danced harder and longer than on other reservations. He also remarked that the dance had a "self-righteous quality," as tribal members endeavored to adhere closely to Sun Dance conventions dating from early in the century.[81] Once again, cultural conservatism was much stronger at Ute Mountain than in Ignacio.

As the century drew to a close, the Sun Dance did not appear to be in danger of going the way of the medicine man in either Towaoc or Ignacio, as the number of dancers appeared to be holding steady, and possibly even increasing.[82] Whereas thirteen Ute Mountain dancers had taken part in the 1966 Sun Dance, fifteen tribal members gathered to dance in the tribe's Sun Dance lodge in 1989.[83] The dance also survived among the Southern Utes, who were led by a new Sun Dance chief in 1994. An aging Eddie Box Sr. passed his title on to Neil Cloud, whom Box described as the "rightful" chief. Neil Cloud was the grandson of the late Sun Dance chief Edwin Cloud. The Sun Dance chieftaincy had languished for several years following Edwin Cloud's death in 1946 before being revived by Eddie Box, and in 1994 this position was finally returned to a member of the Cloud family.[84]

Although it typically did not generate the controversy in Ignacio that peyotism did, the Sun Dance at times divided the Southern Utes into two camps: those who asserted their cultural identity through involvement in this annual event and those who showed little interest in the Sun Dance.[85] In 1961 the catalyst for conflict over the Sun Dance was money. The issue of tribal funding for the dance and the accompanying feast produced a rancorous debate between members of the Tribal Council that year. Martha Evenson demanded to know how tribal funds had been used and complained bitterly that Sun Dance chief Eddie Box had informed her that she should stay out of this issue. Sunshine Smith, an active Sun Dance supporter, agreed that it was not a woman's place to question matters surrounding the dance. This exchange demonstrated the persistence of sharply defined gender roles in at least some aspects of Southern Ute tribal life: even though women were regarded as equals of men in the political arena and they were important participants in the tribe's cultural life as well, some ceremonial leadership matters remained off limits to them. John Baker, who did not take part in Sun Dance observances, questioned the expenditure of tribal funds, asserting that the Sun Dance participants constituted "more or less a private club" from which the tribe as a whole did not derive any benefit.[86]

The Sun Dance and the issue of female participation in such traditionally male-only ceremonies again became a source of controversy in Ignacio in the late 1970s. The traditional prohibition on female dancers was waived, and four women were allowed to dance in their own Sun Dance one summer; but after one of these women died unexpectedly the following year, many tribal members attributed this death to the fact that the female sun dancers had tampered with tribal custom.[87] Women were never again permitted to pérform the Sun Dance in Ignacio.

Another issue pertaining to tribal spiritual life that aroused concern among members of both tribes was the possible intrusion of state or federal law. Uneasiness over this possibility led Terry Knight to attend a 1993 conference on American Indian religious freedom, where he moderated a panel addressing the religious use of eagle feathers and other legally restricted animal and plant materials. And when representatives of the three Ute tribes gathered for a summit meeting in Glenwood Springs, Colorado, in April 1993, a major topic of discussion was the inadequate protection afforded tribal religious practices by the American Indian Religious Freedom Act.[88]

A DIFFICULT CHALLENGE

The Southern Ute and Ute Mountain Ute Tribes of the late twentieth century faced a difficult situation. Saddled with severe poverty and endemic unemployment and a host of related social problems, they were in desperate need of the economic development that could alleviate this bleak state of affairs. And yet to the extent that the two tribes succeeded in developing their reservations, they increased the likelihood that their distinctive way of life—already drastically altered—would be pushed further toward the brink of extinction. To succeed in a modern American economic system characterized by corporate capitalism and high technology, while preserving the tribes' own unique culture, was the imposing challenge confronting the members of the two Ute tribes of Colorado.

CONCLUSION

Many of the issues confronting the Ute people of Colorado during the late twentieth century were highlighted at the annual general meeting of the Southern Ute tribal membership, held on June 18, 1993, in the tribe's Head Start building. Annual meetings such as this, which Chairman Leonard Burch likened to stockholders' meetings, were open to any of the tribe's members, now numbering some 1,259 people. The usual meeting facility, the community center at the Sky Ute Lodge complex, was unavailable for this particular gathering because of construction work on the new Sky Ute Casino. Gaming was clearly the foremost issue in the minds of many of those in attendance, but this topic was not scheduled to be addressed until late in the course of the lengthy assembly, which lasted from 9:00 A.M. until 5:30 P.M. Tribal member Annabelle Eagle suggested that the agenda be changed so that this important item might be discussed earlier in the day, but Chairman Burch denied her motion. "You guys always fix it so we have no time for questions," she complained.[1]

The question-and-answer period regarding the new casino did not arise until about 5:00 P.M., and by this time many of the tired

tribal members had already headed home. Some critics of the
new casino still remained, however. One of these was John E.
Baker Sr., the architect of the tribe's rehabilitation program of
the 1950s and early 1960s. The former rehabilitation director,
councilman, and tribal chairman was seventy-five years old and
nearly blind, but he still followed tribal affairs closely and remained as outspoken as ever. On the subject of the new casino,
Baker acknowledged that Indian people had always gambled, but
not, he claimed, for high stakes. He further asserted that "gambling
is not the answer as far as the Southern Ute Tribe is concerned,"
and he voiced concern about the close proximity of the casino to
the schools and the tribe's offices. Tribal member Mary Chavez
was more emotionally emphatic in her opposition, crying, "I hate
gambling!" and warning that it was the devil's work. Chairman
Burch, for his part, cited the benefits that the casino, slated to
open the following September, would bring the tribe.

A number of other items were addressed at the meeting. Councilwoman Vida Peabody drew attention to the endangered status
of the Ute language among the Southern Utes, referring to the
tradition of speaking in the Ute tongue at general meetings. Although most discussion at such meetings was now conducted in
English, some tribal members still preferred to use the Ute language when speaking before the tribal membership.[2] Peabody
asserted that communicating in their native language spurred
members to speak from the heart, but she also worried that this
practice might seem disrespectful to those tribal members who
could not speak Ute.

Discussion at the meeting also turned to the operations of the
tribal enterprises. Tribal members were told of losses incurred by
Sky Ute Enterprises, a long-standing problem that clearly worried many of those in attendance. Reports concerning the tribe's
oil and gas ventures were much more positive. Leonard Burch recounted the history of tribal energy operations, explaining that
ever since the tribe had begun conducting its own negotiations

with energy companies, it had secured much better deals than the BIA had previously obtained. Tribal officials glowingly predicted future profits from gas wells owned or operated by the tribe's newest and most promising venture—Red Willow Production Company.

A related topic of discussion at the meeting involved hiring policies at the tribal enterprises, long a bone of contention between the Ute people and their council members. Some of those in attendance voiced familiar complaints, asserting that tribal hiring practices failed to give adequate preference to tribal members. Those who rose to assail the practice of giving the best tribal jobs to outsiders clearly struck a chord with others in the audience as these complaints evoked loud applause.[3]

This meeting was typical of many such gatherings held in both Ignacio and Towaoc throughout the latter half of the century. It highlighted issues that had long preoccupied members of both the Southern Ute and Ute Mountain Ute Tribes: rifts between the Tribal Council and the people, with the latter often feeling that their council representatives never listened to them; cultural concerns, such as the diminishing role of the Ute language in contemporary life; and economic development matters, including the performance of tribal enterprises, the availability of jobs for tribal members, and the repercussions of the recent entry into the gaming business.

The decision by both tribes to open their own casinos exposed sharp internal disagreements over questions of economic development. Many concerns about gambling were expressed by Southern Utes at the tribe's 1993 general meeting, and similar questions had often been raised in Towaoc. Whereas some tribal members, particularly those serving on the Tribal Councils, viewed casino gambling as a panacea for the tribal economy, a significant number of tribal members worried about what the opening of casinos would do to their reservation and to their people.

Thus, as the twentieth century drew to a close the two Ute

tribes of Colorado still faced a host of difficulties. Both tribes continued to exist in a dilemma as they sought to both accommodate modern socioeconomic realities and retain their unique tribal identities. Their long and difficult search for a place in modern American society was not over. Ever since the arrival of the Mouache, Capote, and Weeminuche peoples on the Southern Ute Reservation in 1878, they and their descendants had struggled to adjust to new conditions imposed by an outside power that was foreign to their world. These Indians had seen their accustomed way of life taken away as the U.S. government charted a new course for the Ute people. What followed had been a difficult century of adjustment, transformation, and resistance as the Utes were forced to deal with a seemingly endless series of challenges posed by their subordinate position on the periphery of American society. The Southern Ute and Ute Mountain Ute people had been confronted with an economic and cultural revolution directed by the U.S. government and other agents of Euro-American society, and they had been forced to endure the sometimes arbitrary administration of their affairs by an endless array of federal bureaucrats.

The two Ute tribes of southwestern Colorado had not, however, been merely the passive objects of federal Indian policy and socioeconomic forces. They had been active participants in their twentieth-century experience, exerting considerable control over their destiny in the face of many difficult challenges. At times they had embraced new developments and opportunities, and in such cases they adapted such innovations to fit their existing sociocultural system; at other times they had resisted policy changes that they saw as unjustified or incompatible with their situation. Thus, even though the Utes may have been unwilling passengers on the road to a new way of life, they exerted substantial influence over both the route and the pace of this journey.

Along the way, the tribes confronted a number of imposing obstacles. One was the federal government, with its ever-changing policies toward Native Americans. The Ute Mountain Ute and Southern Ute Tribes adapted to a long and sometimes twisting trail of government Indian policies: allotment of tribal lands and the campaign to transform Indians into Christian agriculturalists; tribal reorganization under the Indian Reorganization Act; renewed assault on tribal sovereignty under the termination policy of the 1950s and 1960s; changes in the legal picture surrounding Indian land claims, culminating in large claims judgments at midcentury and the accompanying requirement for tribal rehabilitation plans; and the adoption of new federal programs and legislation in the latter part of the century designed to aid tribes in their quest for self-determination. While frequently exasperated by these wide swings in federal policy, the two Ute tribes successfully weathered these political storms and emerged at the close of the twentieth century with tribal governments that had assumed greater control over their own affairs.

Other obstacles encountered by the Utes of Colorado proved more problematic. Economic pressures were particularly frustrating. Having been forced to abandon their traditional hunting-gathering economy in favor of an agricultural way of life, the Utes at midcentury confronted a modern economy that proved increasingly hostile to small-scale farming and ranching operations in a semiarid region such as southwestern Colorado. Nor did this modern economy provide many jobs for residents of rural areas, such those in the vicinity of Ignacio and Towaoc. Forced once again to adapt to outside economic forces, the two tribes struggled throughout the latter half of the twentieth century to devise a new tribal economy that would provide the necessary levels of revenue and employment. This pursuit of economic autonomy led the two tribes to further develop their energy resources and pursue a number of new economic ventures, such as tourism and casino gambling. Even though oil and gas operations and the new casinos proved lucrative at times, unemployment and poverty remained endemic on the two reservations.

Even more intractable were the various social ills that developed as a by-product of economic development. Crime, suicide, health problems, and, especially, alcoholism exacted a terrible human toll on both reservations. A variety of programs were devised to combat these persistent social maladies, but these modern-day problems showed few signs of abating on either reservation.

In addition to suffering the effects of alcoholism and other ills accompanying modernization, the Utes were also faced with another worrisome by-product of development: the loss of their cultural heritage. With the passing of each generation, more cultural knowledge and more Ute traditions were lost. Traditional band chiefs were replaced by elected councilpersons and chairpersons, the healing practices of the medicine man largely disappeared, extended families ceased playing a major role in Ute society, and fluency in the Ute language became increasingly rare among tribal members. The more successful the tribes were in promoting education and economic self-sufficiency among tribal members, the more tenuous became the existence of their cultural identity.

The preservation of tribal identity was further exacerbated by another challenge facing the leadership of each tribe: the maintenance of tribal unity. Internal strife was seemingly ever present in both Towaoc and Ignacio as political conflict often proved quite volatile. Factional disputes arose frequently, most often over economic matters, such as the size or frequency of per capita payments out of tribal funds, but also at times over cultural issues. Popular distrust of tribal leaders was a constant on both reservations as political squabbles often pitted Tribal Councils and chairpersons against their constituents. Elected leaders were often accused by tribal members of failing to look out for their interests and of ignoring their concerns. A related complaint was that the Tribal Councils conducted much of their business behind closed doors and failed to keep their constituents informed about tribal business. Hotly contested tribal elections, often resulting in charges of impropriety on the part of either candidates or voters, were another source of friction within each tribe.

This, then, was the common dilemma facing the Southern Ute and Ute Mountain Ute Tribes throughout the twentieth century: they were assailed from without by various political and economic pressures and threatened from within by economic deprivation, social and cultural turmoil, and factional conflict. Although both tribes faced the same challenges, their situations were not identical, nor did they always respond to these problems in the same manner.

The contrast between the Ute Mountain Ute and Southern Ute experiences was scarcely perceptible prior to the bands' arrival on the newly established Southern Ute Reservation in the late 1870s, and the divergence of their respective paths did not become clearly apparent until the mid 1890s. Passage of the Hunter Act in 1895 presented the Colorado Ute bands with the prospect of allotment in severalty of tribal lands. The contrasting responses of the three Ute bands to this legislation set the people of the Weeminuche band on a far different course than that followed by the members of the Mouache and Capote bands. Whereas the latter group of Utes accepted allotments and settled in close proximity to non-Indian newcomers on the eastern portion of the reservation, members of the former group rejected allotment and settled instead on commonly held tribal land at the western end of the old reservation. Living in relative isolation on the arid lands surrounding Sleeping Ute Mountain, these Indians, soon to be called the Ute Mountain Utes, did not experience the acculturative influence of regular contact with non-Indian neighbors. As a result, Ute Mountain society became more closed and hostile toward outsiders than was the case in the racially and culturally heterogeneous environment faced by Southern Utes living around Ignacio. Not surprisingly, the latter tribe was more quick to adopt elements of Anglo-American and Mexican-American culture and economy. The Indians at Ute Mountain also experienced acculturation, but at a much slower pace. At the same time, they clung more tenaciously to traditional Ute cultural practices as well as to recently adopted pan-Indian cultural innovations such as the peyote religion and the modern form of the Sun Dance. This acculturation gap, begun following the 1896 allotment, was still in evidence one hundred years later at the close of the twentieth century.

The Southern Ute–Ute Mountain Ute dichotomy also extended at times to the tribes' respective relationships with the federal government. Agency superintendents routinely reported on the generally cooperative attitudes of Southern Ute leaders and of progress made by this tribe, while their comments regarding the Indians at Ute Mountain were much more pessimistic, characterizing these people as apathetic, stubborn, and retrogressive. Superintendent D. H. Wattson's exasperation over his inability to win Ute Mountain Ute support for the Indian Reorganization Act in the mid 1930s was typical. The dissimilar responses of the two tribes to the prospect of reorganization under the IRA are representative of their frequently disparate reactions to ideas emanating from Washington.

This simple dichotomy between Southern Ute accommodation and Ute Mountain Ute resistance in response to federal government policies is, however, misleading. In actuality, each of the two tribes practiced both accommodation and resistance. This was evident at Ute Mountain, where Chief Ignacio led opposition to sending Ute children to distant boarding schools but also welcomed the establishment of a school close by in Navajo Springs, and where Chief Jack House sought to prevent tribal members from voting in an IRA referendum but later served for nearly a quarter century on the Tribal Council that arose out of the subsequent IRA reorganization.

Likewise, Southern Ute leaders did not enthusiastically embrace every initiative emanating from the Indian Office, nor were they hesitant to challenge federal policies that they regarded as unjust or unreasonable. Although tribal members agreed to accept allotments in 1896, they refused to cooperate in the early years of the twentieth century with new annuity and ration distribution policies requiring them to work in order to receive goods from the agency. They also took their grievances all the way to Washington in 1925 and again in 1926, and the earlier delegation journeyed to the capital in spite of the fact that these Ute delegates had not been officially recognized by the Indian Office. And even though Southern Ute tribal leaders of the mid 1930s embraced the IRA much more readily than did their Ute Mountain counterparts, they also clashed more loudly with the BIA in the early 1950s as they sought to devise and then implement their tribal rehabilitation plan.

Thus, the reality of the Ute Mountain Ute and Southern Ute experiences during the twentieth century is not simple but complex. In political affairs, each tribe pursued accommodation at some times and resistance on other occasions. The same is true of the cultural evolution undergone by the two Colorado Ute tribes. Neither tribe was universally "progressive"; nor was either tribe consistently "conservative," rejecting all twentieth-century cultural innovations. Once again, the cultural history of these tribes was much more complicated than can be explained by any simple progressive-conservative dichotomy. True, the Southern Utes acculturated at a more rapid pace than their more isolated cousins at Ute Mountain did, and the latter tribe was able to retain more of its traditional culture; but this does not mean that the Ignacio Utes actively championed assimilation into the dominant non-Indian culture, nor did they simply cast aside their cultural heritage.

The twentieth-century stories of these two tribes are thus both parallel and divergent. The Southern Utes and Ute Mountain Utes have often followed different paths, beginning most significantly with their contrasting responses in the 1890s to the federal government's allotment policy, but they have also faced essentially the same dilemma posed by life in twentieth-century America. Some particular problems may have varied as a result of geographical differences between their two reservations, but the larger challenge posed by both internal and external factors has principally been the same in both Towaoc and Ignacio. And as the two tribes approached the close of the century, the differences tended to fade, while the commonalities loomed larger.

Clearly, the Southern Ute and Ute Mountain Ute tribes made great strides over the course of the twentieth century toward controlling their own destinies. They both advanced substantially toward their goals of political and economic self-determination. As the century drew to a close, the Ute Indians of Colorado had achieved a level of independence scarcely imaginable to their ancestors earlier in the century.

This increased autonomy, however, had come at a substantial cost. In the final decade of the century, Ute Mountain tribal members such as Arthur Cuthair disparaged the impact of millions of dollars in tribal income on traditional Ute society, while others such as Norman Lopez dreamed of escaping the increasingly bustling and noisy environs of Towaoc. Lopez would rather have lived at his more secluded birthplace partway around Sleeping Ute Mountain at Mariano Springs.[4] And in Ignacio Southern Ute elders lamented the rapid disappearance of their native tongue and worried that the tribe's young people were not learning the old ways. The two tribes had undergone a major transformation as they attempted to find their place in modern-day America. It had not been an easy century for the people of the Ute Mountain Ute and Southern Ute tribes.

NOTES

INTRODUCTION

1. John E. Baker Sr., interview by author, June 15, 1993, tape recording. Tapes of all interviews conducted by the author are in the author's possession.

2. Ibid.

3. Ibid.

4. Minutes of Southern Ute General Council meeting, September 28, 1951, 3–7, microfilm roll NA XII, box 4, Tri-Ethnic Project Files (series VII) of the Omer C. Stewart Collection, Western History Collections, Norlin Library, Boulder, Colorado (hereafter, Tri-Ethnic Project Files).

5. Minutes of Southern Ute General Council meeting, December 27, 1951, 5, microfilm roll NA XII, box 4, Tri-Ethnic Project Files.

6. John E. Baker Sr., interview.

7. "Two Ute Leaders in Denver for Yearly Visit to the Bank," *Denver Post*, January 18, 1963. In this article, Jack House is reported to have estimated his age as of this date as being seventy-one or seventy-two. Ernest House Sr., the chief's grandson, believes that Jack House was eighty or eighty-one at the time of his death in August 1971 (Ernest House Sr., telephone interview by author, July 15, 1993, tape recording).

8. Frances Wall, interview by Floyd O'Neil, Winston Erickson, and Charles Root, January 9, 1991, 18, copy of transcript in the possession of Arthur Cuthair.

9. Ernest House Sr., interview by author, June 11, 1993, tape recording.

10. Report of Council Meeting of the Ute Mountain Indians, April 8, 1921, box 10, 44017–064, Southern Ute Agency, Records of BIA, RG 75, National Archives, Rocky Mountain Region, Denver.

11. Ira S. Freeman, A History of Montezuma County, Colorado (Boulder, Colo.: Johnson, 1958), 21. Ernest House Sr. (interview, June 11, 1993) also explains his grandfather's position as being one filled according to individual qualifications as opposed to heredity. Several books and newspaper articles erroneously refer to Jack House as a "hereditary chief."

12. Robert W. Delaney, The Ute Mountain Utes (Albuquerque: University of New Mexico Press, 1989), 119.

13. "Governors Snubbed by Ute," Denver Post, May 8, 1958.

14. "Utes Determined to Block Oilfield Road," Denver Post, June 4, 1958.

15. "$500,000 Awarded for Ute Road Rights," Denver Post, November 18, 1959.

16. It was not until Jack House finally gave his approval—after years of refusing it—that the tribe proceeded with plans to open a tribal park showcasing the Anasazi ruins that dot Mancos Canyon and other nearby canyons (Ernest House Sr., interview, June 11, 1993).

17. Donald Callaway, Joel Janetski, and Omer C. Stewart, "Ute," in William C. Sturtevant, ed., Handbook of North American Indians, vol. 11, Warren D'Azevedo, ed., Great Basin (Washington, D.C.: Smithsonian Institution, 1986), 336; J. Donald Hughes, American Indians in Colorado, 2d ed. (Boulder, Colo.: Pruett, 1987), 22.

18. Joy Leland, "Population," in William C. Sturtevant, ed., Handbook of North American Indians, vol. 11, Warren L. D'Azevedo, ed., Great Basin (Washington, D.C.: Smithsonian Institution, 1986), 608.

19. Ibid., 610.

20. The American Indian Reference Book (Portage, Mich.: Earth Company, 1976), 41–42.

21. Harold Hoffmeister, "The Consolidated Ute Indian Reservation," Geographical Review 35:4 (October 1945): 620.

1. THE SOUTHERN UTES AND
UTE MOUNTAIN UTES PRIOR TO 1900

1. Donald Callaway, Joel Janetski, and Omer C. Stewart, "Ute," in William C. Sturtevant, ed., *Handbook of North American Indians*, vol. 11, Warren D'Azevedo, ed., *Great Basin* (Washington, D.C.: Smithsonian Institution, 1986), 336.

2. David Rich Lewis, *Neither Wolf nor Dog: American Indians, Environment, and Agrarian Change* (New York: Oxford University Press, 1994), 32; Joy Leland, "Population," in William C. Sturtevant, ed., *Handbook of North American Indians*, vol. 11, Warren L. D'Azevedo, ed., *Great Basin* (Washington, D.C.: Smithsonian Institution, 1986), 609.

3. Omer C. Stewart, *Ethnohistorical Bibliography of the Ute Indians of Colorado*, Series in Anthropology, no. 18 (Boulder: University of Colorado Press, 1971), 1; Jan Pettit, *Utes: The Mountain People*, rev. ed. (Boulder, Colo.: Johnson, 1990), 1.

4. Marvin K. Opler, "The Origins of Comanche and Ute," *American Anthropologist* 45 (1943): 155.

5. James Jefferson, Robert W. Delaney, and Gregory C. Thompson, *The Southern Utes: A Tribal History* (Ignacio, Colo.: Southern Ute Tribe, 1972), vii–viii; Callaway et al., 338–340, 365, 366; Marvin K. Opler, "The Southern Ute of Colorado," in Ralph Linton, ed., *Acculturation in Seven American Indian Tribes* (Gloucester, Mass.: Appleton-Century, 1940), 126–127; Stewart, 1. Spelling of band names varies: Weeminuche is spelled in some sources Weminutc, Wiminuch, or Weminuche; Capote is sometimes written Kapota, Kapoti, or Ca-po-tas; and Mouache is variously spelled Mowatsi, Mowatci, Muache, or Muwach. Additional spellings may also be found for the other four Ute bands, but these are the three bands with which this volume is most concerned. Callaway identifies several additional bands that lived in present-day Utah—the Pahvant, Timpanogots, Sanpits, and Moannunts—all of which were subsequently placed on the Uintah Reservation.

6. Omer C. Stewart, *Indians of the Great Basin: A Critical Bibliography* (Bloomington: Indiana University Press, 1982), 18; Callaway et al., 339.

7. Lewis, 29.

8. Callaway et al., 340–345.

9. Ibid., 354.

10. Opler, "The Southern Ute," 126–127.

11. Richard O. Clemmer, "Differential Leadership Patterns in Early Twentieth-Century Great Basin Indian Societies," *Journal of California and Great Basin Anthropology* 11:1 (1989): 35; Callaway et al., 354.

12. Lewis, 27.

13. Opler, "The Southern Ute," 122–128.

14. Frank Gilbert Roe, *The Indian and the Horse* (Norman: University of Oklahoma Press, 1955), 73.

15. Demitri B. Shimkin, "The Introduction of the Horse," in William C. Sturtevant, ed., *Handbook of North American Indians*, vol. 11, Warren L. D'Azevedo, ed., *Great Basin* (Washington, D.C.: Smithsonian Institution, 1986), 517; Opler, "The Southern Ute," 156–157; Stewart, *Ethnohistorical Bibliography*, 1; Roe, 79. Opler speculates that the Utes probably first possessed horses around 1640, and he reports that they were already equestrians by the time they signed their first treaty with the Spanish in 1675. Stewart contends that horses first fell into Ute hands as a result of the 1680 Pueblo Revolt. Roe concludes that these Indians apparently had horses by about 1700 but further mentions the possibility that this might have been the case as early as 1600. Shimkin speculates that Ute captives among the Spaniards learned about horses by 1637–1641, and he asserts that the Utes were using pack horses by the 1650s.

16. Lewis, 29–30. Lewis stresses that, even though the acquisition of horses led to modification of Ute society, it did not change the established diversified subsistence strategy employed by these people.

17. Opler, "The Southern Ute," 156–160.

18. Thomas D. Hall, *Social Change in the Southwest, 1350–1880* (Lawrence: University Press of Kansas, 1989), 127.

19. Quoted in ibid., 154.

20. Ibid., 122.

21. Robert W. Delaney, *The Ute Mountain Utes* (Albuquerque: University of New Mexico Press, 1989), 13.

22. Quoted in Opler, "The Southern Ute," 174.

23. Frances L. Swadesh, *Los Primeros Pabladores: Hispanic Americans on the Ute Frontier* (Notre Dame, Ind.: University of Notre Dame Press, 1974), 3.

24. Ibid., 22–23, 47.

25. Ibid., 2.

26. Gregory C. Thompson, *Southern Ute Lands, 1848–1899: The Creation of a Reservation*, Occasional Papers of the Center of Southwest Studies (Durango, Colo.: Fort Lewis College, 1972), 1; Richard O. Clemmer and Omer C. Stewart, "Treaties, Reservations, and Claims," in William C. Sturtevant, ed., *Handbook of North American Indians*, vol. 11, Warren L. D'Azevedo, ed., *Great Basin* (Washington, D.C.: Smithsonian Institution, 1986), 526.

27. Hall, 99.

28. Ibid., 115–117.

29. Ibid., 242.

30. Ibid., 239.

31. Thompson, 3.

32. Ibid., 4; Hall, 221.

33. Thompson, 4.

34. Joseph G. Jorgensen, *The Sun Dance Religion: Power for the Powerless* (Chicago: University of Chicago Press, 1972), 42.

35. P. David Smith, *Ouray Chief of the Utes* (Ouray, Colo.: Wayfinder Press, 1986), 34, 43; J. Donald Hughes, *American Indians in Colorado*, 2d ed. (Boulder, Colo.: Pruett, 1987), 62; Jefferson et al., 49. This account comes from Smith. Hughes asserts that Ouray's mother, not his father, was a Jicarilla Apache. Smith's contention that Ouray's mother was a Tabeguache would account for his membership in the Tabeguache band since the Utes typically defined kinship matrilineally and followed matrilocal residence patterns (Callaway et al., 352–353). Jefferson et al. concur that Ouray's mother was a member of the Uncompahgre (Tabeguache) band and that his father was half Jicarilla Apache.

36. Hall, 221.

37. Smith, 65, 72.

38. Clemmer and Stewart, 534.

39. Jefferson et al., 21; Thompson, 5; Smith, 72.

40. The Brunot Agreement, negotiated in 1873 and ratified in 1874, was termed an "agreement," rather than a "treaty," as a result of a policy change made by Congress in 1871. To enable members of the House to exert some control over negotiations with Indians, the practice of negotiating treaties, which required only ratification by the Senate before a final

signature from the president, was replaced by the negotiated agreement, which required approval from both houses of Congress (Thompson, 6).

41. U.S. Department of the Interior, Office of Indian Affairs, *Annual Report of the Commissioner of Indian Affairs to the Secretary of the Interior for the Year 1876* (Washington, D.C.: GPO, 1876), 102. The specific title of the Indian affairs annual report varies in later years; subsequent citations will be to the *Annual Report of the Commissioner of Indian Affairs*.

42. U.S. Department of the Interior, Office of Indian Affairs, *Annual Report of the Commissioner of Indian Affairs, 1877* (Washington, D.C.: GPO, 1877), 153–154.

43. U.S. Department of the Interior, Office of Indian Affairs, *Annual Report of the Commissioner of Indian Affairs, 1878* (Washington, D.C.: GPO, 1878), 45.

44. Frances L. Swadesh, "The Southern Utes and Their Neighbors, 1877–1926: An Ethnohistorical Study of Multiple Interaction in Contact-Induced Culture Change" (M.A. thesis, University of Colorado, Boulder, 1962), 2; U.S. Department of the Interior, *Annual Report of the Commissioner of Indian Affairs, 1878*, 154.

45. Swadesh, "The Southern Utes," 4–5.

46. Robert L. Perkin, *The First Hundred Years* (Garden City, N.Y.: Doubleday, 1959), 282.

47. Thompson, 10.

48. Swadesh, "The Southern Utes," 5–7, 21.

49. Jorgensen, 45–46; Hughes, 68.

50. Quoted in Jorgensen, 46.

51. Jefferson et al., 54; Smith, 185.

52. Thompson, 26.

53. Swadesh, "The Southern Utes," 67.

54. Quoted in ibid., 13.

55. Quoted in Thompson, 33–34.

56. Quoted in ibid., 34.

57. Swadesh, "The Southern Utes," 16, 22.

58. Thompson, 39–44.

59. Swadesh, "The Southern Utes," 21–23, 41–44. Some agents, such as Henry Page (1879–1881), are suspected of having hoped to be in an advantageous position to file their own land claims on removal of the South-

ern Utes. Others, such as Christian Stollsteimer (1885–1887), who benefited from a special arrangement allowing him to graze his own stock on
tribal land at no cost to himself, opposed any change in the status quo.

60. Quoted in Marjane Ambler, *Breaking the Iron Bonds: Indian Control
of Energy Development* (Lawrence: University Press of Kansas, 1990), 10.

61. Quoted in Thompson, 50.

62. Robert W. Delaney, *The Southern Ute People* (Phoenix: Indian Tribal
Press, 1974), 74–75; Swadesh, "The Southern Utes," 6; Clemmer, 38; Jefferson et al., 98; Jan Pettit, *Utes: The Mountain People*, rev. ed. (Boulder, Colo.:
Johnson, 1990), 162. Buckskin Charlie's band membership is variously identified in sources: Delaney, Swadesh, and Pettit label him a Mouache; Jefferson and Clemmer identify him as a Capote chief. What is certain is that by
1880 Charlie had become a chief among both of these bands.

63. Jefferson et al., 54.

64. Opler, "The Southern Ute," 183.

65. Thompson, 54.

66. Ralph C. Taylor, "Ignacio Sought Peace as Ute Chief," *Pueblo Chieftain*, May 18, 1969; Swadesh, "The Southern Utes," 23.

67. Thompson, 59; Swadesh, "The Southern Utes," 26.

68. Opler, "The Southern Ute," 183.

69. Swadesh, "The Southern Utes," 33; Clemmer, 38.

70. Thompson, 55; Swadesh, "The Southern Utes," 33–34; Jefferson
et al., 43.

71. "A Wild Rush for Ute Lands," *Denver Times*, May 4, 1899.

2. TWO TRIBES IN A NEW CENTURY

1. U.S. Department of the Interior, Office of Indian Affairs, *Annual
Report of the Commissioner of Indian Affairs for the Year 1879* (Washington,
D.C.: GPO, 1879), 17.

2. U.S. Department of the Interior, Office of Indian Affairs, *Annual Report of the Commissioner of Indian Affairs, 1880* (Washington, D.C.: GPO,
1880), 17.

3. David Rich Lewis, *Neither Wolf nor Dog: American Indians, Environment, and Agrarian Change* (New York,: Oxford University Press, 1994), 17.

4. U.S. Department of the Interior, Office of Indian Affairs, *Annual Re-

port of the Commissioner of Indian Affairs, 1885 (Washington, D.C.: GPO, 1885), 240.

5. Frances L. Swadesh, "The Southern Utes and Their Neighbors, 1877–1926: An Ethnohistorical Study of Multiple Interaction in Contact-Induced Culture Change" (M.A. thesis, University of Colorado, Boulder, 1962), 64.

6. Frances L. Swadesh, *Los Primeros Pabladores: Hispanic Americans on the Ute Frontier* (Notre Dame, Ind.: University of Notre Dame Press, 1974), 98.

7. Ibid., 98, 106–108.

8. Ibid., 128; Swadesh, "The Southern Utes," 111, 159.

9. Swadesh, *Los Primeros Pabladores*, 1–2.

10. U.S. Department of the Interior, Office of Indian Affairs, *Annual Report of the Commissioner of Indian Affairs, 1900* (Washington, D.C.: GPO, 1900), 213–214, 640.

11. Swadesh, "The Southern Utes," 57, 160.

12. James Jefferson, Robert W. Delaney, and Gregory C. Thompson, *The Southern Utes: A Tribal History* (Ignacio, Colo.: Southern Ute Tribe, 1972), 95.

13. U.S. Department of the Interior, *Annual Report of the Commissioner of Indian Affairs, 1900*, 214.

14. Swadesh, "The Southern Utes," 160.

15. "Information Regarding Indian Schools," 1936, Southern Ute Boarding School, Allen Day School, box 1, 8NN 75-91-218, Consolidated Ute Agency, Records of BIA, RG 75, National Archives, Rocky Mountain Region, Denver.

16. Marjane Ambler, *Breaking the Iron Bonds: Indian Control of Energy Development* (Lawrence: University Press of Kansas, 1990), 14–15.

17. Swadesh, "The Southern Utes," 39.

18. Joseph G. Jorgensen, *The Sun Dance Religion: Power for the Powerless* (Chicago: University of Chicago Press, 1972), 97.

19. Ambler, 213–215.

20. Quoted in Swadesh, "The Southern Utes," 34, 91.

21. Ibid., 36.

22. Quoted in ibid., 69.

23. Ibid., 89, 97–98, 149.

24. Quoted in ibid., 95.

25. J. Donald Hughes, *American Indians in Colorado*, 2d ed. (Boulder, Colo.: Pruett, 1987), 93.

26. Quoted in Swadesh, "The Southern Utes," iii–iv.

27. Ute Mountain Tribal Council, "Plan of Operation for Use of the Proceeds from Claims Case no. 47567," March 12, 1970, 3, Tribal Resolutions File, Ute Mountain Ute Agency, Towaoc, Colorado.

28. "Sleeping Ute Legend," *Ute Mountain Ute Echo* (June 1987). This version of the Sleeping Ute legend is based on an account by Russell Lopez.

29. Quoted in "Attitude of the Ute Indians on the Reservation Opening," *Denver Times*, May 14, 1899.

30. Iris Salt, interview by Floyd O'Neil, Winston Erickson, and Charles Root, January 7, 1991, copy of transcript in the possession of Arthur Cuthair. A large number of tribal members were interviewed by this three-man team in January 1991 as part of a project commissioned by the Ute Mountain Ute Tribe. These interviews offer a great deal of information about the character of life on the Ute Mountain Ute Reservation from the 1910s through the middle part of this century.

31. U.S. Department of the Interior, *Annual Report of the Commissioner of Indian Affairs, 1885*, 240.

32. Marvin K. Opler, "The Southern Ute of Colorado," in Ralph Linton, ed., *Acculturation in Seven American Indian Tribes* (Gloucester, Mass.: Appleton-Century, 1940), 183.

33. S. F. Stacher, "The Indians of the Ute Mountain Reservation, 1906–9," *Colorado Magazine* 26:1 (January 1949): 56–57; Iris Salt, interview, 9–11.

34. Stacher, 58–59.

35. Ibid., 53.

36. David F. Aberle and Omer C. Stewart, *Navaho and Ute Peyotism: A Chronological and Distributional Study*, Series in Anthropology, no. 6 (Boulder: University of Colorado Press, 1957), 18; "Information Regarding Indian Schools," Ute Mountain Boarding School.

37. Jan Pettit, *Utes: The Mountain People*, rev. ed. (Boulder, Colo.: Johnson, 1990), 168. Towaoc is pronounced "TOY-ock."

38. Consolidated Ute Agency, Annual Narrative Report, 1923, Section I, Microfilm Publication M1011, Records of BIA, RG 75, National Ar-

chives, Rocky Mountain Region, Denver. Subsequent citations will specify only the agency, the type of report (narrative or statistical), and the year.

39. Jorgensen, 59.

40. Jorgensen, 64; Forbes Parkhill, *The Last of the Indian Wars* (New York: Crowell-Collier Press, 1961), 19–20, 43–44; Swadesh, "The Southern Utes," 88. The Indian Homestead Act of 1884, the Indian Severalty Act of 1885, and Section Four of the Dawes Severalty Act of 1887 permitted Indians to claim allotments of homestead lands on or off reservations.

41. Consolidated Ute Agency, Annual Narrative Report, 1923, Sections III and V; Robert S. McPherson, *A History of San Juan County: In the Palm of Time* (Salt Lake City: Utah State Historical Society, 1995), 160.

42. Clifford Whyte Sr., interview by Floyd O'Neil, Winston Erickson, and Charles Root, January 8, 1991, copy of transcript in the possession of Arthur Cuthair. Several other interviews with Ute Mountain Ute tribal members conducted as part of this oral history project provide much information about the Indians residing in the area of Allen Canyon and, later, White Mesa. These interviews also establish many of the family relationships between the two groups.

43. Stacher, 59.

44. McPherson, 149–150.

45. Parkhill, 70–71, 113–114; Jorgensen, 65–66.

46. Consolidated Ute Agency, Annual Narrative Report, 1923, Section V; McPherson, 159–162.

47. Consolidated Ute Agency, Annual Narrative Report, 1930, Section III.

48. Consolidated Ute Agency, Annual Narrative Report, 1931, Section III.

49. E. Z. Black, "Answers to Questions on Circular no. 2361," November 29, 1927, box 8, 051-055/052, Consolidated Ute Agency, Records of BIA, RG 75, National Archives, Rocky Mountain Region, Denver.

50. Ibid.

51. Consolidated Ute Agency, Annual Narrative Report, 1931, Section III.

52. E. Z. Black, "Farmer's Weekly Report," September 26, 1925, box 8, 051-055/052, Consolidated Ute Agency, Records of BIA, RG 75, National Archives, Rocky Mountain Region, Denver.

53. "Annual School Census Report," Allen Canyon, 1926–1932, box 8, 051-055/054, Consolidated Ute Agency, Records of BIA, RG 75, National Archives, Rocky Mountain Region, Denver.

54. E. J. Peacore, to C. E. Faris, September 25, 1930, box 2, General Correspondence, Consolidated Ute Agency, Records of BIA, RG 75, National Archives, Rocky Mountain Region, Denver.

55. 23d Annual Report of the Board of Indian Commissioners, 1922, 16–17, as quoted in Robert W. Delaney, *The Ute Mountain Utes* (Albuquerque: University of New Mexico Press, 1989), 87–88.

56. Axel Johnson, "A Self-Biography: A Few Happenings in the Eighty Years of Axel Johnson," unpublished manuscript, as quoted in Delaney, 85–86.

57. U.S. Department of the Interior, Office of Indian Affairs, *Annual Report of the Commissioner of Indian Affairs, 1894* (Washington, D.C.: GPO, 1894), 128. This statement is corroborated by the research of Frances Swadesh ("The Southern Utes," 16), who found records indicating that twelve of twenty-seven Southern Ute children attending the Albuquerque Indian School between 1883 and 1885 had died while at school.

58. U.S. Department of the Interior, *Annual Report of the Commissioner of Indian Affairs, 1880*, 240.

59. U.S. Department of the Interior, *Annual Report of the Commissioner of Indian Affairs, 1900*, 640; Consolidated Ute Agency, Annual Statistical Report, 1923.

60. Axel Johnson, as quoted in Delaney, 85–86.

61. Harold Hoffmeister, "The Consolidated Ute Indian Reservation," *Geographical Review* 35:4 (October 1945): 620. The population statistics reported in this article were obtained from the Consolidated Ute Agency.

62. Swadesh, "The Southern Utes," 166–167.

63. Opler, 194.

64. Swadesh, "The Southern Utes," 166–168.

65. Jorgensen, 18–19, 24; Jefferson et al., 64; Pettit, 88.

66. Aberle and Stewart, 16–17. Sam Lone Bear's name is also given in various sources as Sam Roan Bear, Sam Loganberry, and Cactus Pete.

67. Ibid., 18–23; Omer C. Stewart, *Peyote Religion: A History* (Norman: University of Oklahoma Press, 1987), 196; Omer C. Stewart, "The Southern Ute Peyote Cult," *American Anthropologist* 43 (1941): 305–308; Omer

C. Stewart, *Ute Peyotism: A Study of a Cultural Complex*, Series in Anthropology, no. 1 (Boulder: University of Colorado Press, 1948); Marvin K. Opler, "The Character and History of the Southern Ute Peyote Rite," *American Anthropologist* 42 (1940): 468. There is some confusion as to when peyotism was first introduced and accepted at Ute Mountain. Earlier sources—Opler; Stewart, "The Southern Ute"; and Stewart, *Ute Peyotism*—indicate that the peyote ritual was first brought to Ute Mountain by Sam Lone Bear in the 1910s but that the peyote cult was not widely accepted there until the early 1930s following a visit by John Peehart (also written as John P. Hart and John Peak Heart) in around 1931. Stewart provides a different—and more convincing—account of the introduction and widespread acceptance of peyotism in his later works (with Aberle, *Navaho and Ute Peyotism*; and *Peyote Religion*). The more recent explanation, that John Peehart came to Ute Mountain not in 1931 but some time before 1918 and that the peyote ritual gained adherents there almost immediately, rather than twelve to fifteen years later, is based on interviews with a number of Ute Mountain sources. The newer version of events was independently attested to by Jack House, Nathan Wing, Walter Lopez, and Herbert Stacher, all of whom agree that John Peehart came to Ute Mountain before the relocation of the subagency from Navajo Springs to Towaoc, a move that took place in 1918.

68. Stewart, "The Southern Ute," 306. All of the sources cited in the previous note agree on this differential extent of peyote acceptance among the two Ute tribes.

69. Swadesh, "The Southern Utes," 165–166.

70. James Russell, "Conditions and Customs of Present-Day Utes in Colorado," *Colorado Magazine* 6:3 (May 1929): 112.

71. Swadesh, "The Southern Ute," 151.

72. Ibid., 23.

73. U.S. Department of the Interior, *Annual Report of the Commissioner of Indian Affairs, 1894*, 128.

74. Stacher, 57–59.

75. Richard O. Clemmer, "Differential Leadership Patterns in Early Twentieth-Century Great Basin Indian Societies," *Journal of California and Great Basin Anthropology* 11:1 (1989): 38. Clemmer states that "Ignacio seems to have abandoned leadership of his band after 1910 and settled on an allotment" near the town of Ignacio.

76. Ibid., 39.

77. For an excellent discussion of the complex blend of "traditional" and "progressive" tendencies in individual Indian leaders, see David Rich Lewis, "Reservation Leadership and the Progressive-Traditional Dichotomy: William Wash and the Northern Utes, 1865–1928," *Ethnohistory* 38:2 (1991): 125–147.

78. Quoted in Swadesh, "The Southern Ute," 16.

79. Ibid., 20.

80. Ibid., 152.

81. Richard O. Clemmer and Omer C. Stewart, "Treaties, Reservations, and Claims," in William C. Sturtevant, ed., *Handbook of North American Indians*, vol. 11, Warren L. D'Azevedo, ed., *Great Basin* (Washington, D.C.: Smithsonian Institution, 1986), 534; Clemmer, 35–37.

82. Swadesh, "The Southern Ute," 152.

83. Ibid., 153.

84. Ibid., 153–154.

85. U.S. Court of Claims, *The Confederated Bands of Ute Indians* v. *the United States*, no. 30360, decided May 23, 1910, 440, 471, box 10, 44017-173/004, Southern Ute Agency, Records of BIA, RG 75, National Archives, Rocky Mountain Region, Denver.

86. Quoted in Swadesh, "The Southern Ute," 154.

87. Consolidated Ute Agency, Annual Narrative Report, 1925, Section V.

88. Swadesh, "The Southern Ute," 154.

89. Ute delegation to Commissioner of Indian Affairs, November 17, 1925, box 10, 44017-154/064, Consolidated Ute Agency, Records of BIA, RG 75, Rocky Mountain Region, National Archives, Denver.

90. Ute delegation to members of the Senate and House of Representatives, March 24, 1926, box 10, 44017-154/064, Consolidated Ute Agency, Records of BIA, RG 75, National Archives, Rocky Mountain Region, Denver.

91. Swadesh, "The Southern Ute," 109–110.

92. Florence E. Whittier, "The Grave of Chief Ouray," *Colorado Magazine* 1:7 (November 1924): 313–316; Jefferson et al., 52–53.

93. Whittier, 314–315.

94. Jefferson et al., 53.

95. Pettit, 203.

3. RESERVATION LIFE IN THE 1930s

1. Indian agencies such as the Southern Ute Agency had been administered throughout most of the nineteenth century by Indian agents. An act passed in 1893 initiated the transfer of these agents' duties to school superintendents, who, unlike politically appointed agents, were governed by Civil Service regulations. Thus, beginning in 1893 all agents were gradually replaced by "superintendents," who were not necessarily in charge of any school (National Archives Microfilm Publications, Microfilm Publication M1011, Introduction, Records of BIA, RG 75, National Archives, Rocky Mountain Region, Denver).

2. Consolidated Ute Agency, Annual Statistical Report, 1930, Records of BIA, microfilm roll NA VI, box 4, Tri-Ethnic Project Files (series VII), Omer C. Stewart Collection, Western History Collections, Norlin Library, Boulder, Colorado. All Annual Statistical Reports cited in this chapter were found in the Tri-Ethnic Project Files.

3. U.S. Senate, Committee on Indian Affairs, *Survey of Conditions of the Indians of the United States: Hearings Before a Subcommittee of the Committee on Indian Affairs*, 71st Cong., 2d sess., May 13, 1931, 10618–10619.

4. Consolidated Ute Agency, Economic and Social Surveys, Southern Ute Indians and Ute Mountain Reservation, 1934, Records of BIA, microfilm roll NA IV, box 3, Tri-Ethnic Project Files.

5. Frances L. Swadesh, "The Southern Utes and Their Neighbors, 1877–1926: An Ethnohistorical Study of Multiple Interaction in Contact-Induced Culture Change" (M.A. thesis, University of Colorado, Boulder, 1962), 129.

6. Sunshine Cloud Smith, telephone interview by author, June 26, 1995, tape recording.

7. Consolidated Ute Agency, Economic and Social Surveys, Ute Mountain Reservation, 1934.

8. Consolidated Ute Agency, Annual Narrative Report, 1935, 4, Microfilm Publication M1011, Records of BIA, RG 75, National Archives, Rocky Mountain Region, Denver. All Annual Narrative Reports cited in this chapter are from this microfilm publication.

9. Resolution no. 49 of the Southern Ute Tribal Council, March 7, 1940, microfilm roll NA XI, box 4, Tri-Ethnic Project Files.

10. National Association on Indian Affairs, "Investigation of Southern Ute Jurisdiction and Ute Mountain Reservation," 1935, 9, microfilm roll NA XI, box 4, Tri-Ethnic Project Files.

11. Consolidated Ute Agency, Annual Statistical Report, 1930.

12. Quoted in Swadesh, 84.

13. Ibid., 51–53.

14. U.S. Senate, *Survey of Conditions of the Indians of the United States*, 10620–10621; Division of Extension and Industry, Consolidated Ute Agency, Project Report, General Farming, Southern Ute Reservation, February 15, 1935, microfilm roll NA IV, box 3, Tri-Ethnic Project Files.

15. D. H. Wattson to Commissioner of Indian Affairs (hereafter, CIA), February 6, 1934, microfilm roll NA XI, box 4, Tri-Ethnic Project Files.

16. Consolidated Ute Agency, Annual Statistical Report, Southern Ute Reservation, 1931.

17. U.S. Senate, *Survey of Conditions of the Indians of the United States*, 10661.

18. Consolidated Ute Agency, Economic and Social Survey, Southern Ute Indians, 1934.

19. Division of Extension and Industry, Consolidated Ute Agency, Project Report, Sheep, Southern Ute Reservation, February 15, 1935; U.S. Senate, *Survey of Conditions of the Indians of the United States*, 10611.

20. Consolidated Ute Agency, Economic and Social Survey, Southern Ute Indians, 1934.

21. Consolidated Ute Agency, Economic and Social Survey, Ute Mountain Reservation, 1934.

22. Division of Extension and Industry, Consolidated Ute Agency, Project Report, Sheep, Ute Mountain Reservation, December 7, 1932.

23. National Association on Indian Affairs, "Investigation of Southern Ute Jurisdiction and Ute Mountain Reservation," 21.

24. Richard O. Clemmer, "Hopis, Western Shoshones, and Southern Utes: Three Different Responses to the Indian Reorganization Act of 1934," *American Indian Culture and Research Journal* 10:2 (1986): 29; John C. Cameron, Notes for report for Consolidated Ute staff meeting, 10:00 A.M., December 16, 1940, microfilm roll NA XI, box 4, Tri-Ethnic Project Files.

25. Floyd O'Neil, "The New Deal: An Overview," in Kenneth R. Philp,

ed., *Indian Self-Rule: First-Hand Accounts of Indian-White Relations from Roosevelt to Reagan* (Logan: Utah State University Press, 1995), 39.

26. Donald L. Parman, *The Navajos and the New Deal* (New Haven, Conn.: Yale University Press, 1976), 35, 271.

27. National Association on Indian Affairs, "Investigation of Southern Ute Jurisdiction and Ute Mountain Reservation," 22.

28. Elbert J. Floyd to other heads of departments, Consolidated Ute Agency, Address given December 16, 1940, microfilm roll NA XI, box 4, Tri-Ethnic Project Files.

29. David F. Aberle and Omer C. Stewart, *Navaho and Ute Peyotism: A Chronological and Distributional Study*, Series in Anthropology, no. 6 (Boulder: University of Colorado Press, 1957), 33.

30. Elbert J. Floyd, "Ute Indian Agency Farm Agent's 1937 Report Shows Indian Family Earns $514," *Durango Herald-Democrat,* January 24, 1938.

31. The Southern Ute–Ute Mountain Ute delegation of 1925 had included among its grievances the accusation that Superintendent McKean had falsified his reports regarding conditions on the reservation. A similar charge had been made in 1913 by agency farmer S. K. Emerson with respect to reports of agricultural production submitted by Superintendent Charles F. Werner (Swadesh, 85–86).

32. "Ute Indians Seen Dying out Rapidly," *New York Times,* November 24, 1937.

33. Peter Iverson, *The Navajo Nation* (Westport, Conn.: Greenwood Press, 1981), 168–169. Iverson presents an excellent discussion of the role of licensed traders on the Navajo Reservation; his analysis applies equally well to trading post operations on other reservations.

34. Swadesh, 53–56.

35. Cal Queal, "Towaoc Utes Planning Wisely; Lead New Life," *Denver Post,* March 24, 1955.

36. Peggy Strain, "Utes' 1952 Land-Settlement Victory Turned to Defeat," *Denver Post,* September 25, 1977; Arthur Cuthair, interview by author, June 10, 1993, tape recording.

37. Consolidated Ute Agency, Annual Narrative Report, 1935, 13.

38. Consolidated Ute Agency, Economic and Social Survey, Southern Ute Indians, 1934.

39. National Association on Indian Affairs, "Investigation of Southern Ute Jurisdiction and Ute Mountain Reservation," 10.

40. Consolidated Ute Agency, Annual Statistical Report, Southern Ute Reservation, 1931.

41. S. F. Stacher to CIA, October 2, 1937, 8NN 75-91-218 (1970-456015), Consolidated Ute Agency, Records of BIA, RG 75, National Archives, Rocky Mountain Region, Denver.

42. Consolidated Ute Agency, Economic and Social Surveys, Southern Ute Indians and Ute Mountain Reservation, 1934.

43. S. F. Stacher to CIA, September 14, 1938, 8NN 75-91-218 (1970-456015), Consolidated Ute Agency, Records of BIA, RG 75, National Archives, Rocky Mountain Region, Denver.

44. Lucy Wilcox Adams (Director of Navajo Schools) to W. W. Beatty (Director of Education, Office of Indian Affairs), September 12, 1938, 8NN 75-91-218 (1970-456015), Records of BIA, RG 75, National Archives, Rocky Mountain Region, Denver.

45. Marvin K. Opler, "The Southern Ute of Colorado," in Ralph Linton, ed., *Acculturation in Seven American Indian Tribes* (Gloucester, Mass.: Appleton-Century, 1940), 187.

46. Consolidated Ute Agency, Annual Statistical Reports, Southern Ute and Ute Mountain Ute Reservations, 1931.

47. Consolidated Ute Agency, Annual Statistical Reports, Southern Ute and Ute Mountain Reservations, 1931–1940.

48. Consolidated Ute Agency, Annual Statistical Reports, Southern Ute and Ute Mountain Reservations, 1930, 1940.

49. Consolidated Ute Agency, Annual Narrative Report, 1931, Section III.

50. Consolidated Ute Agency, Annual Statistical Reports, Southern Ute and Ute Mountain Reservations, 1934.

51. Consolidated Ute Agency, Annual Narrative Report, 1935, 4, 9, 10.

52. U.S. Senate, *Survey of Conditions of the Indians of the United States,* 10702.

53. Quoted in Opler, 194.

54. National Association on Indian Affairs, "Investigation of Southern Ute Jurisdiction and Ute Mountain Reservation," 23–24.

55. Consolidated Ute Agency, Annual Narrative Report, 1934, Section III.

56. Consolidated Ute Agency, Annual Statistical Reports, Southern Ute and Ute Mountain Reservations, 1930.

57. Consolidated Ute Agency, Annual Statistical Reports, Southern Ute and Ute Mountain Reservations, 1935.

58. Swadesh, 122.

59. Quoted in U.S. Senate, *Survey of Conditions of the Indians of the United States,* 10698.

60. Opler, 198.

61. Interviews of members of both tribes by the author (1993) and interviews of members of the Ute Mountain Ute Tribe by Floyd O'Neil, Winston Erickson, and Charles Root (1991) indicate that this practice continued to be a common one throughout the 1930s and 1940s. Opler (130–134) discusses the original workings of this arrangement during the aboriginal period.

62. Opler, 196.

63. S. F. Stacher to CIA, February 15, 1938, microfilm roll NA XI, box 4, Tri-Ethnic Project Files.

64. Opler, 196.

65. James Jefferson, Robert W. Delaney, and Gregory C. Thompson, *The Southern Utes: A Tribal History* (Ignacio, Colo.: Southern Ute Tribe, 1972), 66–67.

66. Ibid., 70.

67. Jefferson et al., 70–71; Jan Pettit, *Utes: The Mountain People* (Boulder, Colo.: Johnson, 1990), 86–87. This description of the Bear Dance is also based on the author's own observations while attending two days of the Ute Mountain Ute Bear Dance on June 6–7, 1993.

68. Opler, 185.

69. Southern Ute Agency, Annual Narrative Report, 1920, Section 1.5; Minutes of General Council meeting, May 23, 1939, microfilm roll NA XI, box 4, Tri-Ethnic Project Files. As early as 1920, the superintendent reported that the Bear Dance, formerly held in early spring, had been rescheduled so as not to conflict with spring farm work. A similar postponement was decided on by the Southern Ute General Council in May 1939.

70. S. F. Stacher to CIA, August 7, 1939, microfilm roll NA XI, box 4, Tri-Ethnic Project Files.

71. Consolidated Ute Agency, Annual Narrative Report, 1925, Section I.

72. Consolidated Ute Agency, Annual Statistical Report, 1930, 6.

73. Joseph G. Jorgensen, *The Sun Dance Religion: Power for the Powerless* (Chicago: University of Chicago Press, 1972), 17–19.

74. Ibid., 7, 18–19.

75. Quoted in Opler, 198.

76. Omer C. Stewart, *Ute Peyotism: A Study of a Cultural Complex*, Series in Anthropology, no. 1 (Boulder: University of Colorado Press, 1948), 18.

77. Aberle and Stewart, 17.

78. Quoted in Marvin K. Opler, "The Character and History of the Southern Ute Peyote Rite," *American Anthropologist* 42 (1940): 466–467.

79. Quoted in ibid., 465.

80. Quoted in Stewart, 19.

81. Omer C. Stewart, "The Southern Ute Peyote Cult," *American Anthropologist* 43 (1941): 306.

82. Aberle and Stewart, 34; Opler, "The Character and History of the Southern Ute Peyote Rite," 477; Sunshine Cloud Smith, interview.

83. Aberle and Stewart, 35–36.

84. Stewart, "The Southern Ute," 307–308; Terry Knight, telephone interview by author, July 6, 1993, tape recording.

85. "Only in Theory Does Chief Tony Buck Still Lead Southwest Colorado Utes," *Grand Junction Daily Sentinel*, April 9, 1944.

86. National Association on Indian Affairs, "Investigation of Southern Ute Jurisdiction and Ute Mountain Reservation," 19.

87. Ibid., 25.

88. Swadesh, 10.

89. U.S. Senate, *Survey of Conditions of the Indians of the United States*, 10679–10680.

90. Ibid., 10676–10678.

91. Ibid., 10678–10679.

92. Ibid., 10700–10701.

93. Ibid., 10700.

94. Ibid., 10680–10684.

4. THE INDIAN REORGANIZATION ACT
AND PURSUIT OF SELF-DETERMINATION

1. "Buckskin Charley, Chief of Utes, Passes Away Today," *Durango Herald-Democrat*, May 9, 1936.

2. Richard O. Clemmer, "Differential Leadership Patterns in Early Twentieth-Century Great Basin Indian Societies," *Journal of California and Great Basin Anthropology* 11:1 (1989): 39.

3. National Association on Indian Affairs, "Investigation of Southern Ute Jurisdiction and Ute Mountain Reservation," 16, Records of BIA, microfilm roll NA XI, box 4, Tri-Ethnic Project Files (series VII), Omer C. Stewart Collection, Western History Collections, Norlin Library, Boulder, Colorado.

4. Franklin D. Roosevelt to Rep. Edgar Howard, April 28, 1934, in *Congressional Record* (April 31, 1934), U.S. House of Representatives, microfilm roll NA XI, box 4, Tri-Ethnic Project Files.

5. Kenneth R. Philp, "Introduction," in Kenneth R. Philp, ed., *Indian Self-Rule: First-Hand Accounts of Indian-White Relations from Roosevelt to Reagan* (Logan: Utah State University Press, 1995), 16–17.

6. Buckskin Charlie and Tribal Council to Commissioner of Indian Affairs, February 12, 1934, Wheeler-Howard File 1011 066-1934, box A894 1-B, Records of BIA, RG 75, National Archives, Washington, D.C.

7. D. H. Wattson to CIA, February 2, 1934, Wheeler-Howard File 1011 066-1934, box A894 1-B, Records of BIA, RG 75, National Archives, Washington, D.C.

8. Floyd A. O'Neil, "The New Deal: An Overview," in Kenneth R. Philp, ed., *Indian Self-Rule: First-Hand Accounts of Indian-White Relations from Roosevelt to Reagan* (Logan: Utah State University Press, 1995), 42.

9. Richard O. Clemmer, "Hopis, Western Shoshones, and Southern Utes: Three Different Responses to the Indian Reorganization Act of 1934," *American Indian Culture and Research Journal* 10:2 (1986): 25.

10. Results of Southern Ute tribal election on IRA, June 10, 1935, microfilm roll NA XI, box 4, Tri-Ethnic Project Files.

11. D. H. Wattson to CIA, November 10, 1934, microfilm roll NA XI, box 4, Tri-Ethnic Project Files.

12. D. H. Wattson to CIA, Stenographic transcript of arguments made

by tribal leaders at Ute Mountain IRA election, June 15, 1935, microfilm roll NA XI, box 4, Tri-Ethnic Project Files.

13. Quoted in Oren Lyons, "The IRA and Indian Culture, Religion, and Arts," in Philp, ed., 100. This statement was made by Oren Lyons of the Onondaga Tribe.

14. Wattson indicated in his November 1, 1934, letter to the commissioner that the Ute Mountain Indians had asserted that they would come under the provisions of the act regardless of whether they voted; Wattson had responded to them by saying that if they did not hold an election, they would automatically come under the provisions of the IRA. Assistant Commissioner Zimmerman's letter of reply on December 14, 1934, agreed with the superintendent's interpretation: "Unless a majority vote against IRA, the act will become effective." Both letters in microfilm roll NA XI, box 4, Tri-Ethnic Project Files.

15. Lawrence C. Kelly, "The Indian Reorganization Act: The Dream and the Reality," in Roger L. Nichols, ed., *The American Indian Past and Present*, 3d ed. (New York: Knopf, 1986), 249–250.

16. Allan G. Harper to Mr. Jennings, February 17, 1936, microfilm roll NA XI, box 4, Tri-Ethnic Project Files.

17. John Painter, "Implementing the IRA," and Robert L. Bennett, "Implementing the IRA," in Philp, ed., 81–82, 83, respectively.

18. "Superintendent Raymond deKay," *Southern Ute Drum*, November 17, 1972.

19. Quoted in Kelly, 254.

20. D. H. Wattson to CIA, January 28, 1936, microfilm roll NA XI, box 4, Tri-Ethnic Project Files.

21. Assistant CIA William Zimmerman Jr. to Secretary of the Interior, October 23, 1936, microfilm roll NA XI, box 4, Tri-Ethnic Project Files.

22. Petition for an election and adoption of a constitution, adopted at a general meeting of the Ute Mountain Indians, February 11, 1938, microfilm roll NA XI, box 4, Tri-Ethnic Project Files.

23. S. F. Stacher to CIA, February 15, 1938, microfilm roll NA XI, box 4, Tri-Ethnic Project Files.

24. Minutes of special joint meeting of the Confederated Ute Bands, May 9–10, 1938, 5–6. All minutes of Tribal Council, Joint Council, General Council, or Business Council meetings cited in this chapter, unless

otherwise indicated, are from microfilm roll NA XI, box 4, Tri-Ethnic Project Files.

25. Minutes of Joint Tribal Council meeting, August 16, 1939, 1–2.

26. U.S. Department of the Interior, Office of Indian Affairs, *Constitution and By-laws of the Ute Mountain Tribe* (Washington, D.C.: GPO, 1940), in box 10, Folder 064, Consolidated Ute Agency, Records of BIA, RG 75, National Archives, Rocky Mountain Region, Denver.

27. D. H. Wattson to CIA, November 17, 1936, microfilm roll NA XI, box 4, Tri-Ethnic Project Files. Most secondary sources state that Antonio Buck Sr. was the first chairman of the new Southern Ute Tribal Council; this document shows, however, that John Burch was the initial chairman.

28. S. F. Stacher to CIA, June 5, 1940, Tribal Resolutions File, Ute Mountain Ute Agency, Towaoc, Colorado (hereafter, UMU Agency).

29. Minutes of the Ute Mountain Tribal Council, September 3, 1940, 1.

30. Petition for Charter, adopted at Southern Ute Tribal meeting, April 20, 1938, microfilm roll NA XI, box 4, Tri-Ethnic Project Files.

31. S. F. Stacher to CIA, October 3, 1938, microfilm roll NA XI, box 4, Tri-Ethnic Project Files.

32. Certification of Election, November 1, 1938, microfilm roll NA XI, box 4, Tri-Ethnic Project Files.

33. Corporate Charter of the Southern Ute Tribe, 3–4, 10, microfilm roll NA XI, box 4, Tri-Ethnic Project Files.

34. Bennett, 84.

35. Quoted in Kelly, 254.

36. Minutes of Southern Ute Tribal Council meeting, August 20, 1940, 2.

37. Minutes of Ute Mountain Tribal Council meeting, April 3, 1941, 1.

38. Minutes of Ute Mountain Tribal Council meeting, March 3, 1941, 2.

39. Floyd E. MacSpadden to CIA, May 21, 1941, Tribal Resolutions File, UMU Agency.

40. Floyd E. MacSpadden to CIA, August 29, 1941, Tribal Resolutions File, UMU Agency.

41. Minutes of Southern Ute Tribal Council, April 15, 1941, 1.

42. Joseph G. Jorgensen, *The Sun Dance Religion: Power for the Powerless* (Chicago: University of Chicago Press, 1972), 233–234.

43. Minutes of Southern Ute Tribal Council meeting, May 27, 1940, 1.

44. Minutes of Southern Ute Tribal Council meeting, September 18, 1940, 2.

45. Ibid., 1.

46. Minutes of Southern Ute Tribal Council meeting, May 15, 1940, 1.

47. Minutes of Southern Ute Tribal Council meeting, August 20, 1940, 2.

48. Minutes of Southern Ute Tribal Council meetings, November 3, 1947, 2, and December 1, 1948, 1.

49. Petition of the Ute Mountain Band of Indians, February 11, 1938, microfilm roll NA XI, box 4, Tri-Ethnic Project Files.

50. Consolidated Ute Agency, Annual Statistical Reports, Southern Ute and Ute Mountain Reservations, 1932, microfilm roll NA VI, box 4, Tri-Ethnic Project Files. All Annual Statistical Reports cited in this chapter are from the Tri-Ethnic Project Files.

51. Consolidated Ute Agency, Annual Statistical Reports, Southern Ute and Ute Mountain Reservations, 1940.

52. Consolidated Ute Agency, Annual Statistical Reports, Southern Ute and Ute Mountain Reservations, 1940–1946; "Southern Ute Veterans, We Salute You for Veterans Day," *Southern Ute Drum*, November 7, 1980.

53. Consolidated Ute Agency, Economic and Social Surveys, Southern Ute Indians and Ute Mountain Reservation, 1934, microfilm roll NA IV, box 3, Tri-Ethnic Project Files; Consolidated Ute Agency, Annual Statistical Reports, Southern Ute and Ute Mountain Reservations, 1945.

54. Report of Council Meeting of the Ute Mountain Indians, April 8, 1921, box 143, 0064/322, Consolidated Ute Agency, Records of BIA, RG 75, National Archives, Rocky Mountain Region, Denver.

55. Consolidated Ute Agency, Characteristics of the Population, Southern Ute and Ute Mountain Reservations, 1940–45, microfilm roll NA V, box 4, Tri-Ethnic Project Files.

56. "Ute Indian Boy Scout Troop at Ignacio Formed," *Durango Herald-Democrat*, December 12, 1942.

57. Floyd E. MacSpadden to William Zeh, December 17, 1946, 8NN 75-91-218 (1970-456015), Consolidated Ute Agency, Records of BIA, RG 75, National Archives, Rocky Mountain Region, Denver.

58. D. H. Wattson to CIA, June 5, 1933, microfilm roll NA XI, box 4, Tri-Ethnic Project Files.

59. Consolidated Ute Agency, Annual Statistical Reports, Southern Ute and Ute Mountain Reservations, 1938, 1945.

60. Eric T. Hagberg to CIA, September 12, 1951, 8NN 75-91-218 (1970-456015), Consolidated Ute Agency, Records of BIA, RG 75, National Archives, Rocky Mountain Region, Denver.

61. Cal Queal, "Towaoc Utes Planning Wisely; Lead New Life," *Denver Post*, March 24, 1955.

62. Elbert J. Floyd to Charles R. Graves, October 1, 1952, Tribal Resolutions File, UMU Agency.

63. Elbert J. Floyd to Francis Griswold, October 15, 1951, 8NN 75-91-218 (1970-456015), Consolidated Ute Agency, Records of BIA, RG 75, National Archives, Rocky Mountain Region, Denver.

64. Queal, "Towaoc Utes Planning Wisely."

65. Resolution no. 8 of the Southern Ute Tribal Council, February 1, 1939; Resolution no. 162 of the Southern Ute Tribal Council, August 2, 1943; both in microfilm roll NA XI, box 4, Tri-Ethnic Project Files.

66. Tentative Budget for FY 1939, Ute Mountain Tribal Council, March 6, 1939; Resolution no. 58 of the Ute Mountain Tribal Council, July 3, 1944; both in Tribal Resolutions File, UMU Agency.

67. Minutes of Joint Council meeting, October 25, 1949, 2.

68. Resolution no. 216 of the Southern Ute Tribal Council, October 1, 1945, microfilm roll NA XI, box 4, Tri-Ethnic Project Files.

69. U.S. Court of Claims, *The Confederated Bands of Ute Indians* v. *the United States*, no. 45585, decided October 4, 1943, 419, Ute Claims Cases microfilm, box 4, Tri-Ethnic Project Files.

70. "Ute Lands Restored," *Montrose Daily News*, June 29, 1938.

71. "Indians Get a New Slice of Colorado," *Rocky Mountain News*, October 12, 1938; S. F. Stacher to CIA, February 3, 1938, microfilm roll NA XI, box 4, Tri-Ethnic Project Files; James Jefferson, Robert W. Delaney, and Gregory C. Thompson, *The Southern Utes: A Tribal History* (Ignacio, Colo.: Southern Ute Tribe, 1972), 96.

72. Charles Clark Johnson, "A Study of Modern Southwestern Indian Leadership" (Ph.D. diss., University of Colorado, Boulder, 1963), 84.

73. Charles F. Wilkinson, "The Indian Claims Commission," in Philp, ed., 151.

74. Ibid., 152–154.

75. "History of the Southern Ute Tribe," *Southern Ute Drum*, November 7, 1969.

76. *The Confederated Bands of Ute Indians v. the United States*, 420–433.

77. Minutes of the Uintah and Ouray Tribal Business Meeting with representatives of the Southern Ute Agency, March 27, 1939, 2.

78. Minutes of Joint Meeting of the Southern Ute, Ute Mountain, and Northern Ute Councils with attorney Ernest Wilkinson, September 6, 1946, 3.

79. Minutes of Southern Ute Tribal Council meeting, November 1, 1946, 2.

80. "Survey Covering Vast Ute Region," *Denver Post*, August 8, 1946.

81. Minutes of Joint Meeting of Southern Ute and Ute Mountain Tribal Councils, May 1, 1947, 7–14. Subsequent quotations from this joint meeting were taken from these same minutes and will not be cited individually.

82. Minutes of Southern Ute Tribal Council meeting, August 2, 1948, 2.

5. THE 1950s: NEW WEALTH AND NEW CHALLENGES

1. U.S. Court of Claims, *The Confederated Bands of Ute Indians v. the United States*, nos. 45585, 46640, 47564, 47566, Judgments entered July 13, 1950, 433–441, Ute Claims Cases microfilm, box 4, Tri-Ethnic Project Files (series VII), Omer C. Stewart Collection, Western History Collections, Norlin Library, Boulder, Colorado; Resolution no. 2 of the Ute Mountain General Council, June 15, 1950, Tribal Resolutions File, Ute Mountain Ute Agency, Towaoc, Colorado; Southern Ute Tribe, "A Report to the Commissioner of Indian Affairs by the Southern Ute Tribe," June 1, 1956, 4, Western History Department, Denver Public Library, Denver.

2. Minutes of Southern Ute Tribal Council meetings, December 12, 1951, 5, and December 27, 1951, 1, Southern Ute Tribal Records and Archives, Ignacio, Colorado (hereafter, SU Archives); John E. Baker Sr., interview by author, June 15, 1993, tape recording.

3. Charles Clark Johnson, "A Study of Modern Southwestern Indian Leadership" (Ph.D. diss., University of Colorado, Boulder, 1963), 86.

4. Frances L. Swadesh, "The Southern Utes and Their Neighbors, 1877–1926: An Ethnohistorical Study of Multiple Interaction in Contact-

Induced Culture Change" (M.A. thesis, University of Colorado, Boulder, 1962), 51, 97–98.

5. Sharon Cloud, "Biography of Sunshine Smith," *Southern Ute Drum*, March 31, 1989.

6. Ibid.; Sunshine Cloud Smith, interview by author, June 17 and 20, 1993, tape recording.

7. Minutes of Southern Ute General Council meeting, September 28, 1951, 4–7, SU Archives. Subsequent quotations from this meeting come from these minutes and will not be cited individually.

8. Minutes of Southern Ute General Council meeting, December 27, 1951, 4, SU Archives.

9. Minutes of Southern Ute Tribal Council meeting, December 12, 1951, 2, 7, SU Archives.

10. Minutes of Southern Ute General Council meeting, December 27, 1951, SU Archives.

11. Johnson, 102–104.

12. John E. Baker Sr., interview. In this interview Baker contended that a sudden shift occurred in the position of opponents of the rehabilitation plan: "The tables turned. Those who had advocated complete dissolvement of the tribe began to think completely in the opposite direction. The pendulum swung completely the other way. . . . They changed so completely, they began to be isolationists. They began to talk Ute. They began to revive the old Indian customs."

13. Minutes of Southern Ute Tribal Council meeting, December 15, 1953, 2, microfilm roll NA XII, box 4, Tri-Ethnic Project Files. All Southern Ute Tribal Council and General Council meeting minutes for 1953–1957 were obtained from this microfilm roll in the Tri-Ethnic Project Files.

14. John E. Baker Sr., interview.

15. Southern Ute Tribe, "A Report to the Commissioner of Indian Affairs by the Southern Ute Tribe," 4.

16. "Ute Land Claims Undecided," *Grand Junction Daily Sentinel*, August 26, 1963.

17. Resolutions no. 194 (October 3, 1951) and 229 (February 4, 1953) of the Ute Mountain Tribal Council, Tribal Resolutions File, UMU Agency.

18. Minutes of Ute Mountain Tribal Council meeting, September 5, 1952, 2–3, Central Classified Files (1907–1959), Consolidated Ute Agency,

Records of BIA, RG 75, National Archives, Washington, D.C. All Ute Mountain Tribal Council meeting minutes cited in this chapter were obtained from this file of the National Archives in Washington, D.C.

19. Minutes of Ute Mountain Tribal Council meeting, February 4, 1953, 1–2.

20. Minutes of Ute Mountain Tribal Council meeting, November 17, 1952, 2.

21. Minutes of Ute Mountain Tribal Council meeting, February 4, 1953, 3.

22. Elbert J. Floyd to Area Director Charles Graves, September 1, 1953, Tribal Resolutions File, UMU Agency.

23. James E. Officer, "Termination as Federal Policy: An Overview," in Kenneth R. Philp, ed., *Indian Self-Rule: First-Hand Accounts of Indian-White Relations from Roosevelt to Reagan* (Logan: Utah State University Press, 1995), 114.

24. Ibid., 118.

25. U.S. House of Representatives, Committee on Interior and Insular Affairs, *Report with Respect to the House Resolution Authorizing the Committee on Interior and Insular Affairs to Conduct an Investigation of the Bureau of Indian Affairs Pursuant to House Resolution 89*, 83d Cong., 2d sess., September 20, 1954, 204, 297–299.

26. Joseph G. Jorgensen, *The Sun Dance Religion: Power for the Powerless* (Chicago: University of Chicago Press, 1972), 137.

27. Southern Ute Tribe, "A Plan for the Rehabilitation of the Southern Ute Tribe," 4, SU Archives; Bill Miller, "Colorado Indians Learn to Live with Money," *Rocky Mountain News*, September 6, 1960.

28. Southern Ute Tribe, "A Plan for the Rehabilitation of the Southern Ute Tribe," 4; CIA Glenn L. Emmons to Area Director W. Wade Head, November 19, 1954, microfilm roll NA XII, box 4, Tri-Ethnic Project Files.

29. Southern Ute Tribe, "A Plan for the Rehabilitation of the Southern Ute Tribe," 1.

30. Minutes of Ute Mountain Tribal Council meeting, August 14, 1953, 1–2.

31. Transcript of meeting of Ute Mountain Tribal Council with Superintendent Elbert J. Floyd, Robert Bennett, Hall Stenz, and Mr. Bovay, spring 1954 (no date on transcript), box 16, 8NN 075-89-052, 5, United Pueblos

Agency, Records of BIA, RG 75, National Archives, Rocky Mountain Region, Denver.

32. John C. Rainer to Wade Head, July 1, 1954, box 16, 8NN 075-89-052, United Pueblos Agency, Records of BIA, RG 75, National Archives, Rocky Mountain Region, Denver.

33. Transcript of meeting of Ute Mountain Tribal Council with Floyd, Bennett, Hall, and Bovay, 8.

34. Resolutions nos. 277, 291, 295, 507, and 508, March 19, 1954–January 6, 1956, Tribal Resolutions File, UMU Agency.

35. Minutes of Ute Mountain Tribal Council meeting, August 13, 1953, 2.

36. Minutes of Ute Mountain Tribal Council meeting, October 26, 1953, 3.

37. Sunshine Cloud Smith, interview.

38. Gene Wortsman, "Ute Mountain Indians' Oil Lease Income Up," *Rocky Mountain News*, September 22, 1956.

39. Resolution no. 324 of the Ute Mountain Tribal Council, September 22, 1954, Tribal Resolutions File, UMU Agency.

40. Resolution no. 324 of the Ute Mountain Tribal Council, September 22, 1954, Tribal Resolutions File, UMU Agency.

41. Consolidated Ute Agency, Tribal program obligations report for the Southern Ute Reservation, September 22, 1955, microfilm roll NA XII, box 4, Tri-Ethnic Project Files.

42. Southern Ute Tribe, "Where We Stand: A Report by the Southern Ute Tribe" (Ignacio, Colorado: Southern Ute Tribe, 1960), 89–90, SU Archives.

43. Minutes of Southern Ute Tribal Council, November 18, 1955, 3.

44. Minutes of Southern Ute General Council meeting, July 21, 1960, 16, SU Archives.

45. Jorgensen, 109.

46. Cal Queal, "Ute Indians Plan New, Richer Life," *Denver Post*, March 23, 1955; Miller.

47. Resolution no. 241 of the Ute Mountain Tribal Council, August 31, 1953, Tribal Resolutions File, UMU Agency.

48. Miller.

49. Resolution no. 196 of the Ute Mountain Tribal Council, November 2, 1951, Tribal Resolutions File, UMU Agency.

50. Resolution no. 342 of the Ute Mountain Tribal Council, November 5, 1954, Tribal Resolutions File, UMU Agency.

51. Robert S. McPherson, A History of San Juan County: In the Palm of Time (Salt Lake City: Utah State Historical Society, 1995), 212–213.

52. Consolidated Ute Agency, "Highlights of Council Activity During the Past Year," October 24, 1955, 8NN 75-91-218, Records of BIA, RG 75, National Archives, Rocky Mountain Region, Denver.

53. Consolidated Ute Agency, "Summary Statement of Withdrawal Status," December 31, 1955, 8NN 75-91-218, Records of BIA, RG 75, National Archives, Rocky Mountain Region, Denver.

54. McPherson, 163, 213. These are 1995 statistics.

55. U.S. Senate, Committee on the Judiciary, Juvenile Delinquency: Hearings Before the Subcommittee to Investigate Juvenile Delinquency of the Committee on the Judiciary, 84th Cong., 1t sess., April 28–30, 1955, 123.

56. Southern Ute Tribe, "A Plan for the Rehabilitation of the Southern Ute Tribe," 55.

57. Southern Ute Tribe, "Where We Stand," 25–26.

58. Robert W. Delaney, The Ute Mountain Utes (Albuquerque: University of New Mexico Press, 1989), 101; Ira S. Freeman, A History of Montezuma County, Colorado (Boulder, Colo.: Johnson, 1958), 21.

59. U.S. Senate, Juvenile Delinquency, 123.

60. Bill Miller, "Education Is Important to Indians," Rocky Mountain News, September 7, 1960.

61. Henry F. Dobyns, "Therapeutic Exercise of Responsible Democracy," in Stuart Levine and Nancy Oestreich Lurie, eds., The American Indian Today (Deland, Fla.: Everett/Edwards, 1965), 174.

62. Fred R. Baker, "All Southern Ute Tribe in New Blue Cross Deal," Denver Post, November 11, 1955.

63. Resolution no. 490 of the Ute Mountain Tribal Council, November 28, 1955, Tribal Resolutions File, UMU Agency.

64. Bill Miller, "Indians Proud of Livestock Progress," Rocky Mountain News, September 11, 1960; J. W. Campbell, "Ute Indians Learn to Operate Large Ranch," Gunnison News-Champion, June 12, 1957.

65. San Juan Health Unit, "Ute Rehabilitation Program, Public Health," 10, accompanying Resolution no. 429 of the Ute Mountain Tribal Council, June 15, 1955, Tribal Resolutions File, UMU Agency.

66. Robert W. Fenwick, "Poverty-Ridden Utes: Tribes Gather to Split $5,752,035 Award," *Denver Post,* September 30, 1951.

67. Elbert J. Floyd to Area Director Charles L. Graves, October 1, 1952, Tribal Resolutions File, UMU Agency.

68. Jorgensen, 115.

69. Miller, "Indians Proud of Livestock Progress"; see also citations in Chapter 4 to statistical reports of the Consolidated Ute Agency.

70. Ibid.; Bill Miller, "Wealthy Indian Tribe Invests Funds Wisely," *Rocky Mountain News,* September 5, 1960.

71. Southern Ute Tribe, "A Plan for the Rehabilitation of the Southern Ute Tribe," 8; Southern Ute Tribe, "Where We Stand," 2.

72. Southern Ute Tribe, "Where We Stand," 55.

73. Jorgensen, 113–114.

74. "Ute Rehabilitation Program, Public Health," 9.

75. Minutes of Southern Ute Tribal Council meeting, February 5, 1954, 2.

76. San Juan Health Unit, "Ute Rehabilitation Program, Public Health," 10–11.

77. Minutes of Ute Mountain Tribal Council meeting, September 4, 1953, 1–2.

78. Southern Ute Tribe, "Where We Stand," 13–14.

79. U.S. Senate, *Juvenile Delinquency,* 121, 123, 130.

80. Resolution no. 390 of the Ute Mountain Tribal Council, April 13, 1955, Tribal Resolutions File, UMU Agency.

81. Resolution no. 538 of the Ute Mountain Tribal Council, February 9, 1956, Tribal Resolutions File, UMU Agency.

82. Tom Johnson, interview by Floyd A. O'Neil, Winston Erickson, and Charles Root, January 8, 1991, 21, copy of transcript in the possession of Arthur Cuthair.

83. "Durango Official Denies Poor Treatment of Utes," *Rocky Mountain News,* August 24, 1955.

84. Bill Miller, "Cortez Works to Aid Indian Neighbors," *Rocky Mountain News,* September 10, 1960.

85. Minutes of Southern Ute Tribal Council meeting, September 7, 1955, 3.

86. Sunshine Cloud Smith, interview; Bertha Grove, interview by author, June 21, 1993, tape recording.

87. Bertha Grove, interview; Sunshine Cloud Smith, interview; Johnson, 18. The recollections of Bertha Grove and Johnson's report of seeing six Sun Dance poles standing on the dance ground in 1960—a new pole is erected for each year's dance—both indicate that the dance was first revived around 1955. Both Smith and Grove talk of the revival of the sweat ceremony. Grove recounts Sunshine Smith and her sisters instructing Eddie box in the ways of the Sun Dance chief.

88. John E. Baker Sr., interview.

89. Johnson, 127.

90. David F. Aberle and Omer C. Stewart, *Navaho and Ute Peyotism: A Chronological and Distributional Study*, Series in Anthropology, no. 6 (Boulder: University of Colorado Press, 1957), 17.

91. U.S. House, *Report with Respect to the House Resolution Authorizing the Committee on Interior and Insular Affairs to Conduct an Investigation*, 139; Sunshine Cloud Smith, telephone interview by author, June 26, 1995, tape recording; Bertha Grove, interview. The House committee report states that there were fifteen peyote users in 1954. Johnson (21–24) estimates "two dozen" peyotists in the Ignacio area in the early 1960s. Sunshine Smith and Bertha Grove both mention the Cloud family's opposition to the peyote rite and the controversial nature of peyote use on the Southern Ute Reservation at this time.

92. Omer C. Stewart, "The Peyote Religion," in William C. Sturtevant, ed., *Handbook of North American Indians*, vol. 11, Warren L. D'Azevedo, ed., *Great Basin* (Washington, D.C.: Smithsonian Institution, 1986), 673.

93. Consolidated Ute Agency, "Summary Statement of Withdrawal Status," April 16, 1956, Southern Ute, 5, Ute Mountain, 4, 8NN 75-91-218, Records of BIA, RG 75, National Archives, Rocky Mountain Region, Denver.

94. Albert Wing Sr., interview by Floyd A. O'Neil, Winston Erickson, and Charles Root, January 8, 1991, 1–10, copy of transcript in the possession of Arthur Cuthair.

95. Ibid., 16–23; Bill Miller, "New Wealth Permits Recreation Program," *Rocky Mountain News*, September 8, 1960.

96. Johnson, 115, 135, 148.

97. Harold Hoffmeister, "The Consolidated Ute Indian Reservation," *Geographical Review* 35:4 (October 1945): 623.

98. Freeman, 20–21; Miller, "Colorado Indians Learn to Live with Money."

99. Minutes of Ute Mountain Tribal Council meeting, October 30, 1951, 1–2.

100. Minutes of Ute Mountain Tribal Council meeting, September 6, 1951, 2.

101. John E. Baker Sr., interview; Sunshine Cloud Smith, interview, June 17 and 20, 1993.

102. Minutes of Southern Ute Tribal Council meeting, March 1, 1954, 3.

103. Minutes of Southern Ute Tribal Council meeting, February 26, 1954, 1.

104. Minutes of Southern Ute Tribal Council meeting, January 10, 1956, 1.

105. Dobyns, 175, 180, 182.

106. Minutes of Southern Ute Tribal Council meeting, April 27, 1956, 2.

107. Johnson, 124–125.

108. Ibid., 98.

109. Ute Mountain Ute Agency, Listing of Council Members, Superintendent's Office, UMU Agency.

110. "Women Hold 2-1 Voting Majority on Southern Ute Tribal Council," *Denver Post*, October 11, 1960.

111. Johnson, 134–135.

112. Southern Ute Tribe, "Where We Stand," 86–87.

113. Sunshine Smith, interview, June 17 and 20, 1993.

114. "Utes to Get Community Building," *Denver Post*, July 5, 1960.

6. TRIBAL ECONOMY AFTER 1960

1. Minutes of Southern Ute General Council meeting, July 21, 1960, 3, Southern Ute Tribal Records and Archives, Ignacio, Colorado.

2. Ibid., 4.

3. Ibid., 15–16.

4. Joseph G. Jorgensen, *The Sun Dance Religion: Power for the Powerless* (Chicago: University of Chicago Press, 1972), 121.

5. Sharon Cloud, "Southern Ute Fair Rich in History," *Southern Ute Drum*, September 5, 1986.

6. Mary B. Chavez, Letter to the editor, *Southern Ute Drum*, March 19, 1993.

7. Quoted in "Irrigation an Issue at General Council," *Southern Ute Drum*, March 4, 1977.

8. Southern Ute Tribe, "Progress and the Future: A Report by the Southern Ute Tribe" (Dallas: Taylor, 1966), Agricultural Resources Committee section, SU Archives.

9. "Ute Mountain Tribal Lands and Allotted Indian Lands," *Ute Mountain Ute Echo*, January 16, 1981.

10. Ute Mountain Tribal Council, "Plan of Operation for Use of the Proceeds from Claims Case no. 47567," March 12, 1970, 4, Tribal Resolutions File, Ute Mountain Ute Agency, Towaoc, Colorado.

11. Jim Carrier, "Ranch's Chief Cowboy Rounds up Cattle, Prepares for Winter," *Denver Post*, October 2, 1989; Clifford Whyte Sr., interview by Floyd O'Neil, Winston Erickson, and Charles Root, January 8, 1991, 17, copy of transcript in the possession of Arthur Cuthair.

12. Alan L. Sorkin, *American Indians and Federal Aid* (Washington, D.C.: Brookings Institution, 1971), 18–19, 66.

13. "Layoffs Won't Hurt Economy Says Ute Mtn. Tribal Official," *Southern Ute Drum*, July 21, 1977.

14. "Ute Mtn. Tribe Makes Large Economic Impact in Local Area," *Ute Mountain Ute Echo* (March 1993).

15. Quoted in Kathleen Brown, "Tribal Games Are a Profitable Business," *Southern Ute Drum*, April 30, 1993.

16. Ibid.

17. Quoted in John T. Rehorn, "1993 General Meeting: Gaming the Big Issue," *Southern Ute Drum*, June 25, 1993.

18. Southern Ute Tribe, "Progress and the Future," Tribal Land Assignment Program section.

19. Southern Ute Tribal Council to tribal members, memo, "Explanation of Per Capita Payments," April 22, 1988, Council Meeting Minutes File, SU Archives; John T. Rehorn, "Gas Market Slump Affects Tribal Income," *Southern Ute Drum*, March 3, 1995.

20. Jim Carrier, "Utes Learn, Too Late, to Watchdog Oil," *Denver Post*, November 12, 1989.

21. Minutes of Southern Ute Tribal Council meeting, September 12, 1967, 2, SU Archives; Resolution no. 1755 of the Ute Mountain Tribal Council, July 10, 1968, Tribal Resolutions File, UMU Agency.

22. Resolution no. 1931 of the Ute Mountain Tribal Council, November 24, 1970, Tribal Resolutions File, UMU Agency.

23. "Ute Tribal Award Is Overturned by Court," *Grand Junction Daily Sentinel*, April 26, 1971.

24. Southern Ute Tribe, "Where We Stand: A Report by the Southern Ute Tribe" (Ignacio, Colo.: Southern Ute Tribe, 1960), 89–90, SU Archives.

25. Minutes of Southern Ute Tribal Council, July 1, 1960, 2, SU Archives.

26. Minutes of Southern Ute Tribal Council, September 26, 1960, 1, SU Archives.

27. Southern Ute Tribal Council to tribal members, notice, "Special Information to All Tribal Members from the Tribal Council," August 1963, Council Meeting Minutes File, SU Archives.

28. Southern Ute Tribal Council, "Explanation of Per Capita Payments"; "Meeting Held with Tribal Council Regarding Additional Dividend Payment," *Southern Ute Drum*, August 4, 1989.

29. Resolution no. 1337 of the Ute Mountain Tribal Council, August 18, 1964, Tribal Resolutions File, UMU Agency.

30. Ute Mountain Tribal Council, "Plan of Operation for Use of the Proceeds from Claims Case no. 47567," 3, 6, 7–8.

31. Ibid., 12, 13.

32. Sorkin, 137–138.

33. Area Director Walter O. Olson to Chairman Albert Wing, September 27, 1971, Tribal Resolutions File, UMU Agency.

34. Resolution no. 2035 of the Ute Mountain Tribal Council, December 14, 1971, Tribal Resolutions File, UMU Agency.

35. Peggy Strain, "Utes' 1952 Land-Settlement Victory Turned to Defeat," *Denver Post*, September 25, 1977; Peggy Strain, "Tribe Leaders Accused of Fund Drain," *Denver Post*, September 20, 1977.

36. Resolutions no. 2947 and no. 2948 of the Ute Mountain Tribal Council, October 19, 1982, and November 24, 1982, respectively, Tribal Resolutions File, UMU Agency.

37. Resolutions no. 3730 and no. 3739 of the Ute Mountain Tribal Council, November 23, 1990, and December 14, 1990, respectively, Tribal Resolutions File, UMU Agency; Vance Gillette, "Story of the Golden Goose," *Ute Mountain Ute Echo* (December 1990).

38. Clem Work, "Drumbeat of Progress Goes on," *Rocky Mountain News,* May 29, 1969.

39. Minutes of Southern Ute General Council meeting, April 7, 1972, SU Archives.

40. Ute Mountain Tribe, "Ute Mountain Ute Pottery," brochure; Resolution no. 1960 of the Ute Mountain Tribal Council, March 25, 1971, Tribal Resolutions File, UMU Agency.

41. "Ute Mountain Utes Use Pottery Project as Tribal Hallmark," *Rocky Mountain News,* September 17, 1989; "Ute Mountain Ute Pottery a Smash in Supermarkets," *Ute Mountain Ute Echo* (December 1987–January 1988).

42. Minutes of Ute Mountain Tribal Council meeting, February 21, 1953, 1, Central Classified Files (1907–1959), Consolidated Ute Agency, Records of BIA, RG 75, National Archives, Washington, D.C.

43. Ernest House Sr., interview by author, June 11, 1993, tape recording.

44. Ibid.

45. Arthur Cuthair, interview by author, June 10, 1993, tape recording.

46. Ibid.; "Ute Mountain Tribal Park," *Denver Post,* September 25, 1985.

47. "Financial Report, Ute Mountain Tribal Park," *Ute Mountain Ute Echo* (July 1987); Joanne Ditmer, "Ancient Mystery: Kiva to Divulge Its Secrets with a Fund-raiser's Help," *Denver Post,* July 31, 1993.

48. "Utes Fear Tourist Bucks to End if Misrouted Road Corrected," *Denver Post,* September 27, 1987.

49. "Ute Tribal Park May and June 1987," *Ute Mountain Ute Echo* (July 1987).

50. "Ute Mountain Ute Tribe, National Park Service to Study Tourism Related Growth on Tribal Land," *Ute Mountain Ute Echo* (May 1988).

51. Resolution no. 3102 of the Ute Mountain Tribal Council, January 17, 1985, Tribal Resolutions File, UMU Agency.

52. "Ute Mountain Ute Tribe Annual Report 1987," *Ute Mountain Ute Echo* (August 1987); "Ute Mtn. Tribe Makes Large Economic Impact."

53. Jim Carrier, "City's Siren Song Lures Few off Reservation," *Denver Post,* November 20, 1989.

54. Resolution no. 3063 of the Ute Mountain Tribal Council, June 14, 1984, Tribal Resolutions File, UMU Agency; "Indian Tribe Set for Bingo," *Rocky Mountain News,* July 7, 1984; Resolution no. 3261 of the Ute Mountain Tribal Council, February 20, 1987, Tribal Resolutions File, UMU Agency.

55. Southern Ute Tribe, *Progress and the Future*, History of Lake Capote section.

56. "Horse Training Center Begins," *Southern Ute Drum*, September 20, 1974.

57. Minutes of Southern Ute Tribal Council meeting, May 20, 1975, 6, SU Archives.

58. "Sky Ute Country Store Opens," *Southern Ute Drum*, April 4, 1986.

59. Philip S. Deloria, "The Era of Indian Self-Determination: An Overview," in Kenneth R. Philp, ed., *Indian Self-Rule: First-Hand Accounts of Indian-White Relations from Roosevelt to Reagan* (Logan: Utah State University Press, 1995), 196–197.

60. Alfonso Ortiz, "The War on Poverty," in Philp, ed., 220–221.

61. Robert Burnette, "The War on Poverty," in Philp, eds., 226. Burnette, a former director of the National Congress of American Indians, points to mismanagement of grant money, saying, "This grantsmanship business became a disease."

62. "Pino Nuche to Quit 'Soda Pop Business,'" *Southern Ute Drum*, September 17, 1976.

63. Ibid.

64. Minutes of Southern Ute Tribal Council meeting, March 2, 1982, 1, SU Archives.

65. Minutes of Southern Ute Tribal Council meeting, March 5, 1980, 2, SU Archives.

66. Minutes of Southern Ute Tribal Council meeting, June 16, 1987, 1, SU Archives.

67. Minutes of Southern Ute Tribal Council meeting, July 31, 1987, SU Archives.

68. Minutes of Southern Ute Tribal Council meeting, July 14, 1989, 2, SU Archives.

69. Larry Burt, "Western Tribes and Balance Sheets: Business Development Programs in the 1960s and 1970s," *Western Historical Quarterly* (November 1992): 485.

70. Leonard C. Burch, "Chairman Burch Clarifies A-LP Alternatives and Motives," *Southern Ute Drum*, January 22, 1993.

71. Ibid.

72. Leonard C. Burch, "Briefing Paper on Animas–La Plata Project Al-

ternatives," *Southern Ute Drum*, March 19, 1993; "Benefits of the Colorado Ute Indian Water Rights Settlement Act to the Ute Mountain Ute Tribe," *Ute Mountain Ute Echo* (February 1988); Deborah Frazier, "$572 Million Pact Includes Water for Utes," *Rocky Mountain News*, July 1, 1986.

73. "Annual Report to the Colorado Commission of Indian Affairs," *Ute Mountain Ute Echo* (February 1991).

74. "Farm and Ranch Enterprise Harvests First Cash Crop," *Ute Mountain Ute Echo* (November 1987).

75. "Interior Secretary Lujan Announces $31 Million Contract for Dolores Project Canal Construction," *Ute Mountain Ute Echo* (February 1992).

76. "Dolores Project Brought Major Impact to Ute Life," *Ute Mountain Ute Echo* (March 1993).

77. Leonard C. Burch, "Money No Substitute for A-LP," *Southern Ute Drum*, April 30, 1993; "History of a Project," *Denver Post*, July 12, 1995.

78. Mark Obmascik and Adriel Bettelheim, "Animas–La Plata 'Not Cost Effective,'" *Denver Post*, July 12, 1995.

79. Quoted in ibid.

80. Burch, "Chairman Burch."

81. Kit Miniclier, "Tribe to Sue or Redo Water Deal," *Denver Post*, December 30, 1994.

82. Marjane Ambler, *Breaking the Iron Bonds: Indian Control of Energy Development* (Lawrence: University Press of Kansas, 1990), 54–55.

83. Ibid., 85–86.

84. Ibid., 56.

85. Ibid., 91–92, 266.

86. Ibid., 251–252.

87. Ibid., 242.

88. Bob Zahradnik, "Southern Ute Tribe Closes Historic Natural Gas Deal," *Southern Ute Drum*, January 22, 1993; Janet Day, "Tribe Buys 51 Natural Gas Wells," *Denver Post*, January 21, 1993.

89. Zahradnik.

90. Rehorn, "1993 General Meeting."

91. Kit Miniclier, "Feds See Jackpot in Tribal Casinos," *Denver Post*, April 11, 1994.

92. Brown.

93. Ibid.; Kit Miniclier, "Indian-Owned Casino Opens Its Doors To-day," *Denver Post*, September 4, 1992; Kit Miniclier, "Ute Mountain Casino Bustles on First Night," *Denver Post*, September 6, 1992.

94. Joe Garner, "Ute Mountain Casino Pays off Big Time," *Ute Mountain Ute Echo* (July 1993).

95. John T. Rehorn, "The Tribal Gaming Controversy," *Southern Ute Drum*, April 16, 1993; John T. Rehorn, "Sky Ute Downs' General Manager Predicts Financial Turnaround," *Southern Ute Drum*, July 23, 1993.

96. Arnold Santistevan, "Sky Ute Lodge to Get Face-lift in Preparation for Gaming," *Southern Ute Drum*, June 11, 1993; Brown; Kevin McCullen, "Indians Open Second Colo. Casino," *Rocky Mountain News*, September 2, 1993.

97. John T. Rehorn, "Casino's First Year Finds It in Excellent Health," *Southern Ute Drum*, September 2, 1994.

98. John T. Rehorn, "Expansion Begins at Sky Ute Casino," *Southern Ute Drum*, February 17, 1995.

99. "Future Economic Development," *Weenuche Smoke Signals* (March 1994).

100. Jim Carrier, "Tribe Mulls Nuclear Dump," *Denver Post*, April 14, 1993.

7. TRIBAL POLITICS AFTER 1960

1. Minutes of Southern Ute General Council meeting, October 6, 1961, 4, Southern Ute Tribal Records and Archives, Ignacio, Colorado.

2. Charles Clark Johnson, "A Study of Modern Southwestern Indian Leadership" (Ph.D. diss., University of Colorado, Boulder, 1963), 93.

3. John E. Baker Sr., interview by author, June 15, 1993, tape recording; Sunshine Smith, interview by author, June 17 and 20, 1993, tape recording; minutes of Southern Ute General Council meeting, October 7, 1960, 2, SU Archives.

4. Bill Miller, "Utes Make Progress Towards Modern Life," *Rocky Mountain News*, September 12, 1960.

5. Biographical information pertaining to Albert Wing Sr. was obtained from the transcript of the interview of Wing by Floyd A. O'Neil, Winston Erickson, and Charles Root, January 8, 1991, copy of transcript in the possession of Arthur Cuthair.

6. Minutes of Southern Ute Tribal Council meeting, November 6, 1962, 2–3, SU Archives.

7. "Meet the Candidates," *Southern Ute Drum*, October 15, 1993; Robert W. Delaney, *The Southern Ute People* (Phoenix: Indian Tribal Press, 1974), viii.

8. James Jefferson, Robert W. Delaney, and Gregory C. Thompson, *The Southern Utes: A Tribal History* (Ignacio, Colo.: Southern Ute Tribe, 1972), 53.

9. Information pertaining to dates of service of Southern Ute council members and chairmen was obtained from minutes of various Tribal Council and General Council meetings from this period, SU Archives; and also from articles in the tribal newspaper, the *Southern Ute Drum*.

10. John E. Baker Sr., interview.

11. Information pertaining to dates of service of Ute Mountain council members and chairpersons was obtained from a "Listing of Council Members," Superintendent's Office, Ute Mountain Ute Agency, Towaoc, Colorado; from various resolutions of the Ute Mountain Tribal Council, Tribal Resolutions File, UMU Agency; and from articles in the tribal newspaper, the *Ute Mountain Ute Echo* (name changed to *Weenuche Smoke Signals* in May 1993).

12. Kit Miniclier, "First Woman Indian Tribal Leader Wages War Against Status Quo," *Denver Post*, November 25, 1979.

13. Jim Carrier, "Subsurface Anger Helps New Ute Mountain Leader Do Her Job," *Denver Post*, October 21, 1989.

14. Miniclier.

15. "Elections," *Ute Mountain Ute Echo* (November 1992).

16. Quoted in "Burch-Baker Team Reelected," *Southern Ute Drum*, November 15, 1974.

17. Minutes of Southern Ute Tribal Council meetings, January 29, 1964, 1, and March 3, 1964, 3, SU Archives.

18. "Utes' Complaints of Bias Heard," *Southern Ute Drum*, April 21, 1972.

19. "Southern Ute Tribal Council Press Release," *Southern Ute Drum*, November 17, 1972.

20. Kenneth R. Philp, ed., *Indian Self-Rule: First-Hand Accounts of Indian-White Relations from Roosevelt to Reagan* (Logan: Utah State University Press, 1995), 194, 221; Alan Sorkin, *American Indians and Federal Aid*

(Washington, D.C.: Brookings Institution, 1971), 166; Larry Burt, "Western Tribes and Balance Sheets: Business Development Programs in the 1960s and 1970s," *Western Historical Quarterly* (November 1992): 492.

21. Resolutions no. 1072 and no. 1046 of the Ute Mountain Tribal Council, May 10, 1961, and January 25, 1961, respectively, Tribal Resolutions File, UMU Agency.

22. Resolution (no number given) of the Ute Mountain Tribal Council, July 8, 1964, Tribal Resolutions File, UMU Agency.

23. Quoted in Peggy Strain, "Utes' 1952 Land-Settlement Victory Turned to Defeat," *Denver Post*, September 25, 1977.

24. Minutes of Southern Ute Tribal Council meeting, November 7, 1967, SU Archives.

25. Ernest House Sr., interview by author, June 11, 1993, tape recording.

26. Resolution no. 2638 of the Ute Mountain Tribal Council, 1978 (no exact date given), Tribal Resolutions File, UMU Agency; Jim Carrier, "Tribe Fights to Protect Sovereignty," *Denver Post*, November 12, 1989.

27. Resolution no. 2541 of the Ute Mountain Tribal Council, December 6, 1977, Tribal Resolutions File, UMU Agency; Robert W. Delaney, *The Ute Mountain Utes* (Albuquerque: University of New Mexico Press, 1989), 103–106.

28. Steve Garnaas, "Battle Brewing over Ute Gaming," *Denver Post*, November 2, 1991; Amy Malick, "State Approves Gaming Compact with the Southern Ute Tribe," *Southern Ute Drum*, August 7, 1992.

29. Minutes of Southern Ute Tribal Council meeting, February 5, 1980, 2, SU Archives.

30. "Town Board Rejects Petition; Mayor Backs off 'Investigation,'" *Southern Ute Drum*, August 8, 1975; "Tribe, Town Cool It on Water Hassle," *Southern Ute Drum*, September 5, 1975; "Water Bond Issue Rescinded," *Southern Ute Drum*, April 30, 1976.

31. "Ute Mountain Tribe Selected as Citizen of the Year," *Ute Mountain Ute Echo* (February 1987); "Utes Seek to Lift 'Invisible Curtain,'" *Rocky Mountain News*, December 6, 1986.

32. "Ute Mountain Tribe Files Lawsuit Against School District," *Ute Mountain Ute Echo* (July 1989); "Court Orders Change in Election System for Cortez School Board," *Ute Mountain Ute Echo* (May 1990).

33. Quoted in Jim Carrier, "Ugly Rumors, Petty Promises Found in Tribal Elections, Too," *Denver Post*, October 9, 1989.

34. Jim Carrier, "Subsurface Anger Helps New Ute Mountain Leader Do Her Job," *Denver Post*, October 21, 1989.

35. Espeedie Ruiz to Area Director, Memo accompanying Resolution no. 1997 of the Ute Mountain Tribal Council, July 28, 1971, Tribal Resolutions File, UMU Agency.

36. Resolution no. 2341 of the Ute Mountain Tribal Council, May 29, 1975, Tribal Resolutions File, UMU Agency.

37. Resolutions no. 3730 and no. 3739 of the Ute Mountain Tribal Council, November 23, 1990, and December 14, 1990, respectively, Tribal Resolutions File, UMU Agency.

38. Minutes of Southern Ute Tribal Council meeting, April 23, 1986, 1–2, SU Archives.

39. "Statement Made Regarding Petitions to Tribal Council," *Southern Ute Drum*, May 16, 1986.

40. Ibid.; Minutes of Southern Ute Tribal Council meeting, March 24–25, 1987, 6–8, SU Archives.

41. Southern Ute Tribal Council to tribal members, memo, "Explanation of Per Capita Payments," April 22, 1988, Council Meeting Minutes File, SU Archives.

42. Ray C. Frost, "Editorial," *Southern Ute Drum*, September 29, 1989.

43. "Constitution of the Southern Ute Indian Tribe," as amended and approved by an election of September 26, 1975, SU Archives.

44. Minutes of Southern Ute Tribal Council meeting, September 14, 1970, 2, SU Archives.

45. Minutes of Southern Ute Tribal Council meeting, September 30–October 1, 1975, 1, SU Archives.

46. Resolution no. 3087 of the Ute Mountain Tribal Council, November 26, 1984, Tribal Resolutions File, UMU Agency.

47. Minutes of Southern Ute Tribal Council meeting, December 27, 1972, 1, SU Archives.

48. Michael H. Elkriver, Letter to tribal members, *Ute Mountain Ute Echo* (August 1991).

49. Ray C. Frost, "Editorial," *Southern Ute Drum*, September 29, 1989.

50. Minutes of Southern Ute Tribal Council meeting, January 14, 1986, 5, SU Archives.

51. Arthur Cuthair, interview by author, June 10, 1993, tape recording.

52. Quoted in John T. Rehorn, "1993 General Meeting: Gaming the Big Issue," *Southern Ute Drum*, June 25, 1993.

53. Sunshine Smith, interview.

54. "Tribal Council Under Fire at General Meeting," *Weenuche Smoke Signals* (July 1994).

55. Ted Delaney, "Tribe's Future—like Its Past—Tied to Water," *Ute Mountain Ute Echo* (December 1987–January 1988).

56. Peggy Strain, "Tribe Leaders Accused of Fund Drain," *Denver Post*, September 20, 1977; Strain, "Utes' 1952 Land-Settlement Victory."

57. Quoted in Strain, "Utes' 1952 Land-Settlement Victory."

58. Joe Lehi, "White Mesa News," and unsigned response, "Another View of Jack Cantsee," *Ute Mountain Ute Echo*, November 9, 1977.

59. Johnson, 224.

60. Minutes of Southern Ute Tribal Council meeting, December 27, 1972, 6, SU Archives.

61. Bertha Grove, "Letter Is Written About Election," *Southern Ute Drum*, September 26, 1969; Bertha Grove, interview by author, June 21, 1993, tape recording.

62. John T. Rehorn, "The Tribal Gaming Controversy," *Southern Ute Drum*, April 16, 1993.

63. Tony Tallbird, Letter to the editor, *Ute Mountain Ute Echo* (September 1987).

64. Bertha Grove, interview.

65. Robert W. Delaney, Review of Nancy Wood's *When the Buffalo Free the Mountains*. *Ute Mountain Ute Echo*, March 11, 1981.

66. Floyd A. O'Neil, "The Indian New Deal: An Overview," in Kenneth R. Philp, ed., *Indian Self-Rule: First-Hand Accounts of Indian-White Relations from Roosevelt to Reagan* (Logan: Utah State University Press, 1995), 42.

67. "Ute Mountain Ute Tribal Goals Fiscal Year 1989," *Ute Mountain Ute Echo* (January 1989).

68. Minutes of Southern Ute Tribal Council meeting, September 14, 1982, 2, SU Archives.

69. John E. Baker Sr., interview.

70. "General Council Meeting Held," *Southern Ute Drum*, February 1, 1980.

71. Region VIII Committee for Indians, Report on the 1960 Ute Indian Workshop on Alcoholism, March 29–30, 1960, 2, Ute Clippings File, Western History Department, Denver Public Library, Denver.

72. Minutes of Southern Ute Tribal Council meeting, December 5, 1989, 1, SU Archives; "206 Sign Recall Petition," and "Incumbents Reelected," *Southern Ute Drum*, November 9, 1989.

73. "Tribal Council Accepts Recall Petition on Five Council Members," *Southern Ute Drum*, January 5, 1990.

74. John E. Baker Sr., interview.

75. Sunshine Smith, interview.

76. Minutes of Southern Ute Tribal Council meeting, November 1, 1989, 3–4, SU Archives.

77. Kit Miniclier, "Southern Ute Recall Voided; Vote Cast Twice," *Denver Post*, February 7, 1990.

78. Bertha Grove, interview. Grove jokingly commented regarding this allegation: "If I knew witchcraft, half of these Southern Ute people would be dead by now. I'd have got rid of them one by one!"

79. Miniclier, "Southern Ute Recall Voided."

80. "Southwest Inter-tribal Court of Appeals Upholds Decision," *Southern Ute Drum*, September 23, 1991.

81. Quoted in T. Delaney.

82. Vance Gillette, "Law on Removal of a Council Member," *Ute Mountain Ute Echo* (March 1991).

83. "Utes Endorse Continued Modernization," *Denver Post*, October 18, 1992.

84. Patrick O'Driscoll, "Ute Board Dismisses Election-Bribery Charge," *Denver Post*, October 21, 1992.

85. Quoted in "Elections," *Ute Mountain Ute Echo* (November 1992).

86. Arthur Cuthair, interview.

87. Tony Tallbird, Letter to the editor, *Ute Mountain Ute Echo* (September 1987).

88. Arnold Santistevan, "Burch, Peabody, Hudson Wins Tribal Election," *Southern Ute Drum*, November 9, 1990; Kit Miniclier, "His Storm Passed, Southern Utes' Leader Looks Ahead," *Denver Post*, November 18, 1990.

89. "Run-off Election to Be Held for Council Seat," *Southern Ute Drum*, November 13, 1992.

90. Dedra Millich, "Frost Wins Council Seat," *Southern Ute Drum*, February 19, 1993.

91. "October Council Election," *Weenuche Smoke Signals* (October 1994).

92. "Elect Guy T. Pinnecoose, Jr.," advertisement, *Southern Ute Drum*, November 26, 1993.

93. Quoted in Arnold Santistevan, "Tribal Voters Elect Burch and Peabody for Three-Year Terms," *Southern Ute Drum*, December 24, 1993.

8. TRIBAL CULTURE AND SOCIETY AFTER 1960

1. "Fire at Towaoc Post Office Building Called 'Suspicious' by Area Fireman," *Weenuche Smoke Signals* (July 1993); Cal Queal, "Towaoc Utes Planning Wisely; Lead New Life," *Denver Post*, March 24, 1955; D. H. Wattson to Commissioner of Indian Affairs, February 2, 1934, Wheeler-Howard Act File 1011, 066-1934, box A894 1-B, Records of BIA, RG 75, National Archives, Washington, D.C.

2. "Fire at Towaoc Post Office Building."

3. "An Old Error, a New Era," *Weenuche Smoke Signals* (July 1993).

4. Ernest House Sr., "To All Tribal Members," *Ute Mountain Ute Echo* (April 1988).

5. Marie Hight, interview by Floyd A. O'Neil, Winston Erickson, and Charles Root, December 7, 1990, 19, copy of transcript in the possession of Arthur Cuthair.

6. Arthur Cuthair, interview by author, June 10, 1993, tape recording.

7. James A. Clifton, "The Southern Ute Tribe as a Fixed Membership Group," *Human Organization* 24:4 (1964): 322.

8. David Rich Lewis, *Neither Wolf nor Dog: American Indians, Environment, and Agrarian Change* (New York: Oxford University Press, 1994), 3, 5–6.

9. Quoted in Jim Carrier, "Modern Medicine Man Works at Being Link Between Old, New," *Denver Post*, October 12, 1989.

10. Southern Ute Tribe, "Southern Ute Comprehensive Plan," March 11, 1974, 11, Southern Ute Tribal Records and Archives, Ignacio, Colorado; Southern Ute Indian Tribe, "Southern Ute Comprehensive Plan Update," January 1982, 15, SU Archives.

11. Ute Mountain Ute Indian Tribe, "Plan of Operation for Use of the Proceeds from Claims Case no. 47567," March 12, 1970, 6, Tribal Resolutions File, Ute Mountain Ute Agency, Towaoc, Colorado; Ted Delaney, "Tribe's Future—like Its Past—Tied to Water," *Ute Mountain Ute Echo* (December 1987–January 1988); Jim Carrier, "Statistics Don't Reveal Spirit, Perseverance of Knight Clan," *Denver Post*, October 5, 1989.

12. "Staff Meeting, August 20, 1985," *Ute Mountain Ute Echo* (September 1985).

13. Larry Burt, "Western Tribes and Balance Sheets: Business Development Programs in the 1960s and 1970s," *Western Historical Quarterly* (November 1992): 478.

14. Colorado Commission on Indian Affairs, Annual Report, 1981, 22, State Publications Library, Denver.

15. Delaney.

16. U.S. Department of Health and Human Services, Indian Health Service, *Trends in Indian Health, 1991* (N.p.: U.S. Department of Health and Human Services, 1991), 22.

17. Ibid., 56.

18. U.S. Department of Health and Human Services, Indian Health Service, *Regional Differences in Indian Health, 1990* (N.p.: Indian Health Service, 1990), 19.

19. U.S. Department of Health and Human Services, *Trends in Indian Health*, 49.

20. Kit Miniclier, "Indian Crime up: Cultural Changes Blamed," *Denver Post*, September 26, 1993.

21. "Disease Hits Pima Hardest," *Denver Post*, June 21, 1992.

22. Clifton, 322, 326.

23. Resolutions no. 3803 and no. 3805 of the Ute Mountain Tribal Council, October 9, 1991, and October 30, 1991, respectively, Tribal Resolutions File, UMU Agency.

24. Southern Ute Indian Tribe, "Southern Ute Comprehensive Plan Update," 172; "Sunrise Youth Shelter Relocation," *Ute Mountain Ute Echo* (April 1990).

25. Minutes of Southern Ute Tribal Council meetings, November 1, 1960, 8–9, and December 16, 1986, 1; "Peaceful Spirit Adds Two New Staff Members," *Southern Ute Drum*, August 9, 1985.

26. Minutes of Southern Ute Tribal Council meeting, April 3, 1984, 6, SU Archives.

27. Delaney.

28. Resolution no. 3894 of the Ute Mountain Tribal Council, April 23, 1992, Tribal Resolutions File, UMU Agency.

29. Arthur Cuthair, interview.

30. Joseph G. Jorgensen, *The Sun Dance Religion: Power for the Powerless* (Chicago: University of Chicago Press, 1972), 237.

31. Minutes of Southern Ute Tribal Council meetings, September 5, 1979, and May 13, 1986, 1, SU Archives.

32. Terry Knight, telephone interview by author, July 6, 1993, tape recording.

33. Berny Morson, "Schools Rich, Also Poor, Utes Claim," *Rocky Mountain News*, March 22, 1983.

34. Colorado Commission on Indian Affairs, Annual Report, 1981, 22; Jim Carrier, "Frustration Marks Relationship Between Indian Kids, Schools," *Denver Post*, October 23, 1989.

35. Southern Ute Indian Tribe, "Southern Ute Comprehensive Plan Update," 16.

36. Carrier, "Frustration Marks Relationship"; Southern Ute Indian Tribe, "Southern Ute Comprehensive Plan Update," 16.

37. Morson.

38. John E. Baker Sr., interview by author, June 15, 1993, tape recording.

39. Quoted in Anthony Polk, "Indians at Crossroads over School System," *Rocky Mountain News*, April 6, 1980.

40. Ibid.

41. "Opinion: Is the Hassle Worth It?" *Southern Ute Drum*, September 15, 1977.

42. James Guinn Fitzgerald, "An Ethnographic Description of the Relations Between the Communities and Schools of Ignacio, Colorado, from 1900 until 1982" (Ph.D. diss., University of Colorado, Boulder, 1982), 153–154, 162.

43. Minutes of Southern Ute Tribal Council meeting, December 7, 1976, 5, SU Archives; Fitzgerald, 188.

44. Minutes of Southern Ute Tribal Council meeting, March 31, 1987, 2, SU Archives.

45. "Ute Mountain Ute Educational Survey Item Respond," *Ute Mountain Ute Echo* (December 1990).

46. James Jefferson, Robert W. Delaney, and Gregory C. Thompson, *The Southern Utes: A Tribal History* (Ignacio, Colo.: Southern Ute Tribe, 1972), 54–56; Rudy Chelminski, "Indian Tradition Becomes History," *Rocky Mountain News*, February 14, 1961.

47. Quoted in "Three Ute Tribes Meet at Language Conference," *Southern Ute Drum*, February 4, 1977.

48. Ernest House Sr., interview by author, June 11, 1993, tape recording.

49. Norman Lopez, interview by author, June 8, 1993, tape recording.

50. Obdulla Box, "Southern Ute's Working Toward Regaining Vanishing Language," *Southern Ute Drum*, November 12, 1993.

51. Minutes of Southern Ute Tribal Council meeting, October 29, 1975, 1, SU Archives.

52. Tom Given, "Ute Dictionary," *Southern Ute Drum*, April 13, 1979; Dedra Millich, "Ute Language Computerized," *Southern Ute Drum*, May 31, 1991.

53. "Ute Language School Topic at General Tribal Meeting," *Southern Ute Drum*, March 30, 1979.

54. Bob Saile, "State Decree to Grant Utes Expanded Hunting Rights," *Denver Post*, February 19, 1978.

55. Dan Partner, "Utes, Comanches Sign Peace Treaty," *Southern Ute Drum*, September 17, 1976.

56. Marvin K. Opler, "The Origins of Comanche and Ute," *American Anthropologist* 45 (1943): 156–158.

57. Partner.

58. Rocky Hayes, "Name Change for Tribal Paper," *Weenuche Smoke Signals* (May 1993).

59. Norman Lopez, interview; Jim Carrier, "Medicine Man Acts as Both Doctor and Minister," *Denver Post*, October 28, 1989.

60. Carrier, "Medicine Man."

61. Arthur Cuthair, interview by Floyd A. O'Neil, Winston Erickson, and Charles Root, January 7, 1991, copy of transcript in the possession of Arthur Cuthair; Terry Knight, interview.

62. Terry Knight, interview.

63. Ibid.

64. Carrier, "Medicine Man."

65. Omer C. Stewart, *The Peyote Religion: A History* (Norman: University of Oklahoma Press, 1987), 328–330.

66. David F. Aberle and Omer C. Stewart, *Navaho and Ute Peyotism: A Chronological and Distributional Study*, Series in Anthropology, no. 6 (Boulder: University of Colorado Press, 1957), 1.

67. Stewart, 331–332.

68. Carrier, "Medicine Man"; Bertha Grove, interview by author, June 21, 1993, tape recording.

69. Terry Knight, interview.

70. Sunshine Cloud Smith, interview by author, June 17 and 20, 1993, tape recording.

71. Jefferson et al., 65.

72. Bertha Grove, interview. Bertha Grove reported that Sunshine Smith, a relative and a friend, had for years refrained from visiting Grove because of opposition to the Native American Church, in which Grove was an active participant.

73. Jorgensen, 237.

74. Jefferson et al., 65.

75. Jorgensen, 285.

76. Ibid., 212, 266–276.

77. Ibid., 145, 177, 247–248.

78. Ibid., 182.

79. Ibid., 188–193, 212.

80. Ibid., 255, 283.

81. Quoted in ibid., 198–201.

82. Terry Knight, interview; Sunshine Smith, interview; Bertha Grove, interview.

83. Jim Carrier, "Dancing to the Sun," *Denver Post*, October 1, 1989.

84. Obdulla Box, "Sun Dance: An Honored Ute Tradition," *Southern Ute Drum*, August 5, 1994.

85. Jefferson et al., 65.

86. Minutes of Southern Ute Tribal Council meeting, August 31, 1961, 8–9, SU Archives.

87. Bertha Grove, interview.

88. "Indian Leaders Holding Conference on American Indian Reli-

gious Freedom Act," *Ute Mountain Ute Echo* (February 1993); Cassandra
Naranjo, "Historic Ute Reunion, 1993," *Southern Ute Drum*, April 30, 1993.

CONCLUSION

1. Quoted in John T. Rehorn, "1993 General Meeting: Gaming the
Big Issue," *Southern Ute Drum*, June 25, 1993. All information pertaining to
this meeting was obtained from this article.

2. John E. Baker Sr., telephone interview by author, February 9, 1994,
tape recording.

3. Rehorn.

4. Arthur Cuthair, interview by author, June 10, 1993, tape recording;
Norman Lopez, interview by author, June 8, 1993, tape recording.

SELECTED BIBLIOGRAPHY

FEDERAL AND OTHER ARCHIVAL SOURCES

Denver Public Library. Western History Department. Denver, Colorado. Southern Ute Clippings File.
  Newspaper articles.
  Report on 1960 Ute Indian workshop on alcoholism.
  "A Report to the Commissioner of Indian Affairs by the Southern Ute Tribe." June 1, 1956.
National Archives. Rocky Mountain Region. Denver, Colorado.
  Consolidated Ute Agency. Records of BIA. RG 75.
    Agency correspondence and reports.
    Annual School Census Report, Allen Canyon.
    Annual Statistical and Narrative Reports, 1923–1935, Microfilm Publication M1011.
    Farmer's Weekly Reports, Allen Canyon, 1925–1926.
    Summary Statement of Withdrawal Status, 1955, 1956.
  Southern Ute Agency. Records of BIA. RG 75.
    Annual reports, 1910–1922, Microfilm Publication M1011.
  United Pueblos Agency. Records of BIA. RG 75.
    Records relating to tribal affairs, 1935–1968, Southern Ute rehabilitation programs.
National Archives. Washington, D.C.

Central Classified Files (1907–1959). Consolidated Ute Agency. Records of BIA. RG 75.

Minutes of Ute Mountain Ute Tribal Council and General Council meetings, 1951–1953.

Wheeler-Howard Files. Records of BIA. RG 75.

Agency and BIA correspondence.

Norlin Library (University of Colorado). Western History Collections. Boulder, Colorado.

Omer C. Stewart Collection.

Tri-Ethnic Project Files (Series VII). Microfilm boxes 3 and 4.

Records of BIA. RG 75. National Archives.

Agency and BIA correspondence.

Agency reports.

Annual Statistical Reports, 1920–1945.

Constitution and By-laws of the Southern Ute Tribe, 1936.

Constitution and By-laws of the Ute Mountain Tribe, 1940.

Corporate Charter of the Southern Ute Tribe, 1938.

Council resolutions and petitions, 1935–1957.

Economic and Social Surveys, 1934.

Minutes of Tribal Council and General Council meetings, Ute Mountain Tribe, 1937–1950.

Minutes of Tribal Council, General Council, and Joint Council meetings, Southern Ute Tribe, 1937–1957.

National Association of Indian Affairs.

"Investigation of Southern Ute Jurisdiction and Ute Mountain Reservation," October 1935.

Southern Ute Tribal Records and Archives. Tribal Affairs Building. Ignacio, Colorado.

Constitution of the Southern Ute Indian Tribe, as amended in 1975.

Minutes of Tribal Council and General Council meetings, 1951, 1960–1989.

"A Plan for the Rehabilitation of the Southern Ute Tribe." 1954.

"Progress and the Future: A Report by the Southern Ute Tribe." Dallas: Taylor, 1966.

Southern Ute Comprehensive Plan, 1974.

Southern Ute Comprehensive Plan Update, 1982.

"Where We Stand: A Report by the Southern Ute Tribe." Ignacio, Colo.: Southern Ute Tribe, 1960.

Ute Mountain Ute Agency. Towaoc, Colorado.

Listing of Tribal Council members, 1949–1989.

"Plan of Operation for Use of the Proceeds from Claims Case no. 47567," 1970.

Resolutions of the Ute Mountain Tribal Council, 1938–1992.

"Ute Rehabilitation Program, Public Health," 1955.

PUBLISHED FEDERAL DOCUMENTS

U.S. Court of Claims. No. 30360. *The Confederated Bands of Ute Indians v. the United States*. Decided May 23, 1910. 45 C.Cls., 440–471.

U.S. Court of Claims. No. 45585. *The Confederated Bands of Ute Indians v. the United States*. (In accordance with the Act of Congress, June 28, 1938, chap. 776. 52 Stat. 1209.) Reporters' Statement of the Case, Syllabus, and Opinion of the Court. Decided October 4, 1943. 100 C.Cls., 413–433.

U.S. Department of Health and Human Services. Indian Health Service. *Regional Differences in Indian Health, 1990*. N.p.: U.S. Department of Health and Human Services, 1990.

U.S. Department of Health and Human Services. Indian Health Service. *Trends in Indian Health, 1991*. N.p.: Indian Health Service, 1991.

U.S. Department of the Interior. Office of Indian Affairs. *Annual Report of the Commissioner of Indian Affairs to the Secretary of the Interior*. Washington, D.C.: GPO, 1875–1905.

U.S. House of Representatives. Committee on Interior and Insular Affairs. *Report with Respect to the House Resolution Authorizing the Committee on Interior and Insular Affairs to Conduct an Investigation of the Bureau of Indian Affairs Pursuant to House Resolution 89*. 83d Cong., 2d sess., September 20, 1954.

U.S. Senate. Committee on Indian Affairs. *Survey of Conditions of the Indians of the United States: Hearings Before a Subcommittee of the Committee on Indian Affairs*. 71st Cong., 2d sess., May 31, 1931.

U.S. Senate. Committee on the Judiciary. *Juvenile Delinquency: Hearings Before the Subcommittee to Investigate Juvenile Delinquency of the Committee on the Judiciary*. 84th Cong., 1st sess., March 11 and April 28–30, 1955.

INTERVIEWS

Baker, John E. Sr. Interview by author. June 15, 1993. Ignacio, Colorado. Tape recording. Additional interviews by author: July 15, 1993, and February 9, 1994. Taped telephone conversations.

Cuthair, Arthur. Interview by Floyd A. O'Neil, Winston Erickson, and Charles Root. January 7, 1991. Transcript in the possession of Arthur Cuthair. Towaoc, Colorado.

———. Interview by author. June 10, 1993. Towaoc, Colorado. Tape recording.

Grove, Bertha. Interview by author. June 21, 1993. Ignacio, Colorado. Tape recording.

Hight, Marie. Interview by Floyd A. O'Neil, Winston Erickson, and Charles

Root. December 7, 1990. Transcript in the possession of Arthur Cuthair. Towaoc, Colorado.

House, Ernest Sr. Interview by author. June 11, 1993. Towaoc, Colorado. Tape recording. Additional interview by author: July 15, 1993. Taped telephone conversation.

Johnson, Tom. Interview by Floyd A. O'Neil, Winston Erickson, and Charles Root. January 8, 1991. Transcript in the possession of Arthur Cuthair. Towaoc, Colorado.

Knight, Terry. Interview by author. July 6, 1993. Taped telephone conversation.

Lopez, Norman. Interview by author. June 8, 1993. Towaoc, Colorado. Tape recording.

Salt, Iris. Interview by Floyd O'Neil, Winston Erickson, and Charles Root, January 7, 1991. Transcript in the possession of Arthur Cuthair. Towaoc, Colorado.

Smith, Sunshine Cloud. Interview by author. June 17 and 20, 1993. Ignacio, Colorado. Tape recording. Additional interview by author: June 26, 1995. Taped telephone conversation.

Ute, Chloe. Interview by Floyd A. O'Neil, Winston Erickson, and Charles Root. January 9, 1991. Transcript in the possession of Arthur Cuthair. Towaoc, Colorado.

Wall, Frances. Interview by Floyd A. O'Neil, Winston Erickson, and Charles Root. January 9, 1991. Transcript in the possession of Arthur Cuthair. Towaoc, Colorado.

Whyte, Clifford Sr. Interview by Floyd A. O'Neil, Winston Erickson, and Charles Root. January 8, 1991. Transcript in the possession of Arthur Cuthair. Towaoc, Colorado.

Wing, Albert, Sr. Interview by Floyd A. O'Neil, Winston Erickson, and Charles Root. January 8, 1991. Transcript in the possession of Arthur Cuthair. Towaoc, Colorado.

TRIBAL NEWSPAPERS

Echo (renamed *Weenuche Smoke Signals* in 1993). Ute Mountain Ute Tribe, Towaoc, Colorado.

Southern Ute Drum. Southern Ute Tribe, Ignacio, Colorado.

NEWSPAPERS

Denver Post. Denver, Colorado.

Denver Times. Denver, Colorado.

Grand Junction Daily Sentinel. Grand Junction, Colorado.

Montezuma Valley Journal. Cortez, Colorado.
Montrose Daily News. Montrose, Colorado.
Pueblo Star-Journal and Sunday Chieftain. Pueblo, Colorado.
Rocky Mountain News. Denver, Colorado.

BOOKS

Aberle, David F., and Omer C. Stewart. *Navaho and Ute Peyotism: A Chrono-logical and Distributional Study.* Series in Anthropology, no. 6. Boulder: University of Colorado Press, 1957.

Ambler, Marjane. *Breaking the Iron Bonds: Indian Control of Energy Development.* Lawrence: University Press of Kansas, 1990.

The American Indian Reference Book. Portage, Mich.: Earth Company, 1976.

Bennett, Robert L. "Implementing the IRA." In *Indian Self-Rule: First-Hand Accounts of Indian-White Relations from Roosevelt to Reagan,* ed. Kenneth R. Philp, 83–86. Logan: Utah State University Press, 1995.

Burnette, Robert. "The War on Poverty." In *Indian Self-Rule: First-Hand Accounts of Indian-White Relations from Roosevelt to Reagan,* ed. Kenneth R. Philp, 226–227. Logan: Utah State University Press, 1995.

Callaway, Donald, Joel Janetski, and Omer C. Stewart. "Ute." In *Handbook of North American Indians,* ed. William C. Sturtevant. Vol. 11, *Great Basin,* ed. Warren L. D'Azevedo, 336–367. Washington, D.C.: Smithsonian Institution, 1986.

Carriker, Robert C. "The American Indian from the Civil War to the Present." In *Historians and the American West,* ed. Michael P. Malone, 177–208. Lincoln: University of Nebraska Press, 1983.

Clemmer, Richard O., and Omer C. Stewart. "Treaties, Reservations, and Claims." In *Handbook of North American Indians,* ed. William C. Sturtevant. Vol. 11, *Great Basin,* ed. Warren L. D'Azevedo, 525–557. Washington, D.C.: Smithsonian Institution, 1986.

Delaney, Robert W. *The Southern Ute People.* Phoenix: Indian Tribal Press, 1974.

———. *The Ute Mountain Utes.* Albuquerque: University of New Mexico Press, 1989.

Deloria, Philip S. "The Era of Indian Self-Determination: An Overview." In *Indian Self-Rule: First-Hand Accounts of Indian-White Relations from Roosevelt to Reagan,* ed. Kenneth R. Philp, 191–207. Logan: Utah State University Press, 1995.

Dobyns, Henry F. "Therapeutic Experience of Responsible Democracy." In *The American Indian Today,* ed. Stuart Levine and Nancy Oestreich Lurie, 171–185. Deland, Fla.: Everett/Edwards, 1965.

Freeman, Ira. S. *A History of Montezuma County, Colorado.* Boulder, Colo.: Johnson, 1958.

Hall, Thomas D. *Social Change in the Southwest, 1350–1880.* Lawrence: University Press of Kansas, 1989.

Hughes, J. Donald. *American Indians in Colorado.* 2d ed. Boulder, Colo.: Pruett, 1987.

Iverson, Peter. *The Navajo Nation.* Westport, Conn.: Greenwood Press, 1981.

Jefferson, James, Robert W. Delaney, and Gregory C. Thompson. *The Southern Utes: A Tribal History.* Ignacio, Colo.: Southern Ute Tribe, 1972.

Jorgensen, Joseph G. *The Sun Dance Religion: Power for the Powerless.* Chicago: University of Chicago Press, 1972.

Kelly, Lawrence C. "The Indian Reorganization Act: The Dream and the Reality." In *The American Indian Past and Present,* ed. Roger L. Nichols, 3d ed., 242–255. New York: Knopf, 1986.

Leland, Joy. "Population." In *Handbook of North American Indians,* ed. William C. Sturtevant. Vol. 11, *Great Basin,* ed. Warren L. D'Azevedo, 608–619. Washington, D.C.: Smithsonian Institution, 1986.

Lewis, David Rich. *Neither Wolf nor Dog: American Indians, Environment, and Agrarian Change.* New York: Oxford University Press, 1994.

Lyons, Oren. "The IRA and Indian Culture." In *Indian Self-Rule: First-Hand Accounts of Indian-White Relations from Roosevelt to Reagan,* ed. Kenneth R. Philp, 100. Logan: Utah State University Press, 1995.

Marsh, Charles S. *People of the Shining Mountains.* Boulder, Colo.: Pruett, 1982.

McPherson, Robert S. *A History of San Juan County: In the Palm of Time.* Salt Lake City: Utah State Historical Society, 1995.

Officer, James E. "Termination as Federal Policy: An Overview." In *Indian Self-Rule: First-Hand Accounts of Indian-White Relations from Roosevelt to Reagan,* ed. Kenneth R. Philp, 114–128. Logan: Utah State University Press, 1995.

O'Neil, Floyd A. "The Indian New Deal: An Overview." In *Indian Self-Rule: First-Hand Accounts of Indian-White Relations from Roosevelt to Reagan,* ed. Kenneth R. Philp, 30–46. Logan: Utah State University Press, 1995.

Opler, Marvin K. "The Southern Ute of Colorado." In *Acculturation in Seven American Indian Tribes,* ed. Ralph Linton, 119–206. Gloucester, Mass.: Appleton-Century, 1940.

Ortiz, Alfonso. "The War on Poverty." In *Indian Self-Rule: First-Hand Accounts of Indian-White Relations from Roosevelt to Reagan,* ed. Kenneth R. Philp, 220–222. Logan: Utah State University Press, 1995.

Painter, John. "Implementing the IRA." In *Indian Self-Rule: First-Hand Accounts of Indian-White Relations from Roosevelt to Reagan,* ed. Kenneth R. Philp, 80–82. Logan: Utah State University Press, 1995.

Parkhill, Forbes. *The Last of the Indian Wars.* New York: Crowell-Collier Press, 1961.

Parman, Donald L. *The Navajos and the New Deal.* New Haven, Conn.: Yale University Press, 1976.

Perkin, Robert L. *The First Hundred Years.* Garden City, N.Y.: Doubleday, 1959.

Pettit, Jan. *Utes: The Mountain People.* Rev. ed. Boulder, Colo.: Johnson, 1990.

Philp, Kenneth R., ed. *Indian Self-Rule: First-Hand Accounts of Indian-White Relations from Roosevelt to Reagan.* Logan: Utah State University Press, 1995.

Prucha, Francis Paul. *The Great Father: The United States Government and the American Indians.* Lincoln: University of Nebraska Press, 1984.

Rockwell, Wilson. *The Utes: A Forgotten People.* Denver: Sage, 1956.

Roe, Frank Gilbert. *The Indian and the Horse.* Norman: University of Oklahoma Press, 1955.

Shimkin, Demitri B. "The Introduction of the Horse." In *Handbook of North American Indians,* ed. William C. Sturtevant. Vol. 11, *Great Basin,* ed. Warren L. D'Azevedo, 517–524. Washington, D.C.: Smithsonian Institution, 1986.

Smith, P. David. *Ouray Chief of the Utes.* Ouray, Colo.: Wayfinder Press, 1986.

Sorkin, Alan L. *American Indians and Federal Aid.* Washington, D.C.: Brookings Institution, 1971.

Stewart, Omer C. *Ethnohistorical Bibliography of the Ute Indians of Colorado.* Series in Anthropology, no. 18. Boulder: University of Colorado Press, 1971.

———. *Indians of the Great Basin: A Critical Bibliography.* Bloomington: Indiana University Press, 1982.

———. "The Peyote Religion." In *Handbook of North American Indians,* ed. William C. Sturtevant. Vol. 11, *Great Basin,* ed. Warren L. D'Azevedo, 673–681. Washington, D.C.: Smithsonian Institution, 1986.

———. *Peyote Religion: A History.* Norman: University of Oklahoma Press, 1987.

———. "Southern Ute Adjustment to Modern Living." In *Acculturation in the Americas,* ed. Sol Tax, 80–87. Chicago: University of Chicago Press, 1952.

———. *Ute Peyotism: A Study of a Cultural Complex.* Series in Anthropology, no. 1. Boulder: University of Colorado Press, 1948.

Swadesh, Frances L. *Los Primeros Pabladores: Hispanic Americans on the Ute Frontier.* Notre Dame, Ind.: University of Notre Dame Press, 1974.

Thompson, Gregory C. *Southern Ute Lands, 1848–1899: The Creation of a Reservation.* Occasional Papers of the Center of Southwest Studies. Durango, Colo.: Fort Lewis College, 1972.

Wilkinson, Charles F. "The Indian Claims Commission." In *Indian Self-Rule: First-Hand Accounts of Indian-White Relations from Roosevelt to Reagan,* ed. Kenneth R. Philp, 151–155. Logan: Utah State University Press, 1995.

Wood, Nancy. *When the Buffalo Free the Mountains: The Survival of America's Ute Indians.* Garden City, N.Y.: Doubleday, 1980.

THESES AND DISSERTATIONS

Baker, Augusta. "The Ute Indians." M.A. thesis, University of Denver, 1926.

Covington, James Warren. "Relations Between the Ute Indians and the United States Government, 1848–1900." Ph.D. diss., University of Oklahoma, 1949.

Fitzgerald, James Guinn. "An Ethnographic Description of the Relations Between the Communities and Schools of Ignacio, Colorado, from 1900 until 1982." Ph.D. diss., University of Colorado, Boulder, 1982.

Johnson, Charles Clark. "A Study of Modern Southwestern Indian Leadership." Ph.D. diss., University of Colorado, Boulder, 1963.

Mills, Lawrence Wilson. "A Study of the Ute Indians." M.A. thesis, Ohio State University, 1929.

Swadesh, Frances L. "The Southern Utes and Their Neighbors, 1877–1926: An Ethnohistorical Study of Multiple Interaction in Contact-Induced Culture Change." M.A. thesis, University of Colorado, Boulder, 1962.

Tyzzer, Robert Neal III. "An Investigation of the Demographic and Genetic Structure of a Southwestern American Indian Population: The Southern Ute Tribe of Colorado." Ph.D. diss., University of Colorado, Boulder, 1974.

ARTICLES

Beauvais, Fred. "Comparison of Drug Use Rates for Reservation Indian, Non-reservation Indian, and Anglo Youth." *American Indian and Alaska Native Mental Health Research: The Journal of the National Center* 5:1 (1992): 13–31.

Burt, Larry. "Western Tribes and Balance Sheets: Business Development Programs in the 1960s and 1970s." *Western Historical Quarterly* (November 1992): 475–495.

Clemmer, Richard O. "Differential Leadership Patterns in Early Twentieth-Century Great Basin Indian Societies." *Journal of California and Great Basin Anthropology* 11:1 (1989): 35–49.

———. "Hopis, Western Shoshones, and Southern Utes: Three Different Responses to the Indian Reorganization Act of 1934." *American Indian Culture and Research Journal* 10:2 (1986): 15–40.

Clifton, James A. "The Southern Ute Tribe as a Fixed Membership Group." *Human Organization* 24:4 (1964): 319–327.

Hoffmeister, Harold. "The Consolidated Ute Indian Reservation." *Geographical Review* 35:4 (1945): 601–623.

Lewis, David Rich. "Reservation Leadership and the Progressive-Traditional Dichotomy: William Wash and the Northern Utes, 1865–1928." *Ethnohistory* 38:2 (1991): 124–147.

O'Neil, Floyd A. Review of *When the Buffalo Free the Mountains,* by Nancy Wood. *Western Historical Quarterly* (January 1982): 75–76.

Opler, Marvin K. "The Character and History of the Southern Ute Peyote Rite." *American Anthropologist* 42 (1940): 463–478.

———. "The Origins of Comanche and Ute." *American Anthropologist* 45 (1943): 155–158.

Parman, Donald L., and Catherine Price. "A 'Work in Progress': The Emergence of Indian History as a Professional Field." *Western Historical Quarterly* (May 1989): 185–196.

Russell, James. "Conditions and Customs of Present-Day Utes in Colorado." *Colorado Magazine* 6:3 (May 1929): 104–112.

Stacher, S. F. "The Indians of the Ute Mountain Reservation, 1906–9." *Colorado Magazine* 26:1 (January 1949): 52–61.

Stewart, Omer C. "The Southern Ute Peyote Cult." *American Anthropologist* 43 (1941): 303–308.

———. "The Ute Indians: Before and After White Contact." *Utah Historical Quarterly* 34:1 (1966): 38–61.

Whittier, Florence E. "The Grave of Chief Ouray." *Colorado Magazine* 1:7 (November 1924): 312–319.

INDEX